How to Find
Almost Anyone,
Anywhere

How to Find Almost Anyone, Anywhere

Norma Mott Tillman
Private Investigator

Rutledge Hill Press
Nashville, Tennessee

Published in Nashville, Tennessee, by Rutledge Hill Press, Inc., 211
Seventh Avenue North, Nashville, Tennessee 37219.
Distributed in Canada by H. B. Fenn & Company, Ltd., 1090 Lorimar
Drive, Mississauga, Ontario, L5S 1R7.

Typography by D&T/Bailey, Nashville, Tennessee.
Design by Bruce Gore, Gore Studios, Nashville, Tennessee.

Library of Congress Cataloging-in-Publication Data

Tillman, Norma Mott, 1938–
    How to find almost anyone, anywhere / Norma Mott Tillman.
        p.   cm.
    Includes bibliographical references.
    ISBN 1-55853-294-3 (hardcover)
    1. Missing persons—United States—Investigation. 2. Birthparents—
United States—Identification.   I. Title.
HV6762.U5T55 1994   94-40470
363.2'336—dc20   CIP

Printed in the United States of America
2 3 4 5 6 7 8— 99 98 97 96 95 94

How to Find
Almost Anyone,
Anywhere

This book and other projects represent many hours of
neglect to my family,
especially my grandchildren,
which I intend to make up for as soon as possible.
I appreciate the support and encouragement
that have made this book possible.
This book is dedicated to my family.
I love each of you more than you will ever know.

Contents

Preface

I AM OFTEN ASKED "What made you become a detective?" Because I did not actually plan it, I believe I was destined to become a detective. Fate must have intended for me to become a private investigator, because it seems that everything in my life prepared me for what I refer to as being "M.A.D.E. in the USA," M.A.D.E. being my acronym for Mystery, Adventure, Danger, and Excitement.

Nothing has ever been dull, boring, or routine for me. Early on I was curious and adventurous, always exploring the world around me. Living on the edge has been my way of life since childhood, and mysteries have always fascinated me. As you might suspect, other children my age did not share my interests. In addition, I have always been independent, which allows me to do what I want to do, when I want to do it. Of course, because investigators spend so much time alone, on the road tracking down clues, this sense of independence has served me well.

I attribute my creative and innovative qualities to my parents, who possessed many talents. Before becoming a police officer and detective, my father was trained as a mechanical engineer. There was nothing he could not fix, nothing he couldn't take apart and put back together. His nature was to be suspicious of everyone and I remember him joking that "everyone is guilty until proven innocent." When he came home for dinner, I would sit in his car and listen to the police dispatcher. His homicide reference books fascinated me, and by the age of ten I was familiar with such terms as *point of entry, decapitation, angle of attack, rape, homicide, death,* and *evidence*. My father had the patience of Job—another must for a detective. I do not think he ever imagined that I might follow in his footsteps.

My mother was an outgoing person who was also persistent, self-motivated, confident, and determined—more great qualities for an investigator. She taught her family the three R's that matter most to me: respect, responsibility, and religion.

I inherited many qualities from my parents (who died before seeing me become an investigator) that have contributed to my success as an investigator, and I attribute many of my skills, such as the ability to improvise, finding my way around a new place, and surviving in the outdoors to the years I spent in Girl Scouts and summer camps.

After graduating from East High School in Nashville, I went to work for the federal government in Washington, DC. Eventually I was transferred back to Nashville with the Internal Revenue Service. While attending school at night, I met my husband, Sonny, an outstanding athlete who thought he was marrying June Cleaver. Much to his disappointment, he soon found out that I was not even her distant cousin! We have three wonderful daughters, Vicki, Terri, and Lisa, of whom I am extremely proud, and three wonderful grandchildren, Chelsea, Nicole, and Sydney.

After my youngest child started school, I wanted something to do with my time. I started out as a volunteer police dispatcher in the small town in which we lived, and I have never looked back. Later I went to work with the Metro Police Department in Nashville and attended the Metro Police Academy, one of the biggest challenges of my life. On the first day, one of the training sergeants told me that he would break my spirit, that he wished I weren't there. While running through tires during physical training, I fell and broke my foot. He ordered me to get back in formation, even though I asked to be excused. But I survived, and I learned a great deal about the following: shooting a gun; performing emergency medical training; criminal law;

accident investigation; hostage negotiation; officer survival skills; and self-defense. I worked with law enforcement for eleven years.

After leaving the police department, I worked as an insurance fraud investigator and obtained my private investigator's license in 1987. That same year I opened my agency, U.F.O., Inc. (Unlimited Facts Obtained, or, as I sometimes joke, "U Figure it Out," or "Unique Female Operative").

As a result of experiencing so many obstacles and difficulties, and because no one really encouraged me in my pursuits as a private investigator or taught me how to search for information, I decided that I needed to share my knowledge, experience, and resources with others; to become a role model for aspiring private investigators; and through my seminars, a teacher. This is why I wrote this book.

The basic desire to help others has always been my motivation for most everything I do. My faith in God keeps me going, realizing that I can accomplish nothing without the help of God, and believing that He has a purpose for me: helping others find missing loved ones.

One of the greatest gifts of all is being able to locate and reunite loved ones. It is one of the most rewarding experiences of a lifetime.

I wish each of you much success with your searches.

How to Find
Almost Anyone,
Anywhere

1

Searching for the Seed to the Solution

Dear Norma,

I am forty-two years old and have never met my father. I am happily married and the mother of two grown children.

My mother is now deceased, but before her death she revealed the name of my real father, Edward Stevenson. She would never discuss this with me although I asked her for information when I was sixteen and learned that the name of the man on my birth certificate was not my real father.

During the war, in 1943, my mother worked at a plant in Ohio. A co-worker named Edward Stevenson took my mother out one night. They went to a local bar and had a few drinks, then went for a drive. I was conceived that night. By the time my mother found out she was pregnant, she had discovered Edward Stevenson was married. She was ashamed, embarrassed, and humiliated. She felt cheap and dirty. She could not tell anyone. Instead, she quit her job and moved away. She never told Edward Stevenson that he had fathered her child.

1

Her high-school sweetheart came home from overseas and they got married when she was two months pregnant. She did not tell him she was pregnant. He left and went back overseas. When I was born, she put his name as the father on my birth certificate. Of course, he found out about me and knew I was not his child and he divorced my mother. At least that made it appear to everyone that my mother was divorced, not an unwed mother. She never told anyone her secret.

At age sixteen, I wanted to meet my father. At that time, my mother had to admit to me that the man listed on my birth certificate was not my father. At that time, she refused to give me any other information. One day, as my mother lay dying, she told me that my biological father's name was Edward Stevenson and that he was very handsome—6'5" tall, with dark hair and dark eyes. He was a supervisor at the plant and a Union representative. She did not tell me much more. By this time, her speech and memory were failing. She died soon after telling me my father's name. I did not have much to work with.

After my mother's death, I asked her sister if she knew who my father was. She told me she thought he was from New Jersey. I wrote to the New Jersey Office of Vital Statistics for a birth certificate for Edward Stevenson. Because I did not have his age or date of birth, I asked them to search for all persons with that name born from 1900 to 1930. They sent me a copy of a 1911 birth certificate with the name I was looking for. For the next two years, I searched for the man on the birth certificate. I even went to New Jersey myself. I spent several thousand dollars and several years searching for my father, without success.

I want to assure you—and him—that I seek only information. I do not want to cause him problems or embarrassment. I need my medical history as well as other genealogical information pertaining to my heritage. I want to know all I can about this man, but I do not expect a relationship, nor do I want anything from him. He need not fear me, because I do not mean any harm.

Please help make my life complete. Help me find my father.

—JAN

≈ ≈ ≈

Dear Jan,

Based on the information you furnished, I too thought New Jersey would be the logical place to begin. After going to New Jersey and verifying the information you were given, I discovered that the birth certificate you were given was in error. The child whose certificate you were given was actually the child's father. The name of that child's father had mistakenly been entered in the space provided for the child's name. Because the child's name was entirely different, I realized the man you had been searching for was not the right person. Once I discovered this mistake, the obvious place to begin the search was at the plant in Ohio.

Unfortunately, the plant had been closed for years, so how could I find anyone to ask? I decided to begin at the local public library. I went to the reference section to look for 1943 directories. There was a city directory for that year, which contained the names of two men with the same name as your father. One of the names appeared in the current city directory. I drove to the address listed in the directory and talked to a man named Edward Stevenson. He was not the right one. I asked him if he happened to know the whereabouts of the other man and he responded, "I heard he lived in Alabama." I thanked him and gave him my name and phone number, in case he wanted to contact me in the future with additional information. (Norma's Note: Always leave your name and phone number so that you may be contacted easily.)

After returning home, I received a phone call from Edward Stevenson of Ohio. He remembered that the other Edward Stevenson had moved to Tuscaloosa, Alabama.

All I had to do was ask directory assistance in Tuscaloosa, Alabama, for a number for Edward Stevenson. I dialed the number and a man answered. My heart was pounding.

"Is this Edward Stevenson?"

"Yes," he said.

"Are you by any chance the same Edward Stevenson who worked at the Bridge plant in Cincinnati, Ohio, in 1943?"

"Yes, I am."

"Were you 6'5", with dark curly hair and were you a Union representative?" "Yes."

"Mr. Stevenson, may I speak to you about something very personal, very confidential? If this is not a convenient time, I will be glad to give you my phone number and you may call me back, or I can call you back."

"Honey, you go right ahead and ask me anything you want to."

"Do you happen to remember a co-worker named Jane Vaughan?"

"No, I don't believe I do. That was a long time ago."

"Well, Mr. Stevenson, to make a long story short, Jane Vaughan became pregnant by a co-worker named Edward Stevenson. She never told Mr. Stevenson about their daughter."

Dead silence! Then a voice said, "It wasn't my husband; he was married to me then." His wife had been listening the entire time. She took over and did all the talking, convincing me I had made a big mistake. She told me of another man named Edward Stevenson who also worked at the plant. Of course, I had already visited the other one, who was 5'10", with green eyes and red hair.

I knew I had the right one, I just didn't want to hurt anyone, so I said, "I'm so sorry, I must have made a mistake. I didn't mean to cause anyone a problem." Mr. Stevenson was still on the line, even though he did not say a word. After Mrs. Stevenson hung up, he said, "Would you send me her picture?"

"The mother or the daughter?" I asked.

"Both," he responded. I asked him where he wanted me to send them and he gave me his home address.

"Are you sure?" I asked.

"Yes," he said.

—NORMA

I contacted Jan and she wrote her father a letter and sent pictures of her family. Mrs. Stevenson wrote Jan back and said, "What do you want? Leave my husband alone. Do not contact him again, he is not well." Later Jan learned that Mr. Stevenson confessed to his wife that he had been unfaithful.

Of course, Jan was devastated by Mrs. Stevenson's letter. She did not want anything except to meet her father. She wrote back, begging for a few minutes of his time so that they might actually meet one another. Finally, Mrs. Stevenson wrote that Jan and her husband could meet the Stevensons in Little Rock. She insisted that Jan could spend fifteen minutes with Mr. Stevenson. During their meeting, Mrs. Stevenson did all the talking. Jan brought pictures of her son and daughter. Her son was 6'5", with dark, wavy hair—the very image of Mr. Stevenson. At last, Jan met her father. He was distant, but Jan can live with what she learned. Until she met him, she had to imagine what he was like. Now she knew. And for her, the search had been about information, not a relationship.

You've picked up this book because you want to find someone or find out information about somebody. Perhaps you were separated from your father or mother. Perhaps you gave up a child for adoption. Perhaps you've become romantically involved with a person and want to know something about his or her past before you continue the relationship.

Every person who has lost track of a parent, brother, sister, or other loved one has a void inside that aches with fear, longing, curiosity, and sometimes guilt. This is particularly true when family members are separated from each other by adoption or divorce. But it can also happen to men and women who have lost friends, first loves, or military buddies.

Many people doubt that they can actually find the person or information they want. Let me assure you that in reality, it's not hard to do. It just takes persistence and ingenuity.

Over the past few years, I've located more than one thousand missing persons and I orchestrate more than one hundred televised reunions per year between loved ones who have been separated. I've looked for many kinds of people and information. Your search will take hard work, but I can guarantee you that success is almost always possible.

Understand that most missing persons are not actually missing. They just don't know that anyone is looking for them. Therefore, unless someone is missing because of foul play, deliberate evasion, or participation in a witness protection program, he or she probably can be found. The average American will leave a paper trail seven miles long during a lifetime: credit cards, driver's license, automobile registration, medical records, insurance policies, marriage license(s), divorce and bankruptcy proceedings, bank accounts, and more. In Chapter Four, I list forty-three different records that usually exist on the average American.

As you look for those records on the person you are trying to find, most may lead to dead ends. But you only need one live one. Remember that every problem has a seed to the solution. You just need to find it.

For one person, it may be only an old automobile registration. But that can give you an address where the person you are trying to find used to live. And the landlord might have some information. For another person, it may be a place of employment. You may find only one record on your person, but it can lead to the information you need.

The four pieces of information that will help you most in your search are the person's name, date of birth, Social Security number, and last known address. With these four pieces of information, you will almost be guaranteed success in locating a missing person.

As you read through this book, I'm going to let you take a peek at some of my correspondence. Some of the letters include my answers to the writers; others leave the solution to you and your imagination. I've disguised names and locations, but I think you'll soon realize that if you're searching for someone, you aren't alone.

No matter who (or what) you're searching for, all searches have common threads. For that reason, you'll probably see that, at times, I've repeated some information in the pages that follow. You'll want to read chapters that aren't necessarily about your specific search, because there may be something helpful in them.

For example, searches for fathers and for mothers are similar in many ways as long as you begin with a correct name. And a search for an adoptee is closely related to biological mother and father searches because of one common denominator: the adoption process. It would be wise for you to read all the chapters and to take note of any relevant information, no matter where you find it.

The final chapter of the book contains lists of information, addresses, sample forms, and other information that will be helpful to you. Be sure to check it out—you may find just what you need to locate the seed to your solution. That seed, or piece of information, will allow you to write or call public agencies, research city directories and telephone books, ask revealing questions, and access databases until you find the contact information you need.

Once you've read this book, the best advice I can give you is to start with what you know, and follow it until you've solved your personal mystery.

And let me make one more point before we get started. I am a firm believer in keeping the law. After eleven years of experience with law enforcement, I have a healthy respect for law and order. Remember: You do not have to break the law to find a missing person. I don't break the law in my searches, and I don't want you to either. So if you're interested in wiretaps, breaking and entering, trespassing, or getting information through bribery or other covert means, this isn't the book for you. Instead, this is a book for real people with a real need for a reunion.

> *Every problem contains the seed for the solution.*
> *Your goal is to find the seed in your search.*

Types of Missing Persons and Property

A MISSING PERSON is simply a person whom the searcher cannot find. Most missing persons are actually not missing at all; they simply don't know anyone is looking for them.

There are two basic categories of missing persons: criminal and noncriminal. These two basic categories also can be referred to as voluntary and nonvoluntary.

To find almost anyone, whether criminal or noncriminal, the search must have a starting point. Whatever information you have to work with is your starting point. Your mission is to follow "clues" or "trails" that branch from your starting point.

Although I hate to admit it, there are some missing persons that classify as impossible searches. It is almost impossible to find information on a person if you don't have a correct name. Persons who were abandoned have no paper trails. Therefore without a trail, there is nothing to follow. Persons who disappeared due to foul play may not be located if no body is found. Children are difficult to locate because frequently no paper trail exists. The only information to work with is furnished by a witness or person who knew something of the disappearance. And it may be impossible to find a person whose records have been falsified.

Types of Missing Persons and Property

Abandoned Money and Unclaimed Property

Several agencies of the federal government, as well as every state, hold abandoned money until someone comes forward to claim it. A list of national and state unclaimed property offices can be found in the Reference Section.

Most unclaimed property results when an owner dies and no heirs or beneficiaries collect it. This property can be a bank account, an insurance policy, real estate, a will, or other assets. After seven years, this property is transferred to a state Office of Unclaimed Property and it is held there until the rightful owner claims it. Because most people don't know they have anything waiting for them, they never inquire.

Lists of unclaimed properties are available in every state. Most states allow a "finder's fee" for anyone who locates an heir to unclaimed property. Finder's fees vary by state, anywhere from 10 percent of the amount of the property to an unlimited amount. The problem with collecting a finder's fee is that you must do all the work at your own expense, find the people, and then try to get them to sign a contract authorizing you to receive a percentage. There is no guarantee you will collect a dime. This is a risk you may not want to take. (If you are curious to know if you are an heir, you may want to consult a professional heir finder.)

For unclaimed property to be claimed, absolute proof of identity and ownership is necessary. Each state provides forms to be completed by both the finder and the next of kin.

For a small research fee you may write to see if you or a relative has unclaimed stock certificates:

Stock Search International
16855 West Bernardo Dr.,
Suite 207
San Diego, CA 91217
(800) 537-4523

If you would like to find out if a relative had a life insurance policy, write:

American Council of Life Insurance
Policy Search
1001 Pennsylvania Ave. NW
Washington, DC 20004

This search is free, but it will take several months to receive a reply. The following information should be included in an inquiry about an insurance policy: Information on the policy-holder should include name, birthdate, place of birth, residence when policy was issued, date of policy, place of policy, Social Security number, and occupation; Information on the probable beneficiary should include name, address, and relationship to policyholder; Information on the person inquiring should include name, address, relationship to policyholder, any insurance companies already contacted, reason for inquiry, and signature.

Adoption

I believe the adoption search is the most difficult search of all. Few clues usually exist and most states have closed records, leaving the searcher few trails to follow.

According to the *Congressional Record*, there are an estimated five million adoptees in the United States, and two million adoptees are actively searching for biological families every day. Counting the biological parents, siblings, grandparents, aunts and uncles, and other relatives, it is estimated that approximately 135 million people have been involved in the adoption process.

Adoption searches, like other kinds of searches, must begin with whatever information is known about the person being sought. If the searcher is an adoptee, the search for the birth parents may begin with the medical records at birth. If the searcher is the birth parent, the record may begin with a search of records at a courthouse.

The adoption search is more involved than any other search because the search itself is only part of the process. Both the searcher and the missing person will need to be prepared for their reunion. The approach to the missing person is extremely delicate. An inexperienced searcher could ruin a person's life if he or she does not understand the importance of the approach and the preparation required. Adoption searches can be very successful, and happy reunions are possible as long as there is a good understanding of the adoption process.

Ancestors

A genealogical search for ancestors can begin with whatever information you know about yourself. If you know who your parents were and where they were born, it is possible to search through libraries, family Bibles, cemetery records, census records, immigration records, and church records.

One of the largest depositories for genealogical records is the Mormon libraries, with branches in every state. These records are primarily more than fifty years old. In addition, the National Archives has regional libraries and may conduct a search for you by written request.

Census records are maintained on microfilm and are released after the records are seventy years old. The records are released in ten-year increments. The last available census is the 1920 census. Most reference sections of public libraries have these records. To search them, you must understand Soundex, a coding system in which vowels and consonants are assigned a numerical code number. If the name you are searching can be spelled several ways, this coding system will allow you to view all possible names. Once you locate the name you are searching for, the census will give you the names and ages of all persons in that household for that year.

Records exist in book form of passenger lists of persons arriving in this country. These lists will also contain the number of persons in this family, which port they entered, which state and county they settled in, and other information. This information may be requested in writing for a fee, from branches of the National Archives libraries. Other public libraries may have this information in their reference sections. Also be aware that each state has an archives library. These libraries are valuable sources of information. Reference librarians are usually very informative regarding material that may be researched. Within each state may be found a historical society or an agency for historical record keeping. Affiliates of these organizations might be able to assist you with your search.

Criminals

A criminal type of missing person is one who has committed a crime and is wanted by law enforcement. This person knows he or she is wanted and probably fears landing in jail. Even though a criminal is hiding or running, that person must continue daily life—eating, sleeping, surviving. All these activities have the potential to provide you with clues.

Criminals may go to great extremes to hide their whereabouts and will leave few, if any, paper trails. The criminal may even change identity either by using the identity of another person or by changing his or her own identity by transposing numbers in a Social Security number or using an incorrect birthdate. Identifying information is often false. The only paper trail criminals may leave may be their criminal history. However, in the attempt to survive, the criminal might have a vehicle, a driver's license, a Social Security number, a family, a job, insurance, bank accounts, and relatives and friends. A criminal may get sick, need to see a doctor or dentist, attend sports games, subscribe to magazines, and buy medicine. Each of these leaves a paper trail.

Criminals may have a pattern or "m.o."—method of operation or *modus operandi.* They are basically creatures of habit. By analyzing their m.o., you can almost predict their actions. The criminal mind is not complicated; it is just on a different track than the noncriminal's. In order to catch a criminal, you must be able to think like one. You have to figure out what you would do if you were in the same situation. The most difficult part of living a criminal life is not having any contact with your family or friends. Most criminals will eventually get in touch with someone they have known. The easiest way to locate a criminal is to find out who he or she is most likely to contact. It may take a while, but it will probably pay off.

On one criminal case I was able to make friends with the mail carrier of the criminal's parents and found out from what locations the person's parents received mail. On another case, I met the criminal's ex-girlfriend, who opened up to me and told me what I wanted to know. Finding an ex-spouse or ex-girlfriend/boyfriend can be one of the best sources of information about criminals.

With ex-cons, I have received information from a parole officer, a jail guard, and a bondsman. Anyone involved in the process of an arrest can provide information of some type. The criminal court clerk's office may have a copy of a warrant. An arrest record may reveal an attorney.

Because most criminals have a *history* of crime, you will want to analyze previous arrests. How about a bondsman? Who put up the money? By finding out who paid the bond and what the collateral was (maybe a piece of property, which would lead you to the property owner, which might lead you to the person you are looking for), you can find additional information that may lead to the whereabouts of your criminal. By finding out who visited the criminal while he or she was incarcerated, you will have some contacts. Just because they are criminals does not mean there is not a trail. The trail is different and difficult, but it is there.

Divorce

About 50 percent of all children in the United States are reared by single parents, primarily the mother. The absent parent may owe child support or, in the case of a man, may not even know he fathered a child. Probably the most requested search for a noncriminal type of missing person is the request to find a father.

If the parents are divorced, the divorce record is very important. In some states a divorce record will reveal the full names, dates of birth, Social Security numbers, and last known addresses of the parties involved. Also included on the divorce record may be an employer, a place of birth, a list of property, a disposition, and an attorney who represented each party.

For the person who is searching for a parent who was divorced, the first step is to obtain a copy of the divorce record.

Heirs/Beneficiaries

Heirs are persons to whom an estate has been left after a death. An heir to unclaimed property may not be aware of the estate. It takes at least nine months for an estate to be probated after a person's death. Once all debts are paid, if there is no will, the estate is divided among living heirs. If the next of kin is dead, the estate may be handed down to the survivors, who may not be aware of it.

Every state has an Office of Unclaimed Property. This office takes care of unclaimed property such as estates, insurance policies, and bank accounts until the proper owner, an heir or beneficiary, claims it.

The unclaimed property may not be turned over to the state until after seven years because, in the case of a bank or insurance policy, the executor of the estate must make every effort to locate and contact the heir. After all efforts have failed, the estate is then turned over to the state to be held in trust for the owner. States do not have on-staff investigators assigned to find these persons. Therefore almost anyone can conduct these types of searches, and most states do not require licensing. It may be fun to search for other people's heirs, but the risk of doing it without getting paid was discussed in the section in this chapter labeled "Abandoned Money and Unclaimed Property." Start by checking the laws in your state.

Persons who are heirs or beneficiaries probably do not know anyone is looking for them. They may not know they are due money or property. The searcher often does not have much to start with other than a name, and usually only the name of the deceased party. The deceased may have died several generations back and left his estate to a sibling or a sibling's children. By the time the searcher begins, perhaps fifty years have passed. The person's brother may be deceased and have left seven children. The seven children may be deceased and have left thirty grandchildren. Now the searcher must find the thirty grandchildren. Heir searching may be time-consuming and costly, with no guarantee of any repayment of expenses.

Homeless

A homeless person may be classified as a noncriminal type of missing person. However, a homeless person may not leave a paper trail because he or she may not work, pay taxes, own a vehicle, possess a driver's license, or draw a paycheck. A homeless person may draw a welfare check, an unemployment check, food stamps, or receive Medicaid. Most homeless people will have a Social Security number even if they do not use it.

Many homeless people have been released from mental institutions. Some homeless persons have families they choose not to contact. And some homeless people choose this way of life.

A homeless person will probably have a birth certificate and a Social Security number. If the homeless person stays at a Salvation Army facility, a record may exist. The Salvation Army maintains a computer list of persons who stay at or are otherwise in contact with its many locations. Of course, the homeless person may not use his or her true identity. Therefore, any records that exist may not be 100 percent accurate. For information, contact:

> Salvation Army Social Services
> Dept.
> Missing Persons Bureau
> 120 West 14th St.
> New York, NY 10011

It is possible for homeless people to sell or trade their identities. Birth certificates and Social Security numbers may be illegally sold. If the missing person does not work, pay taxes, draw a paycheck, have a bank account, or otherwise leave a paper trail, it will be very difficult to find him or her.

Military

Military searches can be difficult if the searcher is not the next of kin. If the searcher is a relative, there is a slim chance that writing to the National Personnel Records Center in St. Louis, Missouri, will provide information on the missing person. If the person is active military, there are military locating services available. If the person is inactive, there are many organizations that may be contacted. The Veterans' Administration (VA) has regional offices in which a searcher may inquire if the missing person has ever filed a claim for benefits. If a claim such as medical, retirement, disability, or death exists, the VA will verify the claim and provide the claim number. Depending on the year the claim was filed, the claim number may represent either the service I.D. number or the Social Security number.

New Identity

To be truly undiscoverable, a person must change both internally (patterns and survival techniques) and externally (appearance).

To issue a Social Security card, a local Social Security office requires only a minimum level of proof that you are who you say you are, and that you were either born in the United States or are here lawfully. If the evidence you present looks good to the individual helping you, a card will be issued. Recently, it has become more difficult to obtain a card if you are over eighteen, because you have to have a good reason for not having needed a card earlier. The Social Security office is on guard for adults applying for cards. I understand that obtaining a card for a child is not questioned and can be done through the mail. If the child is deceased, the Social Security office may not even know. Once the card is issued, no one really checks to see the age of the person the card was issued to. Therefore anyone could possibly use the card on a very limited basis, without getting caught. Social Security does not perform a background check to confirm information.

An interesting observation is that the law only requires you to have a Social Security number to work and receive income in the United States. You are not required to use this number on any other document other than revenue-producing documents (Privacy Act of 1974). Voluntarily giving your Social Security number on medical forms, on insurance forms, and for credit purposes is unnecessary.

The person who has created a new identity will leave a trail, usually a false one, including credit cards and hotel records. Perhaps the most difficult aspect of creating a new identity is to sever all ties with the past. The past is the one link that can catch up with someone who does not wish to be found. Contact with a relative, friend, or associate; continuing a habit, hobby, or recreational pursuit; frequenting a business establishment; being on a mailing list; or following a pattern of any kind can cause someone who is hiding to be located. This is the ultimate game of "hide and seek."

Relatives

To find information about a missing family member, it may be necessary to talk to older family members. Try to talk with anyone who might have researched the family tree, because chances are that person will have already searched libraries, newspapers, and other reference sources.

Social Security records are confidential and not available for public or even law enforcement review. In some instances, the Social Security office may provide certain limited information to the next of kin. Usually the office will verify whether a death claim is on file. On occasion, the Social Security office will forward a letter to the next of kin. The searcher will not receive any information. However, the letter will be returned if the person did not receive it. Therefore it is worth the effort to try this method.

The Internal Revenue Service also maintains an Office of Disclosure, which will forward a letter to the next of kin if the next of kin has filed an income tax return. Again, if the letter is returned to the sender, it never reached the intended party.

Runaways

A runaway can be classified as a noncriminal type of missing person. However, a runaway is probably hiding from a certain individual. Therefore a runaway may go to extremes not to leave a paper trail. In many instances a runaway is running from a very unhappy situation. A runaway may possess a driver's license and have a Social Security number. A young runaway may not have anything but a birth certificate. Usually, runaways become street survivors.

Witnesses

Attorneys need to locate witnesses to accidents as well as for other litigation purposes, both civil and criminal. Often the case is several years old by the time the attorney needs to actually depose or subpoena the witness, and by then the witness may no longer reside at the address given on the original report. Because of the time periods involved, it is not unusual for witnesses to move, which can make them extremely difficult to locate. A witness who is wanted only for a civil action lawsuit may be hiding from bill collectors and may not leave many trails, not even a forwarding address when moving.

3

Starting Your Search

~

REGARDLESS OF the type of search you are conducting, there is almost always a way to follow a trail of information. The beginning of the trail is the factual information you know about the person you are trying to find.

Profile the person you are searching for. Is the person missing because of: marital problems; financial problems; medical problems; career problems; or criminal problems? Does it appear the person is missing voluntarily or involuntarily? Is the missing person a criminal or noncriminal?

It is best to begin a search with a correct full name. However, many times searchers do not know the name of the person they seek. If you do not have a correct name to begin with, your first objective is to find the name.

The most important pieces of information needed to find almost anyone are: correct full name; date of birth; Social Security number; and last known address.

Write down the answers to these questions: Who am I searching for? Do I have a correct full name? If not, what do I know about this person? Where can I find this person's date of birth? Do I know where this person was born or do I have a last known address?

By using the sample checklists found in Chapter Fourteen, take a few minutes to write down whatever you do know about the person you want to find, where you need to go, and what you need to do. Don't weed out anything at this point. By making these checklists first, you will have specific goals to maintain and you will not waste valuable time or money.

Before you leave home to begin your search, refer to your checklists and make any necessary notes, such as directions to a building or office. If you are not familiar with the city in which you are searching, obtain a good street map. Always be prepared. Have plenty of change for parking meters, photocopy machines, and other incidentals. Carry a pen and paper at all times. Get in the habit of writing down everything you learn and experience, including dates, times, locations, phone numbers, people's names, and conversations.

Assuming you have a correct full name, is this last name (surname) a common or uncommon spelling? Believe it or not, the more uncommon a name is, the easier it is to find. Understand that many people change the spelling of their last name. A name may change an "i" to "y" or drop an "e." There may be many variations of the name over the decades. It is not unusual to find brothers who spell their last names differently, maybe by dropping a double letter or changing a vowel. Realize that women may be harder to locate than men because they are likely to change their names through marriage.

What if the person is hiding deliberately? Depending on why someone is missing, the person may deliberately change his or her name, either by switching the middle name and the first name, or by using a misspelled version. Someone who is running from the law or from bill collectors may try to throw off the pursuers in a number of ways.

It is difficult to exist in our society without leaving a paper trail. Even though a person may be hiding, he or she must have the basic necessities of food, clothing, and shelter. It is likely that the person will also have some form of transportation. But is anything on paper in his or her name? How about a telephone? Is the person on a mailing list?

Most people will have some form of identification, even if it is not authentic. Maybe it's a driver's license. Perhaps the person has health, life, or automobile insurance. Don't missing people get sick, need medicine, file medical claims? Missing people (criminals and noncriminals alike) may work, have hobbies and recreational interests, take vacations, and do almost anything the rest of us do.

If someone owes a lot of back child support or has a lot of bad debts and is wanted in order to be served with civil process, that person is going to take precautions to avoid being located. But it's doubtful that all family ties can be broken completely. A sister may receive a check and cash or deposit it for the person who is hiding. A relative may be helping the person hide.

Try to imagine what the person you are searching for must do with his or her time. Is he employed? Does he have hobbies? How does he spend his time? Does he have relatives? Does he visit them on holidays? Does he pay bills? If so, how? Does he buy food and other supplies? Does she have a car? Does she go to a dentist or doctor? Is she ever sick? Does he take prescription medicine? How does he pay for it? Is she drawing some type of unemployment check, disability, aid to dependent families, or other type of welfare?

No matter why someone is missing, there are certain basic needs that must be met. Your challenge is to determine what some of those needs might be, and to try to follow the clues that those needs will produce.

If you do not have a correct full name, perhaps you know a city or state in which your missing person may have lived or where the individual was born. If you know a city or state, do you know the year your missing person resided there? If not, can you estimate the time? If so, what schools existed then? This is the way a trail begins, with whatever information you have at your fingertips or can obtain easily. Think about what the person might have been doing at a certain time. School? Work? A church, club, or organization? What relevant directories might exist? Is there a family cemetery? Are former neighbors still in the old neighborhood? Does the same mail carrier deliver the mail?

During a lifetime, the average American will leave a paper trail that extends approximately seven miles long.

It is important to write down each "clue" because once you begin searching, each piece of information—no matter how insignificant it may seem at the time—may represent an important step in locating your missing person. Imagine that each clue is a piece of a puzzle, and as you find new clues you find new pieces. Little by little you finally have a complete picture—you locate your missing person.

Start with a notebook in which pages may be inserted. As you continue looking, you will locate various documents that relate to your search. Put your checklists in the front of the notebook for easy access.

As you search through information, remember that every state and every jurisdiction may have different ways of recording information, different laws, and different names of courts.

Be prepared to ask effective questions, and act confident when you ask them. Look neat and professional in appearance, and don't overdress or underdress. Don't be offensive in your approach, and remain nonthreatening. No matter where you go or with whom you speak, probably the most important quality you can possess is a good attitude. Be cheerful, confident, and positive when conducting your investigation. Most of all, believe in yourself, and believe in your search.

Basic Investigative Techniques

In most cases of looking for someone, the searcher will have some information to begin with. By listing each fact or rumor you have heard, along with the name of the person you heard this from, you can begin an information log. This log is merely a way of keeping up with information in an orderly fashion. If your subject has no reason to evade you and doesn't realize you are searching for him or her, that person is probably going to be easy to find. You may not be in a hurry and can afford to write letters and wait for replies. On the other hand, if you are in a hurry and do not care about cost, you might want to consider using an information broker, in which case you must have a correct name, Social Security number, or last known address in order for the computer to find information about your subject. The more information you have, the easier it is to locate the person by computer. (For a list of information brokers, send a self-addressed, stamped envelope with your request to U.F.O., Inc., P.O. Box 290333, Nashville, TN 37229-0333.)

In case you do not have a name, date of birth, Social Security number, or last known address, you may want to register your search in a computer registry. I operate such a nationwide missing persons registry that is capable of matching two or more persons who are searching for each other (For more information, write Nationwide Locating Services, U.F.O., Inc, P.O. Box 290333, Nashville, TN 37229-0333). Thanks to technology, finding a missing person is possible without leaving your desk through computer databases and CD-ROMs. It is possible to find a missing person in fewer than thirty days for under $100.

Before you decide which method suits your particular search, study all the methods available and determine what will help you most. Follow these seven guidelines to get started:

1. Identify the problem on paper, preferably using checklists, with all known persons who may be involved, what

you know about each person, what you need to find out about each person, and so forth (see sample checklists in Chapter Fourteen).

2. Evaluate the information assembled on the checklists and decide who may have additional information about the person you are searching for.

3. Plan where you need to go to obtain the information you need: library, courthouse, federal building, neighborhood. Identify where the data may be located.

4. Get into the habit of writing down everything. A daily log of each new clue will make searching easier. Always include date and time, who you spoke with, what was said, and what information you learned.

5. Practice asking questions. Become aware of how you ask questions that get you results—useful information. With practice, you will be able to conduct an interview with a total stranger, making the interviewee feel comfortable and relaxed. The secret to asking questions that produce results is a combination of good attitude, controlled tone of voice, nonthreatening mannerisms, and awareness of your appearance.

6. Learn to be a good listener. To get someone to tell you what you need to know, you may have to listen to unrelated matters. Be patient and wait for an opportunity to present itself. The ability to recognize opportunity and to act on the opportunity immediately is a skill that can be developed with practice. Actually, it's best to lead someone in another direction, away from the issue at hand, before asking what you really need to know. You may have to talk about most anything, but if you play your cards right, the opportunity will present itself, you will take advantage of the opportunity, and the person you are talking to will never notice that you asked.

7. Evaluate and analyze each piece of information to be sure that you have not overlooked any clues, and eliminate any information that is not vital to your search. This will allow you to profile your missing person. What do you actually know? What additional information do you need to find this person?

The most important thing to remember as you read this book is not only the techniques, but the underlying principle—that an almost infinite number of angles can be explored to get the information you need. Be creative with your own variations of these techniques as you go along. Mold them to fit your specific needs.

Some typical sources of information to get you started include the following (in no particular order):

Records: marriage, divorce, birth and death, driving, criminal, change of address, insurance, voter registration, real estate, military, alumni, fraternity and sorority, school, cemetery, funeral home, adoption, hospital, census, legal, and immigration.

Directories: cross-reference, city/suburban, and telephone.

Documents: business licenses, birth and death certificates, legal notices, and obituaries.

Organizations: unions, trade, professional, and civic organizations, and religious institutions.

People: friends, family, neighbors, community members, teachers, and co-workers. (When contacting people, look for both current and former relationships.)

Finding missing persons is nothing more than a combination of knowledge, experience, and resources. Once you understand and master the fundamentals of basic investigative techniques, you should be able to find almost anyone.

The foundation of investigation is the ability to analyze your information. Until you are experienced at this, begin by making a list of what information you have to work with and what you can do with it. Now take what you have written and examine it closely. All information can be examined and evaluated. Analyzing is nothing more than taking a closer look. No matter how little you have to start with, there is always something you can do. In order to know where to look for additional information, it is necessary to have a thorough understanding of public records. Whether you are searching for a criminal, an heir or beneficiary, a witness, someone who owes money, someone for civil process, a relative, or a friend, there is always a way.

I assume you are adventurous and like to explore. Think of your search as a new adventure. Pretend this is a treasure hunt and the treasure is the missing person. Consider each obstacle as a new opportunity, and don't get discouraged. If you are not determined to find your missing person, you will probably give up easily. Do not let this happen! Keep a positive attitude and whenever a plan fails, re-examine the plan and try it again, but do something different. This is persistence. As far as I'm concerned, "no" only means "maybe." I don't give up easily and I don't get discouraged. When things don't go like I plan them, I just "back up ten and try again."

Allow for unexpected obstacles, and be prepared to deal with them. Remember that there is usually another way to accomplish your goal. Don't get discouraged if at first you do not succeed—just keep trying.

4

Gathering Information

~

To EFFECTIVELY gather useful information, a workable plan of action is necessary, regardless of what type of information you need: personal profile, business profile, or a court case. The same applies to finding missing persons. The seven guidelines elaborated on in Chapter Three are worth summarizing here:

1. Write down all the information you know about the person you seek (see sample checklists in Chapter Fourteen).

2. Evaluate the information you have and decide who might have additional information.

3. Plan where you need to go to get your missing information.

4. Keep a daily log of everything related to your search.

5. Practice asking effective questions.

6. Learn to be a good listener.

7. Evaluate and analyze each piece of information that is not vital to your search and profile your missing person. What do you actually know? What additional information do you need in order to find this person?

With everything you learn, whether it be from talking to other people, reading newspapers, or looking through records and documents, remember that the purpose of the search is to obtain facts. Never lose sight of your goal. Many of the facts you gather will seem to be irrelevant, but you can never be sure which seemingly irrelevant facts will turn out to be important. Regardless of what you do, the only thing that really counts is the facts you gather.

Data Collection

A fisherman may not catch a fish, but he will continue to try different locations, different bait, and different techniques until he finally catches a fish. You must apply the same strategy of persistence and determination. Select a target such as a sec-retary or receptionist and make a simple phone call. Give this person the opportunity to tell you all about the company, the boss, and whatever else you may need to know, without directly asking for this information. You can easily say, "Oh, by the way, I was just wondering if. . . ."

For example, recently I needed some information from an office that was not allowed to release it. The receptionist told me she could not let me have the list of names I needed and that it was not for the public. It was 3:30 on a Friday afternoon. My time was running out, and I needed that information within the hour.

After refusing to fax me the list of names I needed, I asked the receptionist, "By the way, what building are you in?" She told me. I talked about something completely unrelated to what I actually wanted, just as a diversion, saying something like "that office is in a great location." I thanked her for her help and never let on that her refusal had bothered me.

My first plan had been unsuccessful. Now it was time for another approach. Banking on the sage advice that you should treat people better than they treat you, I didn't burn the bridge

I had just crossed. Who knows? I may have to turn around and cross it again.

At a time like this it really pays to have friends and contacts. The more sources of information, the easier the search. I just happened to have a friend who worked in that same building and owed me a favor. "Would it be too much trouble for you to go to an office in your building and pick up a list of names I need today?" I asked. "Sure," she responded.

My friend went to the office and talked to the receptionist who had told me on the phone that she could not let me see or have a copy of the list I needed. My friend asked how much the list would cost, paid the receptionist $10, and faxed it to me—no questions asked. I made my deadline, without leaving my desk. How many people would have tried to get that list after the receptionist said she could not let anyone have it? How many people would have tried another plan? How many people would have walked away empty-handed? Do you see my point? I don't give up or get discouraged. I realize that obstacles are merely opportunities in disguise. And you must do the same.

Locating Your Missing Person

To find the person you are searching for, it may be necessary to locate a friend or relative of the missing person to get information as to his or her whereabouts. That kind of information about friends, relatives, or associates may be found in such unlikely places as a newsletter, a church directory, a trade journal, school yearbooks, club or organization membership directories, professional associations or licensing boards, or even a newspaper clipping of a funeral. Perhaps a pall bearer at a funeral is the best friend of your target. A former employer or co-worker may provide information. I have even found people and information simply by calling the court clerk's office and asking if my target person ever filed for divorce. This information may not be available with a phone call in every state or jurisdiction, but there is usually a way to obtain information of some type.

As an example, let's name your target Harry Mott. Here's what we know about him: his name is Harry Mott, and his last known city of residence was Nashville, Tennessee. Let's say that is all the information you have to begin your search. From this information alone, here is what you can do:

Analyze and evaluate the data: Recognize that the name Mott is not common. While checking the Nashville phone directory to see how many Motts are listed, you find out that there are only a few and none are named Harry. This tells you several things: he may have moved away; he may have an unlisted phone number; he may be deceased; or he may be related to some of the Motts who are listed.

Eliminate data that are not relevant: What should we do first? It seems that we have two choices: search for a death certificate, or call some of the Motts listed in the phone book. Either of these methods is acceptable.

You can obtain a death record from a computer database. There are 92 million death records available through my computer simply by entering a name. In fact, I can find all persons who have died between 1940 and 1993 with that name. Once I find a record, I will have the person's date of birth, Social Security number, place of birth, and last known address.

How can you obtain a death record if you do not have access to an appropriate computer database? You can request a death record search in writing (cost: about $30 per record) from Nationwide Locating Services, U.F.O., Inc., P.O. Box 290333, Nashville, TN 37229-0333.

You can write or visit the Mormon church library of genealogical records. These records will go back before 1968 (cost: 5 cents per copy or if you have a computer, bring a disk and download for free).

You can write your state Department of Vital Statistics (cost: about $10).

Records

Our government feels that record keeping is a necessity; therefore records exist, both public and private, on just about any subject you might be looking for. Have you ever considered how many records exist on you? Almost all of your activities are recorded somewhere.

Although most of the following records (listed in random order) exist on the average American citizen, not all are available for inspection by anyone except the next of kin.

1. Birth certificate (P in most states)
2. Birth medical records (N)
3. Baptism/church/religious records (P)
4. Pre-school/kindergarten records (N)
5. Activities (swimming lessons; music lessons; art lessons; Girl and Boy Scouts, etc.) (N)
6. Medical records (N)
7. Social Security number (N)
8. Bank account (savings) (N)
9. Health insurance (N)
10. School records (N)
11. Driver's license/traffic tickets/accidents (P)
12. Employment (N)
13. College (N)
14. Checking account (N)
15. Alumni association (N)
16. Fraternal/sorority organizations (N)
17. Loan/debts/credit cards/credit (N)
18. Vehicle/vehicle insurance (P/N)
19. Voter registration (P, most states)
20. Military service records/enlistment/discharge (N)

21. Marriage(s) (P)
22. Divorce(s)/child custody/child support/alimony (P)
23. Utility/electricity/water/gas/phone (N)
24. Hobbies/clubs/organizations (P)
25. Professional licensing (P)
26. Business license (P)
27. Taxes (real estate) (P)
28. Bankruptcy (P)
29. Lawsuit/judgment/lien (P)
30. Mortgage (P)
31. Property/real/tangible/other (P)
32. Investments/stocks/dividends/other (N)
33. Insurance/homeowners/life/accident/vehicle/
    other (N)
34. Disability claims (N)
35. Workers' compensation claims (P)
36. Unemployment records (N)
37. Employment tax records (N)
38. Income tax records (N)
39. Retirement/CDs/annuities (N)
40. Corporate records (P)
41. Death certificate (P)
42. Funeral/burial (P)
43. Will (P)

(P = public record, N = nonpublic record but the next of kin
may have access)

I hope your brain is clicking with ideas of what public
records you can look for. As you can see, the paper trail seems
to be unending, even after death. Use your imagination and see

how many records you can find, both public and nonpublic, on your missing person. Here are a few to consider:

Credit Information

The Fair Credit Reporting Act provides that credit information may be requested from a consumer reporting agency only for certain permissible purposes, including:

- In response to the order of a court having jurisdiction to issue such an order;
- In accordance with the written instructions of the consumer to whom it relates (a signed release);
- To use the information in connection with a credit transaction involving the consumer on whom the information is furnished;
- To use the information in connection with the extension of credit to the consumer;
- To use the information in connection with the review or collection of an account of the consumer;
- To use the information for employment purposes;
- To use the information in connection with the underwriting of insurance involving the consumer; or
- To use the information in connection with a determination of governmental instrumentality required by law to consider an applicant's financial responsibility or status.

Credit information may be purchased by the consumer involved or any person who meets the above criteria. It is best to have permission in writing from the person for whom you are requesting the information. In case of a dispute over the legality of your request, you will be able to prove that you had permission to run the report. Otherwise, you might find yourself liable for a lawsuit involving invasion of privacy, among other things. Credit information is not something to be taken lightly. Federal laws are very serious, and persons found guilty of obtaining credit information without a legitimate, permissible purpose may be fined and imprisoned.

If you need information on someone and do not have a permissible reason for obtaining the full credit report, you may consider obtaining only the "header" or "footer" information from the report (available through information broker/computer databases), which does not include accounts, only vital information such as name, address, age, Social Security number, employer, spouse, and names of other persons who have inquired about the report previously. This information can be invaluable. I once found a man as a result of contacting a car dealer who had inquired on the footer information of the credit report. By contacting the car dealer and talking to the salesman who had sold the man a car, I was able to locate his current employer and new address. At his office I asked to speak to him, was told he was "in the field," and was given his beeper number.

Almost everyone you give personal information to sells it to someone else for a profit, especially credit bureaus. Credit bureaus know not only your accounts but also all inquiries made about you by other people. They sell your Social Security number, your date of birth, your spouse's name, every address you have used with credit information, and even your employment information. They even allow their information to be available through databases.

Medical Records

The Medical Information Bureau collects physician and hospital records on more than 12 million Americans and Canadians and is the largest computerized repository of available medical records. The files also contain information on drug and alcohol dependency, psychological tests, and HIV test results.

Medical records may be stored in another state and recorded on microfilm. It is not unusual for medical records to be destroyed after the death of a physician or the closing of a medical facility. Some states destroy records after seven or more years due to lack of storage space.

Each state may have a law regarding requesting medical information, but it has been my experience that all I need is a "medical authorization" for release of medical records, signed either by the person whose records are being requested or that person's next of kin.

You may also want to look for a workers' compensation claim. Anyone who may have been involved in a work-related injury probably filed a report of some type and you should not have any trouble obtaining a copy. Check a telephone book for the state office that handles these claims.

Landlord Evictions

There is a database called Evictalert that contains records of persons reported by their landlords for failure to pay rent or for damage to rental property. Available through National Credit Information (NCI, which is accessible by certain professional legitimate businesses only), it has not been around a long time and is not complete, but it is a database worth checking if you are looking for someone who owes money or has a criminal past.

Financial Records

FINCEN is the federal government's Financial Central Record Database, which contains recorded financial transactions of every American citizen. FINCEN is fed information from your bank account, credit card, taxes, and any other transaction that appears on paper. Accessible only to authorized personnel, it is said to be the "granddaddy of all databases."

Where Do You Find Information?

From courthouses to churches, directories to death certificates, there is a wealth of information just waiting to be tapped.

Here are a few of the more common—and helpful—places to begin.

Courthouses

If you are searching for records related to property, try the tax assessor's office for property tax records, or the registrar of deeds office for deeds to property including the history of ownership. (While you're at it, why not search for other persons with the same last name and see if any of them are related to the person you seek?)

If the family you seek still owns the house, the registrar of deeds will show no record of a transaction transferring ownership of the property. If your missing person has sold the property outright, or is holding a second mortgage, the county recorder will almost always have a record of it. In the latter case, the county recorder and the present owner should both have the seller's new address. If the property was sold outright, look for the real estate office that handled the transaction, the mortgage company that arranged the loan, a bank, a notary, or an attorney. Contact the new owner and/or neighbors and ask for the name of friends or relatives who might know what happened to the person you seek.

Department of Motor Vehicles

Every state has a Department of Motor Vehicles (DMV), which maintains current and historical records of all drivers and their automobiles. Most states' records are accessible through a database. A quick look at your own driver's license shows how useful these records can be. Your full name, current address, date of birth, possibly a Social Security number (in some states this is the driver's license number), and your physical description are all right there. A check of your driving history will reveal accidents, tickets (even in other states), and dates of any violations or arrests. Although these records may not be considered public information in every state, most

DMVs will release this data if there is "good cause." Most states require as little information as the person's name and date of birth. Databases also allow vehicle license plates and/or vehicle identification numbers to be traced. Information brokers may have access to records using a name only.

Libraries

Finding information in a library is like finding a buried treasure. It's there, but it's up to you to uncover it. The reference librarian can direct you to the source that will be the most helpful. Of course, the main branch will have more information than a smaller branch.

Always be prepared for unanticipated expenses, making sure to have plenty of change for parking and photocopies, a pen and tablet to take notes with, and a checklist of what to look for.

Before visiting the library, call to see if it has current, as well as older, editions of city/suburban directories, and cross-reference directories or other materials you anticipate needing. Ask what information is available on CD-ROM, microfilm, and microfiche. Are the photocopy machines working? How much do they charge for making photocopies? What are the library hours? Are researchers available, and if so are they volunteers or do they charge a fee? How much? It may be cost effective to pay someone to do your work for you. If the public library doesn't have what you need, consider a university library.

The reference section of a public library, especially the main library, contains valuable reference material in book form, on computer, on microfiche, and on microfilm. Older records and documents may be found at the state archives. Local courthouses also maintain some form of storage for old records and may also have archives. Seldom are records completely destroyed.

The reference librarian is extremely knowledgeable and will assist you if you ask for help. If you are unable to visit a library in person, you may request information by mail. Some libraries have volunteers who can research for you. Call and ask for the price of photocopies and the name of the person you should contact.

Telephone books, cross-reference (crisscross) directories, yearbooks, and city/suburban directories may go back thirty or more years. If you have an old address of a missing person, check the year before and after the person resided there. Are the same neighbors still there? Are they listed in a current directory? Finding a former neighbor could be the key to finding your missing person.

Computers may be available to access an index to old or new newspaper articles, such as birth and death notices, marriages, and divorces. Check with your library about what databases or other computer services might be available. Mormon church libraries are great for genealogical research.

One of the leading database vendors is Dialog Information Services, Inc. DIALOG offers more than 400 academic, business, and newspaper/periodical databases containing more than 200 million records. Another large vendor is Mead Data Central, which offers LEXIS, a vast database system for lawyers, and NEXIS, a system of newspaper, periodical, and business-oriented databases. Online searches can be costly, however. Some will offer lower rates during specific time periods, but you will need to check out the details before choosing this route.

Trade and professional associations and other nonprofit organizations are almost always willing to help you. To find the most relevant group for your search, look in the subject and location guides of the *Encyclopedia of Associations* and the *National Trade and Professional Associations of the United States*. Then contact the research director or newsletter editor of the group. *The Directory of Experts, Authorities & Spokespersons* is the annual volume used by radio and TV talk-show hosts to find people to appear on their shows. It contains a number of offbeat specialties not found in other directories.

Maps, telephone books, city/suburban directories, historical publications, professional directories, who's who directories, newspaper articles, and census records are but a few of the sources of information that should be available at a public library.

For example, assume that you have the last name of the person you're looking for. While researching old city directories, you notice that a particular individual disappeared after a certain year. This could mean he did not have a telephone, perhaps he died, or maybe he moved away.

If you have an address, try making a few calls to the neighbors (using city and cross-reference directories). After locating a neighbor who remembered the family, you may find that your missing person has moved. Now what?

Five things are possible: the house was sold outright; the house was sold but the owner holds the mortgage; the owner may be renting out the house; the missing person was a renter himself; or a relative may occupy the house.

In any case, what you have uncovered thus far will lead you to the courthouse, another helpful source discussed earlier in this chapter.

Mailing Lists

Private companies offer mailing lists of Americans divided into almost any category imaginable—age groups, professions, businesses, households, consumers, geographic regions. They can be categorized as to people who buy insurance, people who hunt or fish, people who own cars, or people who order from catalogs. Mailing lists are available to anyone who wants to pay for them. You may order lists on disks or printed labels.

To request information about mailing lists, look in your yellow pages under direct marketing or mail services. Or see if your main public library has phone and address directories available on CD-ROM.

State Archives and Libraries

Every state maintains archival information for that state, which includes old newspapers, telephone books, current (and past) city directories from every major city in the state, and state and county courthouse documents. Records are available of all persons from that state who actively served in the military during each war. Most of the records will be at least twenty years old. This is not the place to go for current information. But if you need to trace back many years, this is definitely where you should look. Records are indexed, microfilmed, microfiched, and kept in original condition. State archives and libraries are excellent for genealogical and adoption information. Some states have birth indexes, which list everyone born in those states.

The Library of Congress

The Library of Congress, located in Washington, DC, is the largest library in the United States. The National Reference Service will help you over the phone: (202) 707-5522. If you need research from the Library of Congress, there are private researchers who will help you, for a fee.

National Archives

The National Archives is a federal repository whose records date back to the 1700s. It provides a wealth of information, including military, census, older FBI investigations, and family background records. In addition to the national headquarters in Washington, DC, there are twelve regional branches located across the United States.

There is a request for information form that may be completed and sent to one of these libraries. For $10, they will research a name for you.

Contact information for the National Archives and its regional branches can be found in Chapter Fourteen.

Telephone Books

The logical place to begin looking for someone is in a telephone book; but of course you will not find someone with an unlisted number, who has remarried and has a name you do not know, or who has moved to another city. Nevertheless, the telephone book can provide names of family members who live in the same city.

Old telephone books are valuable because the person you are looking for may have been listed previously. Therefore you may find a former address, which will lead you to the neighbors. Possibly a neighbor who remembers your missing person can provide you with information as to the individual's whereabouts.

If you are an adoptee searching for your birth parents, use a directory for the year before, the year of, and the year after your birth. One of the listings may be your grandparents. Perhaps your parents were still living at home at the time of your birth and did not have a phone listed in their name. If you know the city where your birth parents once lived, check directories for the surrounding cities within a one-hundred-mile radius.

Looking up a last name is easy. If you find more than a few that match, you might want to write one letter, photocopy it, and mail it to all of the people with the right last name. This would keep you from making numerous phone calls.

However, if you have only a partial name or a nickname, you may not recognize the name that is listed because it is not the one you are looking for. Over the years I have learned to look for any name that contains the initial of the name I had.

For example, say I needed to locate Edward Tillman. The phone book does not list an Edward Tillman; however, there is a C. E. Tillman. Edward might be his middle name.

Ask directory assistance to check for a listing in the entire area code you want checked, not just the city. You may at least determine if the person has an unlisted number.

Computer Database Information Services

It is not necessary to own a computer or even to be computer literate to obtain information by computer. Information broker services are available to sell you information from their computer databases. There are thousands of information brokers and search services. Most of these services provide the same information at competitive prices, ranging from five to fifty dollars.

In this Information Age, a surname search is possible throughout the United States with a computer database. Nationwide Locating Services provides millions of phone records, addresses, name searches, death record searches (1940-1994), and a world of other information that may be requested by phone, fax, or in writing. Payment in advance is accepted with a credit card, check, or money order.

Most professional brokers who provide information to attorneys, private investigators, collection agencies, credit services, property managers, and for pre-employment screening use a gateway service called National Credit Information (NCI). Through this one service, access to the following information is available: Consumer credit information from more than 1,000 credit bureaus containing more than 350 million files; Social Security number tracing and verification, for name and address identification, more than 300 million files; Address identification and updates, including information on Social Security numbers, employer information, present and previous addresses, more than 250 million files; Nationwide crisscross for cross-referencing names, phone numbers, and addresses, including searches for identifying neighbors' addresses and phone numbers, more than 92 million files; Nationwide driving record information, providing validity of license, moving violations, arrests, and reported addresses assigned to the license number you provide; Nationwide driver's license number search, provided from only the subject's name, date of birth, and the state you wished searched; Nationwide alpha name search, provided from the subject's name, last known address or state you want searched, to determine the driver's license number, record, and vehicle ownership; Nationwide license plate identification search, provided from any plate/tag number you request and the state to be searched, to determine the ownership of the vehicle and all addresses assigned to that plate number and its vehicle identification number; Commercial business profiles describing a business's credit history, profit and loss history, length of operation, type of business, officers, banking and loan references, payment trends, number of employees, sales volume, and more; Nationwide workers' compensation claim searches on your subject by state, to determine number and type of any claims filed; Nationwide business crisscross cross-referencing business phone number, name, and address information, containing more than eight million files; Nationwide criminal history record searches, providing any criminal convictions from the county you wish searched on the subject, or state you wish searched, or any federal criminal convictions at the county or state level (not all criminal records are available by computer at this time); Federal Aviation Administration searches by tail number or pilot name for owner registration information; and Death record searches through the Social Security Administration's Master Death Record File, more than 41 million records.

Not everyone will qualify to use NCI, which constantly adds new databases to its offerings. You must be a legitimate business with a legal reason for needing the information. If you qualify, you will be allowed access immediately. There is a one-time payment ($795 at the time this book went to press) to sign up, then monthly payments of $20 will be charged if you do not use the service. If you use the service, $10 of the monthly charge will be applied to whatever reports you request. There is a fee for each report you receive, ranging from $5 to $50. If you ask for information about someone and no information is available, you will be charged the same fee as if you had received a report. You may try a free online demonstration if you have a computer and a modem. Call (513) 521-4420 and use DEMO53 as your password. If you would like additional information regarding this service, write: U.F.O., Inc., P.O. Box 290333, Nashville,

TN 37229-0333. (U.F.O., Inc., is a representative of the NCI computer network.)

Public Records

Each court and each jurisdiction should have basically the same types of records available; however, each state, county, parish, township, city, or court may call the public offices by different names. Types of public records available at local court-houses and city halls include:

- Registrar of Deeds: Property deeds recorded; Liens/judgments against property/owner;
- Property Tax Assessor: Appraisals; Maps; Properties owned by individuals or businesses listed by name and location; History of ownership of property;
- County Court Clerk: Vehicle license information; Marriage records; Business licenses; Business taxes;
- Voter Registration: Election records; Registered voters;
- Circuit Court Clerk (or equivalent): Divorce; Adoption; Name changes; Child support enforcement; Lawsuits;
- Chancery Court Clerk (or equivalent): Litigation; Judgments; Lawsuits; Divorce; Adoption;
- Probate Court Clerk (or equivalent): Wills; Estates; Committals; Property deeds; Name changes;
- Trustee: Collection of property taxes;
- Criminal Court Clerk: Criminal arrests; Warrants; Court dates; Court costs;
- County Health Department: Records relating to health; Vital records; Birth certificates; and
- Traffic Violation Bureau: Traffic tickets.

Check the telephone book for public offices available in your city or the city of your search. Don't hesitate to call a public office and ask what records are available and if there is a charge for obtaining copies of their files. Ask if the office is computerized. If you want to write a letter requesting the information by mail, you will need the correct mailing address and contact person, as well as information regarding any costs. It is not always necessary to obtain information in person.

State records that might be available to the public include (not all records in every department are public in every state): driver's license history and vehicle registration and title; corporations' annual reports and charters; UCC filings: secured collateral for loans; birth certificates; death records; birth index; marriage licenses; unclaimed property; education department; election commission; parole board; employment security; health department; human services department; mental health department; military department; public service department; revenue department; personnel department; state bureau of investigation; department of transportation; veterans' affairs department; and professional licensing boards.

Federal records you might be able to access include: U.S. Bankruptcy Court; Department of Defense, military branches/locating services; Federal Bureau of Investigation (some investigations are available through the Freedom of Information Act; others can be found at National Archives); Housing and Urban Development; Internal Revenue Service (the Office of Disclosure may forward a letter to a relative); Department of Labor; Transportation Department; Treasury Department; U.S. Postal Service; Social Security (may forward a letter to next of kin); Veterans' Affairs Department (veterans' claims for benefits); and Department of Agriculture.

A list of federal agencies that might help you in your search can be found in the Reference Section.

Post Office Records

The U.S. Postal Service will no longer allow you to request copies of change of address cards filed by other people. Instead, you should mail a letter to the last address you have for the person, being sure to write "Address Correction Requested" on the envelope. It should be returned to you with the current information.

Voter Registration Records

The person you're looking for may be a regular voter. If so, a voter registration card can be a simple way to locate vital information. These records may be located at the county courthouse and should contain the following information: full name, address, date of birth, place of birth, employer, and voting district.

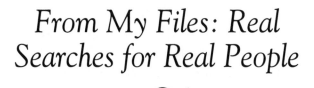

From My Files: Real Searches for Real People

SEARCHES FOR missing loved ones are endless. Many searches result from curiosity about one's heritage; some from necessity; some for medical reasons; and some for identity.

Regardless of the reason for the search, the need to fill a void, the need to feel complete, the need for information is vital to human development. To supress the desire to find a missing loved one only causes problems that may surface in other forms.

Let me encourage you to find your missing loved one and live with the truth instead of the unknown. Whatever you find is better than not knowing. Be prepared to accept whatever you find, because your life will change forever. You can let go of any feelings of anger or frustration that often accompany the unknown, allowing you to feel complete at last.

Sample Cases

A Mother Searches for Her Kidnapped Daughter

   Dear Norma,

> My daughter Bonnie was only six when I last saw her fifteen years ago. I had custody of my daughter

after a bitter divorce. My ex-husband had visitation rights and I was ordered by the court to allow him visits. Fifteen years ago he took Bonnie for a visit and disappeared with her. At first he would let her call me, but would cut her off before she could tell me where they were. After a few months, she was not allowed to contact me again.

I reported Bonnie's disappearance to the local sheriff's office. I called my ex-husband's relatives. I contacted schools and did everything I could think of. Nothing helped. The sheriff's office entered my daughter into a national computer for missing children. The local law enforcement agency contacted the F.B.I. Warrants were issued for the arrest of my ex-husband. I called them regularly, but they never had any news. Eventually I gave up. I never expected to see Bonnie again. I did not believe anyone was trying to find her. No one cared.

I remarried and had other children. One night, my ex-husband returned and set my house on fire with all of us inside. Fortunately, we were unharmed. This man was very vindictive. I feared for the safety of my daughter.

Even though I have exhausted all known means of locating my daughter, when I saw you on television, my hope was renewed. I thought I had done all that I could do, but something made me write you. Can you please help me?

—SANDY

~ ~ ~

Dear Sandy,

Unfortunately your situation is very common. Thousands of children have disappeared as a result of noncustodial parental kidnapping. In order to disappear completely, the kidnapper must totally break all ties with existing family members, friends, associates, and employers and begin a new identity. This is very difficult. To begin a new life with no ties to the old life requires a lot of planning and preparation. It helps to have a lot of money available, because no paper trails to bank accounts can be left behind. How can someone disappear and not leave a paper trail? No more insurance, no checking or savings accounts, no mortgage, no credit, no driver's license, no vehicle registration, no voter's registration, and no contact with anyone.

Choosing to disappear and change identities is a tedious task. A new birth certificate, Social Security number, and resume are issued. You are purged of your name, your history, your friends and your family. You will live among strangers in a place quite your own.
—NORMA

> **Analyze the problem and look for the seed for your solution.**

Bonnie's father is running from law enforcement. He was a known criminal, guilty not only of kidnapping, but also of arson. More than likely he had several aliases and had changed Bonnie's identity by assuming the name of someone who died who was approximately Bonnie's age. (A common way to change one's identity.) Regardless of who he claimed to be and who he claimed Bonnie to be, he made a mistake. When Sandy wrote me, I sent her one of my missing person questionnaires to complete. I was surprised to see that she entered Bonnie's Social Security number. The father had inadvertently neglected to apply for a new Social Security number for Bonnie. At twenty-one, Bonnie was still using the same Social Security number that was issued to her under her real name. This was the seed to the solution.

Bonnie was unaware that she was a kidnapping victim. Her father told her that her mother did not love her or want her any more and that was why she was living with him. Even though her heart was broken, at age six, Bonnie believed her father. She remembered wondering if her mother ever thought about her.

She grew up a victim of kidnapping and child abuse. Her father did not love her and did not really want her; he took Bonnie only to hurt her mother. He was very abusive, physically and mentally. He left Bonnie with strangers and disappeared. A criminal who was running from the law, he was arrested for other offenses; the kidnapping warrant never surfaced.

At the time I located Bonnie, she was living with her boyfriend in Dallas, Texas, and attending college. She was fearful of her father finding her, even though the boyfriend's family was very protective of her. Bonnie thought I was playing a cruel joke on her and that her father had actually hired me to locate her.

When I convinced Bonnie that I was looking for her on behalf of her mother, she was ecstatic. For the first time in fifteen years she was told that her mother loved her and wanted to find her.

A television show had contacted me to arrange a reunion for the Thanksgiving holidays. They requested an emotional situation with a happy ending. This was the perfect choice. Bonnie agreed to surprise her mother on live television.

Getting Sandy to go on television to talk about her daughter's disappearance was not easy. She could not talk about Bonnie without crying and thus was embarrassed. I suggested that she might give hope to other mothers in similar situations and possibly could appeal to Bonnie, if she were watching, or to someone who might know of her whereabouts. Reluctantly, Sandy agreed to discuss her daughter's kidnapping on television.

During an emotional interview, Sandy was asked on camera what she would say to Bonnie if Bonnie were watching. She buried her face in her hands and cried, "Just let me know you are alive."

The host then exclaimed, "Today is your day; here is your baby!"
Bonnie then rushed out from the wings to meet her mother. Needless
to say, there was not a dry eye in the studio. Chances are, there
weren't many in the viewers' homes, either.

Bonnie and Sandy had a lot of catching up to do. Thirty mem-
bers of the family gathered for Thanksgiving dinner, bringing gifts to
Bonnie to welcome her home. She met brothers and sisters she did
not know she had.

After the reunion, Bonnie returned to Dallas and married her
boyfriend. I attended the wedding. A year later, Bonnie gave birth to
a daughter.

A Sister Looks for Her Brother

Dear Norma,

Seventeen years ago my brother and his wife separated. They had two small children. While my brother was home for a visit, he was notified that his year-
old-baby had drowned in the bathtub. The last time I
saw my brother was when I took him to the airport to
return for his daughter's funeral. He was never heard
from again. He was deeply depressed over his failed
marriage, and the death of the baby was devastating. I
do not know whether my brother is dead or alive. I do
not know why he never contacted our family again. I
have tried to locate him, but no one has seen or heard
from him since the baby's funeral. I do not know
where to turn. I want to find my brother. His family
loves him and misses him very much. I am enclosing
his full name, date of birth, Social Security number,
and last known address.

—DIANE

≈ ≈ ≈

Dear Diane,

Seventeen years is a long time for someone not to contact his family. I suspect that there must have been a family problem you failed to mention. Ordinarily, people do not leave a happy, well-adjusted home. I understand your brother's depression, and possible guilt, surrounding his child's death. As hard as it is, you must consider that your brother might have suffered a nervous breakdown or has amnesia. He might even be dead. If those extreme possibilities are not proven, he may be on file in a computer database.

The average person will leave a paper trail. Your brother probably has a vehicle and a driver's license. He may be located with only his Social Security number. If he is not deliberately hiding, your brother can probably be located easily.

—NORMA

Because this woman provided me with her brother's full name, date of birth, last known address, and Social Security number, I was able to search a computer database. Of course, not every searcher will have a computer. A simple letter or phone call to an information broker might be all that is necessary for your missing person. For a list of information brokers, send a self-addressed, stamped envelope, to U.F.O., Inc., P.O. Box 290333, Nashville, TN 37229-0333. Be sure to note what you are requesting.

An Abandoned Son Searches for His Mother

Dear Norma,

The youngest of six children, I am a thirty-year-old married man who has not seen or heard from my mother since I was ten. My father was very abusive and an alcoholic. My mother married him when she was sixteen. I love my mother very much and I miss her every day.

I worry whether she is alive. I wonder what happened to her. She did not tell us anything and has not contacted us since her disappearance. She worked as a waitress and did not return home after work one night. Living with the unknown has almost driven me crazy. I have had three nervous breakdowns as a result.

My father's mother raised us. My father, who is now deceased, abused us. My grandmother loved us and was good to us, but she could not take the place of our mother.

Even though everything has been done that can be done as far as reporting my mother as a missing person to the police, in twenty years no one has found out anything. There has not been a trail to follow. I want to believe she is alive. I must know what happened to her. Please help me!

Enclosed is a copy of her birth certificate, a copy of her Social Security card, a photograph, and her father's death notice (he died last year and I assume she does not know).

—JERRY

～ ～ ～

Dear Jerry,

Of all the missing persons I have received letters about, yours is one of the saddest. I know it has been traumatic living with the unknown. Your imagination has probably run from one extreme to another.

I can understand your mother wanting to get away from an abusive, alcoholic husband, but I cannot imagine her leaving six children to be abused by him.

This makes me wonder whether your mother left voluntarily or involuntarily.

If she left voluntarily, she must have thought only of herself, not her children. Based on the information you furnished, it is possible that your father could have murdered her and her body has never been found. I'm sure that thought has also occurred to you.

I'm sure that if your mother is located, you will be healed of all the hurt, frustration, and anger that has resulted from not knowing what happened.

—NORMA

Jerry furnished me his mother's full name, date of birth, last known address, and Social Security number. If she left voluntarily, she probably changed her name. If she left involuntarily, there is probably no paper trail. If there is no trail whatsoever after twenty years, Jerry's mother may be deceased.

If she left voluntarily and changed her identity, did she change her Social Security number? Probably not. The seed for the solution to this problem is the Social Security number. By running this number through my computer database, Jerry's mother was located immediately. Instead of Joan, she is now Jane Brown, married and living in Georgia. (Jerry's mother never divorced her first husband.)

I attempted to contact Jane Brown by phone. I left my name and phone number several times on an answering machine, but no call was returned. Eventually I drove to Georgia and located the house. I spoke to neighbors and showed them the photograph. The neighbors identified the photograph as the woman who lived at that address. I knocked on the door and a man (who turned out to be Jane's husband) stated that Jane was not home from work yet. He did not seem curious about who I was or what I wanted, as are most of the people I encounter. I showed him the photograph. He said he had never seen that woman before.

Did I have the wrong person? If so, why did she have the same Social Security number? He did not invite me in. I asked if he mind-

ed if I waited for her and he said no, so I waited in my car. When Jane arrived, I told her who I was and that her son wanted to find his mother. She denied that she was the right person, even though she had the two moles on her face that Jerry had described and looked like the woman in the photograph (she denied being that woman). She said she did not have any children. This woman was convinced she was the wrong person, but I believed she was the right person. She even showed me her driver's license with the same date of birth as Jerry's mother's birth certificate. I showed her this and she still denied being that person. She showed me her Social Security number and I showed her the one Jerry sent me. She wondered why that "other woman" was using her number. Jerry's mother was in denial. I had never run into a case like this before. Apparently, the woman had begun a new life, pretending the old life never existed. She was in a state of total denial.

Jane never admitted anything. In fact, she was convinced that I had the wrong person and told me not to contact her again. I showed her Jerry's letter, but it did not faze her. I asked if I could take her picture to show Jerry, and she agreed. Of course, this was my proof that she was in fact the right person.

I did not have the heart to call Jerry and tell him that I found his mother, who did not want any contact with him. I decided to call her sister Liz instead. When I contacted the sister and explained the situation, she thought I must have made a mistake. I told her to be quiet while I made a conference call. I called Jane and talked to her while her sister listened. Jane asked me why I was calling, as she had already told me I had the wrong person. I wanted her sister to hear this for herself. Jane said there was no need for me to contact her again, that she was definitely not the right person. I told Jane I just wanted to be sure that she had not changed her mind and offer her my phone number. "I won't need your number," she said.

Liz was convinced that this voice was indeed her sister. She was stunned. After a few weeks, Liz got up the nerve to tell Jerry, who wanted to face Jane and hear her tell him she was not his mother. Liz went to see Jane first, to be sure she was the right person. Jane *denied having ever seen Liz. She cursed her and told her to get off her property and not to come back.*

Liz broke the news to Jerry. Jane was in fact his mother, but was in denial. Jerry believed that if he faced her, she would admit to him she was his mother. Liz drove Jerry and her mother Ruth to Georgia to see Jane again. While Jerry and Ruth remained in the car, Liz knocked on the door. Jane stepped outside and began cursing Liz and ordering her to leave. Ruth got out of the car and confronted her daughter. Jane cursed her and said she had never seen the woman before. Then Jerry got out of the car and said "Hello, Mother." "Don't call me your mother, I never saw you before," responded Jane.

Jerry, Liz, and Ruth returned to Texas in a state of disbelief and shock. Never in his wildest nightmares did Jerry imagine his mother would not know him, or not want to see him. He was heartbroken.

A week later, Liz's phone rang. It was Jane, asking Liz to tell Jerry that she was his mother and for him to come back to see her. When Liz gave Jerry this message, his response was, "Let her come to see me, I'm not going back."

Jerry called me and told me he had accepted the fact that his mother had chosen to leave him and his siblings. He told me that he could live with what he knew now, that he did not have to worry about his mother anymore. He knew the truth and he could accept it. It was better than the unknown! He sounded like a new person, one whose burden had been lifted. Even though this did not turn out the way he dreamed, I knew he could live with what he found out.

A Brother Searches for His Brother

Dear Norma,

I last saw my older brother when I was thirteen years old, some twenty-five years ago. Matt was in the service, stationed in Korea. He came home once in 1968 and told my mother he planned to marry a Korean woman. My mother threw a fit and told him if he did, he shouldn't come back home, that she would disown him. I have not seen him since.

My other brother and sister have not seen or heard from him, either. We know he may not want any contact with us, but we want him to know we love him and care about him.

He does not know our mother died several years ago. Our grandparents have also died. Only my sister and brothers are left and we will never feel complete without Matt. I do not know whether he ever thinks of us, but he is in our thoughts.

I am enclosing Matt's date of birth, Social Security number, his service I.D. number, and the last known address I have for him.
—CHARLES

~ ~ ~

Dear Charles,

Twenty-five years is a long time to wait. I understand how you must feel. Living without a sibling or other relative causes one to feel incomplete. Subconsciously you wonder what is going on in his life. Is he happy? Is he healthy?

I realize you and your siblings have a need to find Matt. I bet he cares very much for you, but was so hurt by your mother that he could not bear to contact anyone from home again. I'm sure he has many happy memories of you. From what you have told me, I believe Matt will be glad to hear from you and I encourage you to find him.
—NORMA

Charles could locate Matt in one day if he knew how. With a full name, date of birth, Social Security number, last known address, and a service I.D. number, almost anyone can be located!

With the name and date of birth, Charles could get Matt's driver's license by writing each state or contacting an information broker.

With the Social Security number, a letter may be forwarded by the Social Security office. Also, the Social Security number can be run through a computer database and chances are he can be located easily this way.

With the service I.D. number, Charles could check with the Veterans' Administration regional office to see if Matt has filed some type of claim.

Divorce Separates a Daughter from Her Mother
Dear Norma,

When I was five, my father returned from Vietnam and took my younger sister and me and left my mother. I never saw my mother again. I am now thirty-three years old and have always resented my father for doing this to us. I have asked him repeatedly to help me find my mother but he refuses to help. He would never allow us to visit or contact our maternal grandparents.

I have been in counseling for five years trying to learn to control my feelings of anger, hurt, and resentment toward my mother and father. I do not know whether my father abducted us or whether my mother abandoned us. I don't know who to blame or why, and I feel guilty. I have trouble trusting anyone. I live alone and I work, but I have few friends and very little interest in anything. I am in a rut and can't get out. I don't want to live the rest of my life this way.

After I severed all ties with my father when I was a teenager, he finally told me that my mother remarried and told me her new name. Apparently my mother had an affair with this man while my father was in Vietnam (he was actually a friend of my father's).

At one time my mother lived in Alabama. However, she does not appear to be there now. I have tried to contact everyone I can think of. Part of the

problem is that I do not have much information about my mother. I know her first name is Kathy.
—LORI

≈ ≈ ≈

Dear Lori,

The seed for the solution to your problem is your parents' divorce. If you could obtain a copy of this divorce, you would have more information about your mother. Do you have a copy of your birth certificate? It may state your mother's correct full name and place of birth, age, and your place of birth. With your birth information you may request your birth records (with a medical authorization). Once you have her place of birth you could check there for her birth certificate, her family, her school yearbook, her school alumni association, death records of her family members, and church records of her family.

Once you obtain the divorce record, you may know some answers as to whether your mother left your father or he left her. The reason for the divorce may be stated.

With your mother's Social Security number, regardless of who she is today, the Social Security Office can identify her. If you contact Social Security, you may be able to have a letter forwarded to your mother for you. But you will not receive any information, other than verification of any death benefits that might have been paid. The Internal Revenue Service has an office of disclosure that will forward a letter to the next of kin if he or she has filed an income tax return.

I believe your mother can be located easily once you get the divorce record.
—NORMA

The parents' divorce record was located and included the mother's Social Security number. When I entered the number into my computer, I located the mother. I contacted her by phone and she said that her new family didn't know anything about Lori and that she would let me know when she was ready to make contact.

About two weeks later, I received a call from the mother saying she had told her family that she had two older children. It appears that this mother left her husband and two children for another man and made no attempt to contact the children again.

Eventually she met another man but did not tell him the truth about her past. When she was contacted by Lori she seemed unconcerned about Lori's problem.

Although Lori now knows the truth, she is having a problem accepting it. Her mother rejected her as a five-year-old child and as a twenty-five-year-old adult. Even in the face of the harsh reality, Lori wants to believe her childhood fantasy, that her mother would embrace and comfort her and tell her how much she loves her when she found her. Isn't that what we all want?

A Mother Looks for Her Son

> *Dear Norma,*
>
> My thirty-two-year-old son, Jeff, disappeared three years ago. His car was found abandoned in the long-term parking lot at the airport. There was no evidence of foul play. I cannot believe my son would leave and never contact me again. The police and other law enforcement agencies have attempted to locate my son, but so far he has not been found.
>
> The last person to see my son before his disappearance was his next door neighbor. According to her, Jeff placed a garment bag in his car. Jeff had a maid who came to his house and cleaned and did his laundry. Jeff told her not to put certain clothes in his drawer the day before he disappeared. It appears he

left of his own accord, but I do not understand why he did not tell anyone what he planned to do. I believe he would have left a note or told his brother or called me and told me he was going on a trip, but he did not.

I have another son who lived with Jeff. The two boys were very different. Jeff was the perfect gentleman, an Eagle Scout. He loved to read and was very quiet. His brother Tim was wild. Tim used drugs and alcohol and was into pornography.

I was married to the boys' father for more than twenty years before we divorced. My ex-husband came from a very wealthy family and inherited a lot of money. He died one year after Jeff disappeared. Jeff stands to inherit half of his father's fortune, which amounts to more than nine million dollars. If Jeff is not located within seven years, the money will be given to another relative. The money is currently in a trust account and I am trying to be appointed as executrix of this estate.

Can you help me find my son?
—RUTH

≈ ≈ ≈

Dear Ruth,

At first, I thought your son's disappearance might be the result of foul play. I realized that the person who had the most to gain by Jeff's disappearance was his brother Tim. With Jeff out of the way, Tim would get the entire estate.

The more I learned about Jeff, the more I became convinced that Jeff was so unhappy with his family that he probably wanted to create a new life with a new identity. Because he was very fond of adventure books, and he was an Eagle Scout, it would not surprise me to find him surviving almost anywhere. He told the maid not to put certain clothes away, including cut-off jeans. I presume that he planned to go to a warm climate. The one thing that I could not understand was why his brother refused to talk to me. It appeared that he knew more than he was willing to tell. Whatever his reason, his behavior was strange. He refused to help me find his brother, including forbidding me to search the apartment. I did find out, however, that Jeff left his camera behind. His hobby was photography and he loved his camera. He would not have left it unless he planned to return soon. It did not appear he left for good. However, an attache case containing thousands of dollars of stock certificates was gone.

Jeff's bank account was not touched and has had no activity since his disappearance. Jeff's medical insurance was still in effect (there were no claims). Jeff's driver's license expired and was not renewed. No paper trails have been found since his disappearance.

The father's computer might contain the stock certificate information, but I was denied access to it. This case was very frustrating because your family, as a whole, was uncooperative. I did whatever I could think of, but without your cooperation, I eventually was forced to give up.

I hope that one day your family will be reunited.

—NORMA

This case took place several years ago and is still an unsolved mystery. In my opinion, the son left of his own accord to escape an unhappy family situation.

A Son Searches for His Mother

Dear Norma,

I was eleven and my brother John was nine when our father left our mother for another woman. We never saw or heard from him again. My mother struggled to support us. This was in 1911. Times were hard, especially for a single mother. We were very poor. Our mother had to work to feed us. We were left at home alone. One day the authorities knocked on the door and took us to an orphanage. They told us that we had to live there because our mother was unable to take care of us.

Every Sunday our mother would come and take us to church and bring us candy. She would stay all afternoon, then catch a trolley and go home. We knew she loved us and that she wanted us to come back home and live with her. Unfortunately, that never happened.

Instead, my brother was sent to live with a family in Tennessee and I was sent to live with a family in Kentucky. I never saw my brother again. My name was changed. Apparently this family adopted me. I learned they paid $2,500 for me.

When I was sixteen, I ran away and returned to Nashville to find my mother. I found the house where we lived, but my mother was not there. I asked everyone, but no one knew what happened to her. I went to the police and the newspaper, but no one could find her. I never returned to the adoptive family. I lived on the streets and worked until I became an adult.

I married and had two sons of my own. As they were growing up, they asked questions about my family that I could not answer. I began searching for my brother until I found him. We kept in touch until his death several years ago. After searching for my mother for over more than sixty years, my sons decided to take over the search. They have tried very hard to find her, but so far she has not been located. I don't expect to find her alive, but I would like to know where she is buried and what became of her while she was alive. I want to know if she had other children.

My sons were able to trace my father to Texas. He died in 1949 and left his estate to his sons. Of course, no one ever notified us. But it would not have mattered, because the orphanage where my brother and I were placed stated on our records that our parents were deceased and they changed our dates of birth. We had no proof or records to show we were his sons. The estate is being held in a trust.

I am now in my eighties. My life has been consumed with the search for my mother. It looks like I will not get my answers before I die. My sons have agreed to continue the search, and their sons after them if necessary. I hope my sons eventually find all the missing pieces and will be able to claim my inheritance.

—ROBERT

$\approx \approx \approx$

Dear Robert,

I researched your records at the state archives library. The books from the orphanage indicated that your birth date was changed. According to the books, your parents were deceased, which obviously was a lie. This is a very unfortunate situation. I have attempted to find a trail for your mother, but the trail ended around 1916. My gut feeling is that your mother either married or moved away. There is no record of her death, marriage, or divorce. She apparently was employed and was listed in several of the old directories. I found a record of her brother also. The family cemetery is located in another county. I believe a county historian or even church records may be located.

I'm sorry your search lasted your entire lifetime. I wish I could have helped more.
—NORMA

Recently a new database has been developed that allows me to search for a missing person using a first name or approximate year of birth only. If I had had this at the time, more progress might have been possible with this case.

6

Finding Your Father

ALTHOUGH I'M not a psychologist, after many years of working with searchers, I've learned that there is a deep psychological need for every child to know his or her birth parents. No matter why the father is absent, his children need to know his identity. They yearn for a role model. They want security and long for love. They wish their father could provide those basic needs and they dream of a long-lost relationship. But even if they will not have those needs fulfilled, mere knowledge about their father will provide the identity that is so vital to human development.

Dear Norma,

My mother came from a very dysfunctional family. She grew up without feeling loved or wanted. She longed for someone to care about her. At age sixteen she got in some minor trouble and was placed temporarily in a juvenile detention home. A counselor was assigned to her. The counselor told my mother that she needed someone to care for and love, that someday she should have a baby, that it would probably be the best thing she could do.

Eventually, my mother left home and went to visit relatives in Nebraska. She met a nice man, Bill, who was older and going through a divorce. Bill was the father of three beautiful daughters. This man was very kind to my mother. My mother thought it would be wonderful to have a baby, someone to love and care for. Bill had beautiful turquoise eyes and my mother thought she would like to have a daughter with this man's eyes. My mother became pregnant, but never told Bill. In fact, she never saw him again after she learned she was pregnant. She moved away and had me.

While I was very small, my mother married and I was raised by a wonderful stepfather, whom I adore. I learned about Bill when I was a teenager. Of course I became very curious and wondered what Bill was like. My mother told me the whole story so I knew I had three stepsisters.

I am now twenty-four years old and I think it is time I found my father and met my stepsisters. Because none of them know I exist, I do not know how to approach them or how to handle the situation so that I do not hurt anyone.

—JENNIFER

~ ~ ~

Dear Jennifer,

Because no one had been told about you, this news could create a major problem for your father if it is not handled properly. Finding people is an awesome responsibility. The approach must be carefully planned and executed. Regardless of what we find, I know you need to find your father and that you have no intention of causing him a problem. I'm sure he will be very proud of you.

Your mother was very young and knew only your father's name and the place he lived when she met him. She knew he was going through a divorce and she had seen his children.

Based on this information I believe the seed for your solution is his divorce record, where we should find his date of birth, and possibly his Social Security number, his employer at the time of the divorce, and his last known address. With this information, he should be located easily with a search for his name, his driver's license, and any vehicles registered to him. Neighbors at his last known address, his former employer, and even his ex-wife probably know his whereabouts. He probably paid child support. Perhaps he still visits his children. Their names should also be on the divorce record, along with that of his ex-wife. All of them may still be in the same state as they were at the time of the divorce. Many people remain within one hundred miles of where they were born and raised.

All the best,
—NORMA

Bill was found. When Jennifer's mother sent him a photograph of his daughter, he was surprised, but delighted. The resemblance between Jennifer and Bill's youngest daughter by his former wife was amazing. Yes, Jennifer has the most beautiful turquoise eyes, just like her father's. Jennifer met her father and her three stepsisters for the first time on television. It was wonderful.

The Most Common Search of All

The most requested search I receive is from adults who never knew their fathers. They either do not know who he is or the parents divorced when the child was young and the father has not been heard from since.

> *Fifty percent of all children are raised by a single*
> *parent (predominantly the mother), and fifty*
> *percent of those children never know the absent*
> *parent (usually the father).*

Reasons fathers are absent include: unwed mothers (approximately 2,500 babies are born out of wedlock every day in the United States); divorce (approximately 3,000 couples divorce every day in the United States); teenage pregnancies; father in military; and/or father unaware of the child's existence.

Living with the Unknown

I've learned from my clients that one of the worst tragedies in life is living with the unknown and suppressing the desire to know. Searchers secretly ask:

Who is my father?
Does he love me?
Does he know I exist?
Do I look like him?
Would he be proud of me?
What is my medical background?
Where did my father's ancestors originate?
Do I have brothers and sisters?
Do I have grandparents?
Would my other family members want to meet me?

Unfortunately, children who live with the unknown fantasize about what they suppress. If they don't know their fathers, they may pretend that their fathers are famous and therefore simply "too busy" for their children. They imagine that they are like their fathers and have talent for something (like ball playing) because their fathers are professionals of some sort. "I'm a good football player because my daddy is a pro," a child might say about his absent father.

Suppressing the desire to know one's father may cause psychological damage that appears in the form of behavioral problems. Children or teenagers are not necessarily bad but sometimes are crying for help. Failure to understand fatherless children's real difficulties may cause additional problems. This may lead to other complications such as criminal behavior.

In Search of Role Models

Nature intended for children to have two parents, and children have specific needs that only a father or a mother can meet, in each one's special ways. When these needs aren't met, development is thwarted and psychological damage may result. Children who have no contact with a missing parent may develop an inability to function normally as adults or to be good parents.

Children who do not have positive role models often do not become positive role models for their own children. Children of absent parents become insecure and have low self-esteem. When they become adults, they realize that for their lives to be "normal" or complete, they must know who their father is. They must find him in order to release their fears and anger.

Cries for Help

Adults searching for a father are not necessarily expecting a relationship with him, although most will hope for a friendship. The search is not meant to cause the father embarrassment, to hurt him, or to seek material gain. Its interest is to allow the child to put his or her need to rest. Once children have information about their fathers, discovering who he is, where he is, what he is like, they can go on with their lives.

The search for a father is a search for the unknown. Regardless of what the child finds, it is better than not knowing. Denying a child the right to information about a father is a form of victimization. The child becomes an innocent victim, and victims need help.

I receive thousands of letters and phone calls from people who want and need to find their fathers. I consider these requests cries for help. I understand the need, and I've learned that understanding is comforting to those searching for a loved one. Knowing that someone understands, is willing to help, and will try to make life better offers them hope and is spiritually uplifting. Finding a loved one, especially a father or mother, is a form of healing—it mends broken hearts.

Getting the Basic Facts Together

To search for your father, it is best to know his name. Only your birth mother, your birth certificate, your parents' divorce documents, or a cooperative relative can provide this information.

Once you have a name to look for, you may find other information or clues, such as what state your father was born in, what type of employment he had, where he lived at the time of your birth, and what school he attended.

Bear in mind that it is easier to find someone with an unusual name than with a common one. Also, it is not unusual for someone to change the spelling of his or her name—"i" may be changed to "e," for example, or "e" to "y."

Begin with whatever information is known. The more information, the better the chances of finding the father.

The four pieces of information that will make the search the easiest are: full correct name; last known address; date of birth; and Social Security number.

If the searcher has these four pieces of information, I can almost guarantee that the father will be found, unless he is deliberately hiding, he is in a government protection program, he is in another country, or he is deceased and his body has not been found.

Tips for Father Searchers

Here are some tips for finding your father:

1. Obtain a copy of your birth certificate.

2. Obtain copies of all your birth medical records.

3. Obtain a copy of your parents' divorce documents, if possible.

4. Assemble on paper all known information, and list all possible places to search. Each piece of information is a clue that should lead to another piece of information. With a name only, a search may begin in a library, courthouse, or computer.

A reference librarian can suggest available search materials and techniques and possibly direct you to volunteer searchers, genealogists, historians, or other interested parties who can assist you (there may be fees involved). Of course, you also have the option of hiring a private investigator. Public records at a local city hall, courthouse, and state or federal government office may be obtained by written request. Consider sending letters to:

- the last known address, with "Address Correction Requested" written on the envelope;
- Social Security, 6401 Security Blvd., Baltimore, MD 21235, with a request that they forward a letter to your father for "humanitarian purposes";
- the IRS "Office of Disclosure," to forward the enclosed letter to your father. (The "humanitarian purposes" rule applies and you must be the next of kin.);
- the National Personnel Records Center, 9700 Page Blvd., St. Louis, MO 63132;
- a state Office of War Records to verify dates of service of enlistment or discharge;
- the county courthouse of father's birth county for a copy of his birth certificate; and/or
- a Veterans' Administration office, which may have a military veteran's claim (claim number is the service I.D. number or the Social Security number).

Ten More Steps in the Right Direction

Depending on the information you have, you should also do the following:

1. Search for death records for members of your father's family. Obtaining a date of death of a grandparent or relative will lead to an obituary that may contain a list of survivors. This may also lead to probate records for a will or settlement of an estate.
2. Check for school records or yearbooks.
3. Consult census records.
4. Check for driver's license and vehicle, property, and voter's registration. (Driver's license and voter's record usually require a name and date of birth.)
5. Check for lawsuits, judgments, liens, and bankruptcies in case he owes money.
6. Check for traffic tickets and criminal histories.
7. Check membership directories for civic organizations or associations.
8. Check professional licensing.
9. Check with a county historian for possible family cemeteries. A small town's historian is usually a great person to ask for help.
10. Check for a divorce; he may have married several times.

Beware of Fantasies

It is vital for you, as an adult searcher, to be prepared for what you may find. Those who have spent their lives fantasizing (a form of denial) about what great guys their fathers are, and how glad they will be to hear from them, often do not foresee rejection or disappointment. Searchers need to be prepared to accept the truth and to understand that whatever they find is better than the alternative—the unknown.

7

Looking for Your Mother

~

TRYING TO find your mother can be one of the most compelling and traumatic efforts imaginable. Because women are likely to change their names when married, this search can be more difficult than looking for fathers. And considering the fact that your mother is actually the one who gave you life, some would say looking for your mother involves more emotional risk as well.

Four facts—seeds of information—will help enormously: the mother's maiden name; where she was born; where she gave birth; and where she lived when the child was born (in addition to the standard information of last known address, date of birth, and Social Security number).

Dear Norma,

I need your help. I'm looking for my birth mother. I'm twenty-four years old and I was a foster child, along with my sister. We went to a nice family when I was about three or four years old. Through the years, until I was about twelve or thirteen, my birth mother kept in touch, calling me about once a week. I lived in Connecticut (all my life) and she lived in Texas then. I had not heard from her for about ten or eleven years until last year on my birthday. I had a message from her on my answering machine saying that she loves me and misses me. (She said the reason I stopped hearing from her was because my foster mother and the Department of Children and Youth Services told her to stop because I missed her and it was making me upset.)

I'm getting married soon and I want my birth mother to be there. I still love her and my dream is to find her. Please, can you help me or send information on how I can find her? My name is Dawn and I'm in Bridgeford, Connecticut. My birth mother's maiden and married names are Hailey and Stevens.

Thank you.

—DAWN

Finding a Paper Trail

In most states, adopted people can obtain their own birth records (with a medical authorization). Once you've obtained your birth record, you have your mother's name, possibly her date of birth and/or a Social Security number, an address at the time she gave birth, and her physician and insurance carrier. For an adoptee looking for a birth mother, the seed for the search is the birth record. If you were separated from your mother because of a marital separation or divorce, the steps to finding her are different. Usually the mother raises the children. If this was not true in your case, a divorce record is the most useful document.

When a child is abandoned, there is usually very little to go on because there are no trails to follow. Only rarely is any sort of document available. These are difficult searches—practically impossible—unless there is some kind of information.

Sources of Information

The most important thing in a mother search is to begin with the correct name. It's not unusual for someone along the way to provide a wrong name, leading to an eventual dead end. Make sure the spelling is right. If the searcher is around sixty years old and the mother is about eighty, the census records may be the most helpful source of information. The most recent records that have been released are from the 1920 census. However, if you are next of kin, you don't have to wait for another census to be released. You can receive information now from the census bureau.

Making the Right Approach

Just as men and women have fantasies about their fathers, they also have them about their mothers. It's important for searchers to hope for the best. But be prepared for the worst when actually making contact.

Careful preparation must be made. This may be a one-shot opportunity; if it is not handled properly, it can be a disaster. The situation may well be irreversible if it is not handled wisely. A life can be ruined and a chance at a relationship destroyed.

Try to put yourself in the mother's shoes. If someone knocked on your door and didn't explain properly what the visit was about, emotions could prove to be overwhelming. Fears may surface, wounds may be opened, and regret and guilt may erupt after having long been suppressed. The mother may be in a state of denial, unprepared for a reunion. Negative emotions are especially possible if rape or other traumatic experience was involved. An abrupt confrontation with a birth mother can cause emotional and psychological problems, even though the searcher did not intend to cause any harm.

The pros and cons of approaching a birth mother must be weighed carefully before any action is taken. I recommend that a third party make the approach, someone who is not involved emotionally, preferably someone who has experience at this sort of thing. Search and support groups are available in almost every city, and many provide free services. They can suggest an experienced third-party intermediary. Otherwise, a minister or therapist may be the best person to reach out and prepare the way. Regardless of who makes the approach, it should be non-threatening.

Approaching a birth mother requires compassion for her feelings, consideration of her current status, and most of all, courage. Do not do this yourself. Get help from a third party, preferably a professional.

Important Tips

Here are some helpful tips for finding your mother:

1. Learn her maiden name.
2. Estimate her age.
3. Learn her date of birth.
4. Discover her place of birth.
5. Find out her last known address.
6. Look for school records and yearbooks.
7. Search for church directories and baptismal records.
8. Get birth certificates—yours and hers.
9. Try to find death records of family members. Check newspaper obituaries.
10. Seek your birth medical records.
11. Check out the reference library's crisscross directory for the years before and after your birth for all families with her last name.
12. Talk to neighbors, current residents, mail carrier, community historian, the town "busybody," teachers, and social workers.

13. While searching, avoid using the word adoption. Substitute *family tree* or *genealogy*.

In Search of a Mended Heart

The search for a mother is a search for a mended heart. One letter from a woman who wanted to find out if her mother was still alive stands out in my memory as one of the most touching I have ever received. It was written to a local television station after I appeared on a show that featured a mother-daughter reunion. Let me share it with you.

Dear Channel 4,

About four to six weeks ago, I was watching your program and you had a lady on your show who united a mother and daughter who had not seen each other in many years. I did not write down the address but would like to search for my mother and half-brother. I have not seen my mother since approximately 1946, but I did receive a letter in 1950 that was not given to me until after my father's death. I do not believe my mother is alive. She was born in April 1909. Enclosed is all the information I have.

Please forward this letter or write and let me know the address of this lady. Maybe she can help me.
—TERESA

Here is the letter Teresa had received from her mother in 1950:

Dearest Teresa and Dawn,

I guess after these many years of not writing I will drop you a line and let you know I still love you and haven't forgotten you kids for one minute of the day. Hope that you are both okay and getting along well in school.

I am remarried again and he is in the army. I have been married to Howard for almost three years. I am very happy and he is really very good to me. You should see your little brother that we have. He is almost two years old. He was born [she provided dates and the name of the hospital in Battle Creek, Michigan]. His name is John. He sure is a good boy and is as sweet as he can be. Howard really loves him.

What grade are you kids in now? What school do you go to? How is Grandpa? How is your new step-mother? I hope she is good to you.

Battle Creek is a real nice town. It isn't as large as one would think with all the factories they have here. We don't live too far away from the Kellogg and Post factories that make Corn Flakes and all kinds of cereals.

There isn't any snow at all but I have heard over the radio that you have had plenty of snow and cold weather. The winter here is very mild and has been all year.

Well, Teresa, you will be fourteen years old.

I hope you are a good girl. Please send me a picture of you and Dawn. I'll send you a picture of John as soon as I get to town to have some taken.

Write me real soon and let me know all the news, that is, if your dad will let you write. I imagine he has really turned you kids against me. I'll write again if you let me know where you are. I am sending this to the old address.

Love to you both,
—YOUR MOTHER.

Adoption: The Decision
of a Lifetime

~

THE ADOPTION search is a trying one, but it can result in some very satisfying reunions. Here's an overview of the adoption process:

Birth mother makes decision to allow baby to be adopted.
Birth mother may enter a home for unwed mothers.
Birth mother chooses a private or public agency to handle the adoption.
Birth mother has baby.
  Birth mother's medical records completed.
  Child's medical records prepared.
  Child's original birth certificate issued.
  Birth mother signs surrender of parental rights after baby's birth. Depending on the year and court of jurisdiction, the birth mother may have two weeks to one year to change her mind.
Agency takes baby from hospital to either a foster home or the adoptive family's home. Agency may provide "home studies."

Child is placed in adoptive family's home. Adoptive family hires attorney to handle adoption proceedings.

Attorney files a petition for adoption with the court of jurisdiction, usually after the surrender is final (two weeks to one year from date of birth).

Usually one year from the time the petition for adoption is filed, a final decree of adoption is issued by the court.

An amended birth certificate with the child's new name is issued.

Records are sealed and sent to the Office of Vital Statistics.

In actuality, there are several different types of adoptions. Some are done through a public agency such as a state Department of Human Services. Some are done through private agencies, usually connected with religious denominations. Some are independent or private adoptions handled through a doctor or a lawyer. In some instances, these professionals' family members are given a child to raise and the mother disappears. And some adoptions are illegal. Unfortunately, certain adoptions are the result of black market and gray market activities. Some are run by greedy private agencies that care only about money. Some actually sell children. If an illegal adoption took place, the paper trail may be nonexistent or false.

Every person involved in the adoption process has a collection of fears: of each other, about their pasts, and about their futures. As always, the most overwhelming fear is the fear of the unknown.

Here are three myths about the key players in adoptions: adoptees remain children forever and are never capable of making decisions as to what is in their best interest; the adoptive family's relationship with the adopted child will not endure if the child meets a member of his or her biological family; and, biological parents are irresponsible and immature and will remain so for the rest of their lives.

Cast those falsehoods aside, and as you begin your adoption search, keep these guidelines in mind:

- Know the rules of the game: state laws. Read the adoption laws for the current year and the year of the adoption. Request identifying information from the state Department of Human Services. Obtain public records from the court of jurisdiction if available (petition/final decree). Obtain court order to have sealed adoption records opened by the court of jurisdiction. Obtain medical records at birth, with medical authorization. Obtain copy of original birth certificate. Everyone involved in the search needs to write the state a letter waiving his or her confidentiality and requesting that he or she receive any letters from anyone who might be searching for him or her. Consider registering in a missing person's registry.

- Know the players: adoptees, birth parents, adoptive parents. Contact adoption agency and attorneys.

- Know what it takes to win: Learn how to conduct a successful search, how to approach the person you are looking for, and how to prepare for the reunion.

- Play fair: Don't obtain information illegally, and don't lie, cheat, or steal when obtaining information. Respect the feelings of all those involved. Don't disrupt their lives, do harm, or cause trouble.

Special Provisions for Native Americans

The Indian Child Welfare Act of 1978 (Public Law 95-608) entitles adoptees of Native American heritage, including Eskimos and Aleuts, to special rights.

Native American Adoptees also retain their rights of inheritance. Section 301(b) reads: "Upon the request of the adopted Indian child over the age of eighteen, the adoptive or foster parents of an Indian child, or an Indian tribe, the Secretary of the Interior shall disclose such information as may be necessary for the enrollment of an Indian child in the tribe in which the child may be eligible for enrollment for determining any right or benefits associated with that membership."

Birth Parents Looking for Their Children

Let me warn you that when it comes to searching for your child, you will probably not receive a lot of sympathy from anyone. There is a slim chance that one of three people might be willing to help you: the social worker who assisted you at the time of adoption; the attending physician; or the attorney who processed the adoption paperwork.

Birth parents usually don't understand the adoption procedure beyond the point of surrender. They are not aware of the process the adoptive family went through to get the child. They do not know what records exist, where the records are housed, how to ask questions, or how to begin. They are usually told that the records are sealed and that they have no rights. The only thing that most birth parents know is that they had a baby and signed a paper.

Imagine being fourteen years old and making a decision that is irreversible—the decision of a lifetime. You may have been a mother who was not old enough to have a driver's license or vote, or a father who was not old enough to join the military. Yet you had to decide the future of a child—yours.

Dear Norma,

I was an unwed mother at the age of seventeen. I came from a very good family. I fell in love with my boyfriend and I became pregnant just before he was sent overseas. He told me we would marry when he returned. My parents were very ashamed of me. They made arrangements for me to go to another city and stay at a home for unwed mothers. They did not want anyone to know I was pregnant. In 1955, an unwed mother was considered "trash." Although I was ashamed, embarrassed, and humiliated, I did not feel like a bad person. I was frightened about having a baby. I did not know what to expect. Arrangements were made for my baby to be adopted. I was given no options. My parents would not hear of my keeping the baby. I could not raise a baby, I did not know how to support myself. My boyfriend knew I was pregnant, but he was unprepared for the responsibility of a family. I felt that I had no options.

Even though I wanted my baby, I wanted to do what was best for her. I was brainwashed into believing that my baby would have a better chance with a family that could give her all the things she would need. Allowing my baby to be adopted was supposed to be in the best interests of my baby. I never even thought that my choice to allow my baby to be adopted was anything other than an act of love. I loved her and wanted her to have all the things I could not provide. She needed a mother and a father, a secure, stable family that would take good care of her. Giving my baby up was out of love, not because I did not want her.

My daughter is now thirty years old. Every year on her birthday I cry all day and wonder where she is, who she is, and if her adoptive family loves her as much as I do. I only saw her for a short time, but I will never forget her. I wonder if she ever thinks of me, if she hates me for not keeping her. I have lived with guilt and regret for thirty long years.

I eventually married another man. We had three other children. I have told them they have an older sister and they also want me to find her. My life will always be incomplete and I will always have a place in my heart for my first daughter. I want her to know how much I love her.

—BETTY

∾ ∾ ∾

Dear Betty,

I have heard similar stories from almost every birth mother who has ever contacted me. There is a pattern to all the requests I receive. I almost know before a birth mother tells me exactly what she is about to say about the hurt, the guilt, and the regret. I know that being an unwed mother is very difficult, both mentally and emotionally.

After talking to hundreds of birth mothers, I think I understand how they feel and the reasons for their searches. I realize that they have no intention of taking their biological child away from the adoptive family. (In fact, I have never met a birth mother who intended to do that.) It appears to me that there is a lot of misunderstanding about adoptees and biological families searching for each other. I see a need for an educational process to take place in which adoptive families understand the need for adoptees to know their identities in order to develop normally. If denied their identity, adoptees may have problems dealing with the unknown.

I know you need to find your daughter.

—NORMA

I found Betty's daughter. She had been adopted by a doctor who worked at the hospital where she was born. The daughter was thrilled to know her mother was looking for her. She had always wanted to know her biological mother and had always thought of her on her birthday. For fear of hurting her adoptive parents, she had not begun her search, although she had planned to do so without telling the adoptive parents. Once I contacted her, she could not wait to meet her mother and her other siblings. The meeting was wonderful. Betty has also visited Sandra and met her three grandchildren. Sandra felt the need to tell her adoptive parents about finding her birth mother. The adoptive family was not upset, especially when Sandra reassured them that they were always going to be her parents. She wanted them to meet her biological mother so they would know that they had nothing to fear. The relationship has filled a void in their lives, allowing all of them to feel complete and rid themselves of the unknown.

From my perspective, giving up a child for adoption is the ultimate act of love. A birth mother has to sign a surrender terminating her maternal rights forever when she makes the choice to put her child up for adoption. This mother gives up her own flesh and blood, not because she doesn't love or want the baby, but because she loves it so much.

Often in the past, birth mothers were not given options. Usually their parents made their decision for them, especially if they were underage. A young girl who gave up a baby may have lived with regret and guilt, made a thousand times worse by knowing that she had no rights to inquire about her child again.

Dear Norma,

During my sophomore year of college I became a father. I had dated Brenda for four years. We both came from wonderful families; in fact, our families were old friends. I had known her since early childhood. She was a cheerleader at another college. Because we were not at the same school, we did not see each other often. I did not know Brenda was pregnant until about the fifth month. By then, her family had arranged for her to "visit Aunt Ruth." When I learned she was pregnant, I was sure it was mine and I wanted to marry her and raise our child.

Pressure from her family and not being ready for the responsibility led Brenda to give the child up for adoption. I was against this but was not allowed to be a part of the decision. I offered to pay medical expenses and do whatever I could. I felt so guilty and responsible. I was hurt and angry because Brenda would not marry me or allow me to have anything to do with this decision. I had no rights, no say-so about the future of my son.

For twenty-one long years I have lived with guilt and regret. Even though I eventually married someone else and had other children, not a day goes by that I don't think about my first son and wonder if he has a loving adoptive family. I worry that he is abused or needs me for something. I cannot bear to live without knowing who my son is and if he is okay. I need to know he has a good family that can provide for him. If he needs anything, I want to give him whatever I can. I want him to know I have always cared, that he has been in my thoughts since he was born. I need to find my son.

—KEN

~ ~ ~

Dear Ken,

Finding a child who was adopted involves much more than you may realize. After a successful search, which may be difficult, there must come planning, preparing, and counseling with you and your son. You don't just go find someone and appear in his life. Locating an adoptee is an awesome responsibility. Consideration must be taken not to disrupt anyone's life and not to create a problem for the adoptee or his family. Careful planning and preparation are essential.

Because you have initiated this search, I recommend you talk to the biological mother to see if she would like to find her son. She can provide you with the names of the hospital, doctor, the city and state of birth, and the adoption agency she chose to place the baby.

All of this information is very important. Each piece of information is like a piece of a puzzle, so the more pieces you have to work with, the easier it is to complete the puzzle. Once you have talked to her I will go to the courthouse (where the seed for the solution rests) in the city in which she relinquished the baby.

—NORMA

Brenda (who had remarried) said she feared that her new husband might not understand about the son she gave up for adoption. Although Brenda did not want to find her son, she understood and supported Ken's search. She provided the basic information, as well as the baby's original name. She even offered to try to obtain a copy of his original birth certificate.

With the information provided by Brenda, the search began at the courthouse of a small town. Looking through the docket appearance books for the eighteen months after the baby was born, I found that ten families had adopted sons and only one had the birthdate provided by Brenda.

In a nearby town, I found the son, David, working in his uncle's store. I told him I was a private investigator working on a case in the area. He was friendly and easy to talk to. I visited the store twice a week and we became friends. He told me about his girlfriend, who had been adopted and was searching for her birth mother. This was my chance to ask if he too was adopted. "Yes," he said, although he was not searching for his birth parents. "I don't have any desire to find them," he said. "I don't believe they would be people I would be proud of."

I asked him why. His adoptive parents had told him his father was in the navy; therefore he concluded that the father probably was on furlough when he impregnated a prostitute. David thought he would be ashamed of his father.

"Would you want to meet your father if he is someone you would be proud of?" I asked.

"Yes," he said. "If my biological parents are not people I would be ashamed of, I might want to know who they are."

During our next visit I told David that I thought I knew who his father was, and that David would be proud of him. "He comes from a fine family, is well educated, has a good job, and is very successful."

David's face lit up. It was the most encouraging thing he had ever heard about his biological family.

"If you ever decide you want to know who your biological father is, I will tell you," I said.

The next week David said, "I've thought about what you said about meeting my birth father," he said. "I want to meet him."

The father was grateful to me for finding his son, and it resulted in a successful meeting. The two of them have become friends, all the while giving careful consideration to the adoptive family. The birth father wanted to know his son, and not hurt the adoptive family, for he was grateful to them for raising the son he could never forget.

Siblings Looking for Siblings

Dear Norma,

I have a younger sister, Jennifer, who was adopted as a baby. I'm sure she does not know about me. I have wanted to find her since I was very young, but of course I did not know where to look or how to go about doing anything. My life will never be complete until I find her.

Many years ago, I began asking a lot of questions and finally traced my sister to a small town in Illinois.

I found adoption records that told me where the adoptive family had lived, but they were no longer there. I was able to find a neighbor who told me that my sister became a hairdresser and had married. She provided me the name of her husband. I thought I could locate her with that much information. I found the location of the beauty salon where she was formerly employed. However, the salon was no longer in business and I could not find anyone else who could help me. I could not find her name or the name of her husband on any records.

I don't want to give up until I find her. I have gotten so close, but it seems all the doors have suddenly closed and I don't know what else to do. Can you help?

—CHRIS

~ ~ ~

Dear Chris,

You did a great search and came very close to finding your sister. With as much information as you provided me, it only took me a few hours to locate Jennifer and make contact with her. I found a new address for her in another city by accessing her forwarding address from her last known address. With the new address I was able to find new neighbors, and when I contacted the next-door neighbor, I was given the name of your sister's current employer. I contacted the employer and was told that she would be given a message to call me.

Jennifer called me as soon as she got a break. She was thrilled to know about her older sister. She knew she was adopted and had been searching for her biological mother, but did not have much information and had been unable to find her. Jennifer wanted to call you immediately, as soon as she learned about you. While we were talking, Jennifer began talking about her upcoming vacation. She said it would be a wonderful time for a family reunion. She was crying tears of happiness.

Helping people find their loved ones is one of the most gratifying pleasures I have experienced. I'm glad your lives are now complete and I wish you much happiness.
—NORMA

Chris and Jennifer ran up about a $1,000 phone bill before the family reunion, talking day and night in an attempt to make up for lost time. Chris later told me the family reunion was wonderful.

Dear Norma,

I am a thirty-two-year-old housewife with four children. For twenty years, I have been searching for my baby sister who was taken from my mother and placed for adoption. My mother has suffered three nervous breakdowns as a result of losing my sister. According to my mother, she never signed any papers relinquishing my sister. Apparently she was tricked by authorities.

My mother was born with bad eyesight, and by the time she was in the second grade she was having so much trouble that her father took her out of school and began working her in his cotton fields. My grandfather abused her for many years. By age fourteen she ran off and got married to get away from her father. She became pregnant with me. My father ran off and left her. We were forced to move in with my grandfather. My father returned the next year and my mother moved back in with him. She then became pregnant with my sister, Molly. When Molly was only a few months old, my father left again. My mother was poor, uneducated, and unable to provide for us. She signed up for welfare. My grandfather called the Department of Human Services and a social worker came to take Molly, supposedly only for a short time, while my mother looked for a job and housing. My mother was told that she could take Molly on the weekends and visit with her. Every Saturday my mother would go to the courthouse, meet the social worker, and bring Molly home. Every Sunday, my mother would take Molly back. The visitation continued for six months. Then, as usual, my mother went to pick up Molly. Instead, the social worker told my mother that Molly had been adopted by a nice family. That was it. No papers signed, no court order issued. Nothing happened before a judge. The social worker had been my mother's only contact. My mother was devastated. I was only a year and a half older than Molly, so I did not know what happened.

When I was twelve, I found a box containing some papers, including Molly's birth certificate. As my mother told me her story, I learned that she had been hospitalized with a nervous breakdown. I knew my mother was sick, but I did not know why until that time. At the age of twelve, I began looking for Molly. I even went to the courthouse in the town where we lived. I asked everyone at the courthouse to help me find my sister, but no one would help. I even located the social worker and asked her what happened to Molly, but she said she did not remember her. As I grew older, I did everything I could think of to find Molly, but no one ever helped. I wrote the state Department of Human Services, and I told them if Molly ever asked, to please give her a letter. My mother did the same.

I do not know what else to try. I have done everything I can think of. After twenty years of searching, I
have spent approximately $20,000 trying to find my
sister. I do not have any more money to spend.
   Please help me find Molly.
—CAITLIN

~ ~ ~

Dear Caitlin,

   I have done extensive research on adoption and
am very sorry to say the adoption laws are unfair.
Unfortunately, the laws were written many years ago
and the primary purpose of the laws was to protect
the birth mother from being identified. Adoptive
families were not counseled and did not realize that
adoptees need to know their identities. Therefore, a
lot of people have suffered needlessly, especially
adoptees.
—NORMA

The problem began when Molly was three months old, so that
served as a date to start with. Were any papers filed giving the state
authority to take Molly? Was the state appointed as guardian ad
litem for Molly? Who was legally responsible for her? The trail had to
begin at the local courthouse.
   If Molly was adopted, the adoptive family must have filed a peti-
tion to adopt in a court, before a judge. Every courtroom keeps a
daily log of who appears, why they appeared, what the court costs
are, and so forth. This is sometimes called a docket appearance
book. The court also must keep records of what happened with each
case, recorded in minute books.
   To find Molly, I had to look in docket appearance books and
minute books. I had to look for all the families who adopted children
the year Molly was taken from her mother. I was looking for a record
involving a three-month-old baby girl. There was only one record

that matched. This baby was probably Molly. Her name had been changed to Angela. I copied the name of the family and found them listed in the phone book. I called the adoptive family and asked for Angela. Her adoptive mother gave me her married name. When I called Molly (Angela), I was surprised to find out that she had been searching for her biological mother for several years. She had written the state, but the state did not give her the letters written by her mother and sister. She had also been to the same courthouse that her sister and mother had visited in hopes that someone might help her.

Caitlin and Molly (Angela) had a wonderful reunion at Caitlin's home and have become the best of friends. Both of them always wished for a sister, and now they have each other.

Write a Letter to Your Child

No one may have told you this: you can write to the agency that handles adoption in the state of your child's birth, waiving your rights to confidentiality. This authorizes the state to release information about you if your child inquires. You may also write a letter to your child, and if the child is trying to locate you, the letter will be given to him or her.

It is disappointing, often devastating, to the adoptee who inquires when he or she comes of age, to find that no letter is waiting. Their already established sense of rejection is only intensified.

A Matter of Public Record

One stop you'll want to make is the public library. See what the law says about adoption in the state where your child was born. More than likely, the adoptive family went to a judge, had an attorney, and filed with an agency—all before the birth occurred. The court probably gave a trial period of one year before the adoption was final. This means there's a paper trail.

Were the records public? Is the court responsible for maintaining a daily log? Yes. There should be a book somewhere

documenting everybody who appears in court. Although it is
not made public in every state, in many states it is public information. This docket appearance book records who appeared in
the local county courthouse, the date, and the reason for the
appearance.

There may be separate books specifically regarding adoptions, just as there may be separate books for divorces, wills, and
other civil issues. Usually only one court in the courthouse
handles adoptions. Find out which one it is.

A relinquishment is required to terminate the parental
rights so the child may be legally adopted. In most courthouses,
a docket book is kept of all people who go before a judge in a
court of law. Similar to a daily log book, it contains names of
the people and the types of cases that are heard in each courtroom. State and county laws differ, so no one rule will apply to
all searchers. In many states, the docket appearance book is a
public record. If so, it is an excellent place to start an adoption
search.

The search for an adoptee begins with the paper trail at the
courthouse. Look at the appropriate time frame in the docket
appearance book (if it is a public record) for all children who
were adopted through the placing agency that you used. Process
of elimination will narrow the possibility of which child is yours
by sex of the child, the adoptive agency, and other specific
facts.

Your chances of finding your child are better if you went
through a private agency rather than a public one. A private
agency may handle only a dozen male and a dozen female adoptions in the adoptee's county of birth per year.

My advice is never to use the word *adoption* when dealing
with county clerks. Substitute the phrases *family tree* or
genealogical research.

Thanks to modern technology, there is an alternative to following paper trails. Now you can sign onto a missing persons
registry that will match up two people who are searching for

each other if there is mutual consent. Both parties must be registered. I operate such a registry, which I call the Nationwide Missing Person Registry. It is capable of matching two people who are both registered whenever a date of birth, agency, or hospital match. The computer does the work for you. (Lists of people in the registry appear in my quarterly newspaper *Missing Persons*, available at newsstands.) To register your search in this computer registry, you need to fill out a Missing Person Questionnaire, obtainable by sending $10 and a self-addressed, stamped envelope to U.F.O., Inc., P.O. Box 290333, Nashville, TN 37229-0333.

Fearing the Unknown

There are many fears and myths associated with adoption. The adoptee fears rejection by birth parents. He may also fear discovering that his parents were criminal, insane, or otherwise objectionable or undesirable individuals. In addition, there is a concern about receiving bad medical news, such as a family congenital condition or a predisposition toward cancer or heart disease.

Adoptees are reluctant to cause pain to their adoptive families by searching for birth parents, thinking that such a search implies that the adoptive family "didn't love enough" or "didn't do a good job." Adoptees may experience "guilt trips" for asking questions about their biological families. Adoptees have a normal, natural curiosity about their identities.

> *Searching for birth relatives is not an insult to adoptive families.*

The adoptive family fears losing the love of the adopted child or having an undesirable person suddenly enter their lives. They secretly suspect that they haven't lived up to their adopted child's expectations and feel wounded because they've tried hard to be good parents.

The birth parent fears rejection by the child, who may be embittered because of the adoption or who feels abandoned. Birth parents may also fear financial complications or that past indiscretions such as unwed parenthood will be revealed to their spouses and children. Often the birth parent blocks the painful memory of relinquishing a child for adoption.

No Surprises, Please!

It is vital that the birth parent understands the importance of the approach to the birth child. Even though the intent is not to disrupt the child or the adoptive family, unpleasant or even traumatic situations can happen if the approach is not handled properly.

One woman, for instance, wanted to contact her daughter on her eighteenth birthday. This "surprise gift" was a shock both to the girl and her adoptive mother. Because the girl dearly loved her adoptive mother, who was extremely upset by the news, the daughter turned against her birth mother.

This birthday surprise was a total disaster. The girl has never spoken to her birth mother again. The birth mother may never have a second chance because her approach was inappropriate and ill-advised.

A third party is invaluable at this sensitive stage. An experienced private investigator, a search group or organization, a minister, or a therapist with experience in this type of work is preferable to an emotional family member or a blundering friend, however well intentioned they may be.

Looking for Birth Parents

If you are on the other end of the adoption search—the one who is looking instead of the one who is being looked for—

examine the information you know about yourself: adoptive name, adoptive parents, date of birth, city and state of birth, placing agency, and city and state in which the adoption took place.

Dear Norma,

I am a thirty-seven-year-old married mother of two grown children. I am a registered nurse. I was adopted at birth and have wanted to know about my biological family all my life. I was never very compatible with my adoptive family. My adoptive mother has refused to tell me anything about my adoption. I actively began my search for my biological family ten years ago, but have not made much progress.

You were referred to me by a mutual acquaintance. I understand you have found many birth families, as well as many adoptees. When I contacted you, you were kind enough to explain the adoption process to me and you also referred me to an attorney who has been very successful at having adoption records opened by court order.

I took your advice and contacted this attorney. Once the petition to have my records opened was filed by the attorney, the judge allowed me to have my records opened. Not only was I able to view my sealed adoption records, I was able to find my birth mother.

I decided that I wanted to contact her by phone. When I called she immediately asked if I was her daughter. She explained that she had searched for me until about ten years ago. She had given up on ever finding me. We were reunited immediately. My birth mother had married someone other than my father and she had two sons by this marriage. She wanted me to meet her husband and my two half-brothers. It was wonderful to finally know who I looked like and have answers to all the questions I had always wanted to know. Most of all, it was wonderful to know that my mother loved me and cared about me. Having her put her arms around me and embrace me was the most comforting feeling I have ever known.

Not only did I meet my mother, but we also became the best of friends. We both had felt a void all these years and we wanted to heal all the hurt and pain from being separated. My mother told me that she never wanted to give me up, that she was young and unwed. My grandmother made all the arrangements for my adoption. My mother was never given any options. She was told by her mother that she could not keep me. In fact, my grandmother arranged for her hair stylist to adopt me. It was a private adoption. My grandmother always knew who had me, where I was, and who I was. In fact, she continued to be a customer in my adoptive mother's beauty salon and watched me grow up without ever letting me know who she was. My adoptive mother always knew who my mother was and would never tell me anything.

My birth mother told me she loved me and wanted to keep me and had grieved for me all these years. My grandmother would never tell her who adopted me. Once we shared our life stories, we realized that we were separated because my grandmother thought it was best, not because my mother chose to give me up. All these years I have been so unhappy and have longed to know the circumstances of my adoption, yet even though my adoptive mother knew everything, she refused to tell me anything. Because of this, I do not plan to be around her again. She made my life miserable.

Finding my birth mother has made me feel complete. I know the story of my adoption, who my father is, and that I have siblings. I'm sure not many people realize how important this is to an adoptee. I'm sure not many adoptees would feel the resentment toward their adoptive family as I do. If my adoptive mother could have understood how important this void was and what it would have meant to me for her to tell me the truth, I would probably not feel so badly toward her now.

Once I met my birth mother and found that she and I are so much alike, I became very close to her and we love each other very much. My birth mother and I agreed that we wanted to begin our relationship again.

—B.N.

~ ~ ~

Dear B.N.,

I have kept in touch with you to see how things are going, and you have told me what an emotional roller coaster this has been. It sounds like you need to have some professional counseling because you still seem very angry and bitter. This can be emotionally draining and you need to release these feelings. Your emptiness and void are gone. You know the truth. You don't have to live with the unknown anymore. You must let go of the hurt. You need to accept the fact that you cannot change the past and you need to go on with the present and future. You can live with what you know; it's what you did not know that was actually causing the problem.

Searching for a birth parent requires a lot of preparation and you did not have this. You were not ready emotionally for the consequences. It sounds like you may have a touch of guilt about the bitterness toward your adoptive family and anger toward your grandmother.

It has occurred to me that at the time your mother was pregnant, your grandmother thought she was doing what was in your best interest and your mother's best interest, and she loved you enough to want you to be raised by someone she knew and trusted. She apparently did not want a stranger to have you and she was able to monitor your childhood at a distance.
—NORMA

Finding her birth mother has made a difference in B.N.'s life, but she is not completely happy. I think adoptees need to be told about their biological families at an early age. It's too bad no one ever told her adoptive family how damaging it was to not tell her the truth about her birth family. I think laws should be passed making it mandatory for an adoptive family to be counseled concerning the adoptee's need to know his or her identity in order to develop normally.

Write to the state Department of Human Services, Adoption Services, authorizing release of identifying information about yourself and requesting identifying information about your birth parents. (This request is referred to as a Waiver of Confidentiality/Request for Identifying Information.) Include all of the information you have about your adoption, as noted above, in addition to your gender and race. If a search is conducted and consent is not given, you will need to make requests to the county and court of jurisdiction, as discussed later in this chapter.

Your letter might read something like this: "If there is currently a letter on file for me from my birth parents or any other relative, I would appreciate your forwarding this to me. My adopted name is Sally Smith. My date of birth is August 8, 1958. My adoptive parents are John and Sue Smith. I would like to request any identifying information you may have regarding my biological parents as provided in (refer to applicable state law here) and any identifying information you may have regarding any siblings as provided in (refer to applicable state law here). Please place this letter in any file held by your agency concerning my adoption. This letter may be used as a Waiver of Confidentiality. This includes the release of any agency records, hospital records, and court records."

With the information you have on hand, ask the courthouse (for the city in which your adoption took place) which court(s) handled adoptions in the year of your birth (probate, county, chancery, or circuit). Different courts may have handled adoptions, not just one, so make sure you know exactly who was responsible for court records pertaining to adoption the years you are interested in.

Once you know what court records you need to examine, understand the laws of your state regarding adoption for the year you were born. (This may be obtained through a state archives and library or law library.)

If the laws for the year you were born stated that a petition must be filed with the county court clerk's office for probate court, then this is the place to begin. Some counties may use circuit or chancery courts. Some states may have other names, so it is necessary to understand exactly what the laws were the year you were born.

Most legal adoptions require the adoptive family to file a petition requesting permission to adopt a child. This information will be recorded in a minute book, which is similar to a diary. Each minute book should also contain an index. (Entries are made daily of each case that goes before a judge, and each case is assigned a number.)

Each court keeps an account of which cases go to court in a docket appearance book, which is similar to an index. Allow for different counties to have different ways of doing this, but generally most counties will have some sort of record-keeping system similar to an index of who goes to court each day.

After all this searching, it is quite possible that you will still not have the information you need. However, if you do not attempt, you will never know.

It may be that the Waiver of Confidentiality/Request for Identifying Information will be all that is necessary. It may take a while because many others are also requesting identifying information. You may have to wait six months, but be patient; it is the best way to find out.

You may be able to obtain your information through Social Security. Others have been successful by requesting information for "humanitarian purposes." Send the information you have to:

Social Security Administration
Location Services
6401 Security Blvd.
Baltimore, MD 21235

You must enclose a letter to the person you want to contact, but do not seal the letter. It will be read to determine if it qualifies for the "humanitarian purposes" rule. Provide a name, place of birth, or any other information you know will be helpful. The letter will be forwarded to the person you are searching for if it qualifies.

Dear Norma,

My parents divorced when I was a toddler. My mother would not tell me anything about my father. She remarried and had my name changed to that of my step-father. All my life I knew this man was not my natural father. I always wanted to know about my biological father, but my mother hated him. I believe I reminded her too much of my father. She was cruel to me, both physically and mentally.

When I was about ten years old, I found a photograph of a man in an army uniform. It had a name and date on the back. At last I knew what my father looked like and what his name was—James Johnson.

I kept the photograph hidden so my mother never knew. When I was twenty, I began looking for him. I traveled to many cities with my job, and the first thing I did when I arrived in a new city was to check the phone book for all the James Johnsons in that city. You can imagine how many calls (maybe thousands) I made and how much money I spent.

I have tried everything I can think of. Please help me fill the void in my life. I will not be complete until I find my father.

—JAMES

≈ ≈ ≈

Dear James,

Unfortunately, when some parents divorce they become selfish, especially when the divorce is bitter. The noncustodial parent is often left out completely. The custodial parent often wants to punish the absent parent.

Even though your mother did not tell you what you asked, the information on the back of the photograph was enough to give you hope. I'm sure you spent many nights dreaming about your father and many days wondering about him.

You may not realize it, but you have enough information to begin your search. You just don't know what to do with the information you have. Don't feel bad—most people don't know what to do with the information they have.

—NORMA

The seed for James' solution is in his letter—his parents' divorce. This is the starting point, not making random phone calls. Because he was born and raised in Nashville, Tennessee, the divorce must have taken place there because you must file for divorce in the city in which you reside (with a few exceptions). The logical place for this search to begin is the courthouse in Nashville. Once the divorce decree is examined, you should have the father's full name, date of birth, possibly a Social Security number, an employer, and a last known address. Once a person has this much information, there are several ways to locate your missing person (in this case, James' father):

- *Write for a driver's license with a name and date of birth.*
- *Write the Social Security Administration or the Internal Revenue Service and ask them to forward a letter.*
- *Run the name through a computer database.*
- *Check the last known address for a forwarding address or neighbors who may remember the person.*
- *Check with the former employer to see if a new employer contacted that office for a reference.*
- *Check with the military records center for a military record. The Veterans' Administration might have a record of a claim for benefits. The state might have a record of an enlistment or discharge.*

Types of Adoption Searches

In response to the hundreds of adoption-related calls I have received over the years, I created the nationwide Missing Person Registry, a computer database that is capable of matching two persons whose information is duplicated, such as a date of birth, a city or state, or a name. I also began publishing the newspaper *Missing Persons*, which is circulated throughout the United States. The chances of being matched by computer or by someone seeing the search in the newspaper will greatly enhance the searcher's chances of finding the person without actually having to search physically. For details on registering, contact: U.F.O., Inc., P.O. Box 290333, Nashville, TN 37229-0333. Be sure to include a self-addressed, stamped envelope.

A professional adoption searcher may charge an hourly rate or a flat rate. Adoption searchers may belong to a group or may be independent. It is not necessary to hire a "certified" searcher. Private investigators may work on an adoption search. However, there are only a few well-trained, experienced adoption search experts. Most private investigators will not take a case they do not intend to solve, and they should turn down or refer any work for which they are not experienced. Don't be afraid to ask for references and find out if other clients were satisfied. Licensed private investigators are governed by a board of regulators, and if they are charging for services in which they are not experienced or knowledgeable, the board may suspend their license if a complaint is received. Check with the board to see if any complaints have been lodged against a private investigator you intend to hire.

Beware of the "underground" searchers, who may get your information illegally, and for a price.

Certain states will not have open records, and finding any public source of information may be impossible. However, there are attorneys who specialize in adoption and are experienced at having court records opened. But if a searcher tells you that he or she can get you this kind of information without a court order or the legal actions of an attorney, watch out. In the states where some information is available through public records, the experienced searcher should be able to do an adoption search in a matter of weeks. It is quite possible to conduct a legal adoption search in one week. One of the secrets to conducting an adoption search is having good identifying information, such as a correct name, to begin with. Those who do not have a name will have to endure many obstacles. Keep in mind, however, that obstacles are merely opportunities in disguise. Based on my knowledge and experience, I estimate that approximately 75 percent of all adoption searchers will find the person they seek if enough information is available.

The adoption search is more involved than any other search because the search itself is only part of the process of being united (or reunited, as the case may be) with a relative. Both the searcher and the missing person will need to be prepared for the meeting. *The approach to the missing person is extremely delicate.* An inexperienced searcher could ruin a person's life if she does not understand the importance of approach and preparation. Adoption searches can be very successful, and happy outcomes are possible as long as there is a good understanding of the adoption process. Adoption search and support groups exist in every state (see Chapter Fourteen for a list). Check your telephone book for these groups, which can serve to encourage and guide you in your search.

> *One out of every fifty people in the United States is adopted.*

Your individual situation will dictate which search techniques work best. And don't forget the paper trail. Besides the sources described in Chapter Four, remember these pieces of paper that might help you: hospital birth records, original birth certificate, adoption petition, adoption final decree, amended birth certificate, nonidentifying information, court order, medical records, sealed adoption records. In addition, here are several sources that many people have found useful in their adoption searches.

Adoption Agencies

Recently, some states have passed laws requesting adoption agencies to conduct searches on behalf of adoptees and birth parents. Agencies may charge a fee for this service. If you're considering letting an agency conduct your search, make sure you understand what they can and cannot do, and what their limitations are. Don't expect more than they can give you. They are bound by law to do only what the law allows.

Both private and public adoption agencies maintain adoption records of the children they have placed. There may be as many as four copies of these sealed adoption records, with the court, the attorney, the agency, and the state. The agency should have the name, age, and general background information about the person you're looking for.

Agencies are not experienced at finding missing persons, but they may have the last known address or other vital information that will help you. Many times an agency search consists of nothing more than writing a letter to the address where the person was living when the adoption was finalized. Keep in mind that this address is as old as the adoptee. If the letter is returned as undeliverable, in most cases the search is over as far as the agency is concerned. Many of the agencies that have begun doing searches are backlogged with requests, so they may not be able to spend a lot of time on any one search.

Adoptees and/or adoptive parents who are considering having an agency do a search should be aware of one more thing. If a birth parent is located and does not react in a highly positive manner, some social workers might interpret that response as negative, and you will probably be told that the birth parent does not want any contact. (If you make contact with your missing person—in any kind of situation, not just adoption—and that person seems hesitant to speak with you, do not force the issue. Simply leave your contact information, including Social Security number in case you move. Your missing person may want to meet you later. People can change their minds when you least expect it.)

If you do not know the name of the adoption agency that handled your case, write the state Department of Human Services. Include any relevant information about your adoption, and enclose a copy of your amended birth certificate.

Classified Advertisements

If you feel certain that you're searching in the correct geographical area, try running a classified ad in the personals. When placing an ad in a public newspaper that is read by the local residents, keep in mind that identifying someone by name could be embarrassing. Here are some examples that have worked in the past:

> "Looking for lost relative. Urgent medical condition. If you have any information about [insert name] family, please contact immediately."
> "Female born on January 31, 1951, urgently seeks any information regarding parents. Please call [insert telephone number]."
> "REWARD: Genealogist searching for Moore family members, especially with the first name of John who lived in Tennessee between 1935 & 1950. Anyone with information, please call collect [insert telephone number]."

Other Sources

The person you are searching for might have belonged to a trade or labor union. Try requesting information contained in these records.

Professional organizations and state licensing offices are another good place to look. *The National Trade and Professional Associations*, published by Columbia Books, is a reference guide to more than six thousand of these organizations. Most libraries, especially those in universities and technical schools, have this book. Once you have identified an occupation (through city directories, friends, neighbors, etc.), contact the appropriate organizations.

If the doctor and/or attorneys involved in your adoption have moved, the state licensing board should be able to give you some clues to their whereabouts. Often, doctors' records are destroyed if they are deceased. However, frequently hospital records are microfilmed and stored. You may want to check the law of the state to see if you are entitled to all medical records pertaining to you. If so, that means you are entitled to your birth records.

Numerous states have a birth index in their state archives, which lists every baby born in the state. Also try looking on microfilm at a state archives and library for old adoption records from every court in the state.

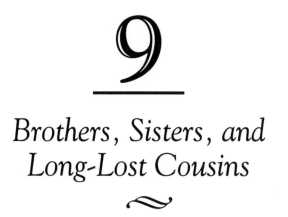

Brothers, Sisters, and Long-Lost Cousins

FINDING A SIBLING requires the same basic information as any other search—a name for which to look. To obtain a name, you'll have to do some groundwork. Start with the information you have. How do you know there is a sibling? Who told you? Is the sibling older or younger than you? Do you know his or her birthday or place of birth?

Begin with a checklist of known information. Once you have the correct full name and date of birth, you can obtain a copy of the birth certificate from the state Office of Vital Statistics. Is your mother, father, or another relative willing to cooperate with you in your efforts?

Depending on the type of search and whether you and your sibling were separated because of adoption or nonadoption circumstances, you may already have the seed for your solution.

Dear Norma,

I am the fourth of six children. Apparently we each had different fathers. Our mother was a prostitute who entertained men in our home.

When I was eight years old, my mother had a boyfriend who told her she had to make a choice—

him or the three younger children. (The others had grown up and moved out.) My mother told me and my brother and sister to get in the back of her boyfriend's pickup truck. They drove us to the country, near our oldest brother's home, where we were told to get out. They drove off without saying goodbye, and my mother did not look back.

We walked to our brother's house. He was married and had a young child with a heart condition. My brother, who did not expect us that night, had a lot of medical expenses to pay. But he took us in and said he would try to raise us. We stayed with him for a few months, but times were tough and my brother could not afford to pay for us. He cried when he told us he would need to call a social worker to take us.

My two younger siblings and I were taken to a home for placement with foster families. It was like an institution. Because of the rejection, abuse, and neglect, I was angry and frustrated. I became rebellious because I felt so unloved and unwanted. I was only a small child, but it seemed no one wanted me. I thought something was wrong with me. I thought I was a bad person. I was classified as a juvenile delinquent and sent to another institution. I never saw my two younger siblings again. That was forty years ago.

Eventually I ran away and enlisted in the military. The discipline was good for me. Even though I became a responsible adult, I could not trust women, and therefore did not enjoy a relationship with a member of the opposite sex. I guess you could say that my mother had ruined my life. As I look back, I realize I was a victim.

When I was eighteen, I decided to look for my mother. I found her, married to the boyfriend. I spent a lot of time and money tracking her down. I knocked on her door and her husband answered. "What do you want?" he demanded. I told him I wanted to see my mother. I was not invited in. He called my mother to the door. "What do you want?" she asked. There was no remorse, no sign of caring, not even a friendly smile. "I just wanted to see the woman who left me on the side of the road and drove off when I was eight years old."

I walked away and never looked back. She did not attempt to stop me, or ask how my life had been, or even ask me to come in and visit. I finally accepted the fact that my mother did not want me. Until then, I think I had been in denial, trying to make excuses for her behavior.

After several years, I met a wonderful woman who understood what I had been through and why I was the way I was. She was the first person I felt loved me unconditionally. I married her and it was the best thing that ever happened to me.

I have continued to look for my two younger siblings, but I could not find them. My wife contacted the home where we were first placed and, by coincidence, my younger brother's wife had contacted them the week before. As a result, my younger brother and I have been reunited, but we cannot find our sister. We want her to know we love her and miss her.

After a lifetime of pain, anger, and hurt, finding my brother was almost a "healing" for me. I know that in order for me to heal completely I need to find my sister, too.

—RICK

≈ ≈ ≈

Dear Rick,

You are fortunate to have a wife who understood your needs and helped you find your brother. I know that you and your brother have done everything you can to locate your sister.

When I am looking for someone, I analyze what has already been done and look for what was not done. In your case, it appears you overlooked one important thing: the foster family that raised your sister may have her Social Security number.

I contacted the foster mother and explained why it was important to find your sister's Social Security number. The foster mother said she had not heard from your sister in years, but she located the information I needed. Once I had the Social Security number, I entered it into my computer and uncovered a new last name. Apparently your sister is married, with her last known address being in Florida.

With that information, I located the neighbors. I did not find a listed phone number, so I could not contact the house directly. The neighbors did not know your sister, but agreed to deliver a message to the house. A short time later, I received a call from a man who said he was divorced from your sister. He thought she was living and working in Georgia, and he provided me with an address.

I attempted to contact your sister in Georgia, but she had moved. Neighbors told me where she had worked, but the former employer did not have any information for me. It appeared that the trail had ended. (I even contacted a private investigator in Georgia and asked her to see if she could pick up a trail, but she was unable to do so.)

Several months later, I was invited to give a seminar in Georgia and decided to drive out to your sister's last known address. It was an apartment complex, and no manager was present. Your sister's apartment was empty, as was the one next door. The only

people available did not speak English. I left my
card in the door of the apartment manager. Several
days later she called to say she was new at the job,
and that she did not have a record of your sister
having lived there. And the post office did not
show a forwarding address. The trail ended once
more.

For now, I'll have to put your case aside. But trust
that I never fully quit looking for anyone, I just don't
actively pursue a search until I have a new clue.
—NORMA

*After several months, it is a good idea to review what had been done
and try again. Never, never give up! I decided to try running the
Social Security number one more time in hopes that an updated one
had been added. Sure enough, this time the sister's number had a
new address in another state.*

*I found the sister, who was in total disbelief that after all this
time her brothers finally had found her. She had lived in many states
and thought that it would be impossible for anyone to locate her. She
had given up all hope of ever finding her brothers. Knowing her
brothers cared about her was the first good thing that had happened
to her in a long time. The reason she was so hard to find? She had
been in jail.*

In Search of Adopted Siblings

If your search is for an adopted brother or sister, what information do you have? Do you know the date and place of birth?
Do you know the hospital? Do you know the city, county, and
state of the adoption? Do you know the adoption agency that
placed the child?

If you are one of the lucky ones who know the placing
agency, and if it is a private rather than a public adoption
agency, you are ahead of the game.

When dealing with a private agency, you may be more likely to find someone who is sympathetic to your cause, such as a social worker. Better yet, the original caseworker may be retired, which means she may feel more free to talk. The social worker who placed your sibling through a private agency may still remember the child and the family that received the child. Furthermore, the agency will probably have a record of the adoption.

Because they deal with such large numbers of babies, and have numerous social workers, public adoption agencies will most likely be less sympathetic to your efforts. (A public adoption agency places several hundred children for every one child placed by a private agency.)

If you know your birth mother, she may be willing to obtain the hospital records of your sibling's birth. The information in the medical records may identify the person who signed the baby out of the hospital, probably the social worker who delivered him or her to the adoptive or foster family. If a foster family was used before placing the baby with an adoptive family, there may be still another trail. (Courts approve and pay foster parents, so records exist.)

Some adoptions are legal and some are illegal, just as some are public and others are private. To identify the adoptive family, a search of the courthouse records of all persons who adopted a child a year or two years after the child's date of birth may turn up names of adoptive families who went through that particular court. Did other local courts also process adoptions in the years of your search? Remember that older children are adopted as well as infants, so you may want to expand the time frame of your search.

Understanding the adoption process is the key to understanding how to find a person who is adopted. (See Chapter Four and Chapter Fourteen for additional information.)

Once the adoptive family is identified, the approach must be planned and executed in such a way as to avoid hurting anyone. Although uniting siblings is not as emotionally risky as reuniting parents with their children, it still requires care and preparation. Consider having a third party make the original approach on your behalf.

If Your Sibling Was Not Adopted

It is not unusual for siblings to be separated because of divorce, and it is fairly easy to find these brothers and sisters. I like to begin with a copy of the divorce decree and obtain information on the custodial parents. It may not be necessary to get your hands on this particular decree if you have a correct name and date of birth. If you know his or her Social Security number, you are almost assured of finding your sibling.

If you are in touch with one of your birth parents, that parent can probably provide additional information, such as the names and addresses of other relatives of the former spouse. The divorced parent probably knows a lot about the person to whom he or she was married. Documents that would include a Social Security number include joint income tax returns, joint bank account statements, insurance policies, and deeds to property.

Once you've located the divorced parent, you may have the seed for solving your search. The former spouse, when found, may know where the sibling is. Finding a half-sibling involves much the same process.

If your sibling is missing because he or she left home and did not return as an adult, your search may not be all that difficult. You have to start with the same four seeds I mentioned earlier: name, date of birth, Social Security number, and last known address. Unless your brother or sister has become a voluntary missing person for some legal or financial reason, is a criminal, or is under protection by the government, or is out of the country, those four pieces of information can take you a long way toward your missing sibling.

If you are searching for a lost brother or sister, you certainly aren't alone. I receive hundreds of letters each year detailing the anguish of separated siblings.

Congratulations! You've Just Inherited . . .

The primary difference between heir or beneficiary search-ing and a normal search for a missing sibling is that you have little information to go on. Usually a name is all there is. In that case, it is up to the searcher to take that name, whether it is common or uncommon, and make the most of it.

The seed for finding the missing person may be contained in the obituary of the deceased. By studying every piece of infor-mation available about the deceased, it is possible to determine the next of kin at the time of death and to get a copy of the death certificate, as well as funeral and cemetery records. (Don't overlook Social Security, census records, insurance, or veterans' benefits that may have paid funeral expenses.)

Back to the Basics

Once you've gleaned everything you can about the per-son in question, you'll need to begin with a plan, and write everything down. Who are you searching for? What do you know about that person? Who can provide additional informa-tion?

Obtain as much information as possible from relatives, fami-ly Bibles, birth certificates, death certificates, obituaries, and other documents.

Write down everything you learn about the missing person in chronological order. As you learn more, add it to your list, which hopefully will include by this time: correct full name; date and place of birth; and last known address.

Explore sources of additional information through various reference resources. For example: public library—city/suburban directory, crisscross reference directory, phone books; state archives and library—old directories, war records, census records, birth records; courthouse—probate records, property records, marriage/divorce documentation; state offices—birth and death records; federal offices—Social Security, military, Veterans' Administration, and Bureau of the Census.

Have a checklist of things to do and places to go. For example: "Call or write for a document, certificate, or other record."; "Go to archives library and look at a 1920 Census microfilm."; "Check public library for obituary in old newspaper."; or "Contact information broker."

10

Best Friends and First Loves

~

WHY DO BEST friends and first loves go their separate ways? There may have been a quarrel, a departure for college, a death, a divorce, a broken heart, a bad decision, or an unplanned journey. Whatever the reason for the separation, the time may eventually come when one or the other longs for a reunion.

To find someone you have not seen for many years, you will have to begin with whatever information you have available. As with any search, this one will be easier if you have a name, a date of birth, last known address, or a Social Security number.

Dear Norma,

I am searching for a lost loved one. I met this man in New Hampshire the summer of 1957. I fell deeply in love with him but lost contact when my aunt and uncle, with whom I was staying, moved from Rye, New Hampshire, to Merideth, New Hampshire. I married and divorced, but never stopped loving this man.

I would like to know if he's married and happy, or even still alive. I want to be able to rest my heart and dreams of knowing one way or another.

I'm sure you've been bombarded with a lot of requests. My family thinks I'm odd and am batting zero here. Maybe I am. Maybe he wouldn't even remember me, but I would like to find out. Thanks in advance for your help.

Sincerely,

—SHANNON

Dear Mrs. Tillman,

I am looking for my first love. He is the father of my oldest son. He was in the Corps of Engineers, U.S. Army, stationed at Ft. Lewis, Washington, in 1941 or 1942.

My son has never seen his father. I am sixty-eight and his father was older than me. He was from Leeville, Louisiana. Please help me find this man.

Yours truly,

—ANN

≈ ≈ ≈

Norma,

To me, friendship is something that should last forever.

When I was a child I went to my grandmother's every summer. She lived in Nashville, Tennessee. I met Sandy and we would stay together the whole summer. When I became a teenager, I still went to Tennessee and Sandy and I would trade clothes, go to the stock car races, and go out on dates with boys. Then we both graduated from high school. Sandy invited me to her wedding and I caught her flowers. I married and she and I saw each other once in a while.

She divorced and married several more times, and we just lost contact. I have found out that she married again and is living somewhere either in North or South Carolina. I have been married to the same man for twenty-nine years.

Maybe if I could find out what her name is now I could find out where Sandy is. Could you tell me how I could find that information?

Oh, by the way, I have two grown boys and am the grandmother of two beautiful grandchildren. So you see, Sandy and I have a lot of catching up to do!

Thank you so much.

—VICKI

Ask Yourself Some Questions

In addition to knowing your missing person's name, there are some other issues to consider:

How did you know this person?
Where did he live?
Where did she work?
Where did she attend school?
Who were your mutual friends?
What do you know about the family?
Is the last name unusual or common?
What was the last year you knew him?

Go to the local library in the city in which your friend lived. If you are no longer living in that city, write or call the library and ask if the reference librarian can look in the crisscross, or cross-reference, directory for the year that you were last in touch with your friend, searching for the last name of the person you seek. Obtain a list of all the individuals with that last name who appear in the directory.

Cities of fewer than fifty thousand people may not have a crisscross directory. If you are dealing with a small town, the library will have old telephone books. Use the reference material that is available. Find out if there are any library volunteers or county historians who could assist you. Almost every town has a historical society with people who enjoy researching families who lived there. There is possibly a genealogist you can call. Small towns often have family cemeteries and the town historian may know where they are located. Someone will help you if you cannot physically do the research yourself.

Who Remembers?

Use your imagination. If nothing else works, you can always place a classified ad in the local newspaper. Ask that anyone with information about this family please contact you.

Here are some other hints:

- School teachers often remember their students.
- Mail carriers remember the people on their routes.
- Church directories list members.
- Cemeteries keep records of all people buried there.
- Funeral homes have records of funerals.
- Courthouses have marriage, divorce, and other records.

Depending on what information you have on this missing person, it is possible in some states to write for a driver's license, vehicle registration, birth records (for an estimated year), and even divorce records. If you remember your friend's former employer, or the school the person attended, try finding someone at either of those places who might give you information. I find neighbors and former neighbors to be excellent sources of information.

First Loves

Your first love may have been in your life many years ago, when you were both very young. You probably have a thousand wonderful memories but precious little information. In most cases, the only thing you know about your first love is a first and last name, possibly a former address, and perhaps a school he or she attended. If it was a girlfriend, her name may have changed more than once since you knew her.

Most people who fall in love when they are very young do not care about personal information and have no need for their lovers' birth date, Social Security number, and, in some cases, even their full name. For some, the meeting may have occurred away from a hometown, during a spring break or a vacation. Often, a first love is a person you know very little about. The less you know, the harder you'll have to work to remember every detail, no matter how insignificant it seems.

Whatever information you can remember is all you'll have to work with. It helps if your first love has an unusual last name, because then you can search the entire United States by computer. (Do this through an information broker if you do not have a computer or if your computer does not have the proper access.)

With only a surname search, it is possible to find the missing person. I have found many people by checking the death records for all persons who died between certain years with the last name of the person I sought. By finding a death record, I find out where the final Social Security payment was made (the last address of the deceased). I also have a date of death, so I am able to check a newspaper for the obituary, which usually lists survivors. By finding survivors, I find the missing person.

No matter what information you begin with, there is *almost* always a trail to follow.

If your first love was someone you went to high school or college with, check with the class representative for the school alumni association. If this does not work, try locating someone who works with school records. Checking old yearbooks and directories may provide a clue. If confidentiality rules prevent you from contacting the person directly, see if someone will relay a message for you, asking your missing person to call or write you. More often than not, someone will cooperate.

Did your first love attend church? Churches maintain records for many years. I have never been turned down for help by a church secretary. As long as you remain nonthreatening to anyone you contact for information, you should not have a problem.

Getting Nowhere Fast?

If you are unable to get information by telephoning, writing, or asking in person, something may be wrong with the way you are inquiring. Practice asking nonthreatening questions in a direct and an indirect manner.

Check your tone of voice. Take note of your mannerisms. Listen to the way you phrase your questions. Polish your charisma. Be as nice as you can be, even if the person does not help. And don't be afraid to smile.

As with any search for a missing person, the approach is important. Disrupting another person's life with an inappropriate approach can be disastrous. Once contact is made, you will be able to determine whether your "best friend" is glad to hear from you, whether your "first love" is now married, and whether you should pursue the possibility of an ongoing relationship.

Helpful Tips

As you look for your first love or an old friend, remember that "no" only means "maybe." Obstacles are opportunities in disguise.

Here are a few more tips:

1. Make sure you have the correct name.

2. Try to obtain his last known address.

3. If you know a birthdate for a man, try looking for a driver's license. (A man will be easier to locate because his name should not have changed as might a married woman's.)

4. If you know a female's father's or brother's name, try looking for him and see if he'll tell you where she is.

5. If you have a last known address, contact neighbors to see if anyone remembers the person or the family. Older neighbors are excellent contacts.

   Ask a librarian, historian, genealogist, or library volunteer to help you research records and find a former address or other information about your missing person.

6. If the person you seek was born prior to 1920, look for a census listing.

   If the person you seek was in the military, try calling the local 800 number for a regional Veterans' Administration (VA) office and ask if the person has filed a claim for any type of benefit. Make up a date of birth if you have to give one. The VA will verify if the person has filed a claim. By asking for the claim number, you will receive either a Social Security number or a service I.D. number. With a Social Security number, an information broker may be able to trace this person through various databases.

11

Men and Women in Uniform: Military Searches

❧

THE MOST COMMON military search is for a father. However, often military friends and buddies who have lost touch over the years decide they want to find each other. Sharing the experience of military life makes service people as close as families. Some would even say that soldiers who fight together in the heat of battle become blood brothers.

If the person you are seeking is on active duty, there are military locating services for every branch of the service. If you know where the person is stationed, perhaps someone there will forward a message to the person you seek.

In one case, I called after 5:00 P.M. on a Friday, needing to speak with someone before Monday. I left a message for the chaplain to call me back, and he did so in about an hour. I asked if he could deliver a message to my missing person. The next day, my call was returned.

> Dear Norma,
>
> My parents divorced when I was six. I have two sisters. My father was a career military officer and was

seldom at home. He lived in other countries and we
hardly knew him. I barely remember him, but I know
I loved him very much and missed him.

After the divorce, my mother remarried and I was
raised by a nice stepfather, although he could never
fill the shoes of my real father.

I am now thirty-three years old, married, and have
three children. My mother died eight years ago.
During this time, someone at the funeral home took a
call from my father, who apparently had been notified
of my mother's death. None of our family was there at
the time and we only got a message that he called.
We were told that he was calling from the Seoul
Garden Hotel in Seoul, South Korea. We never heard
from him again.

I have contacted the military, written Social
Security, and done everything I can think of to locate
my father, but I have not been successful. Can you
please help me find my father?

—ROB

≈ ≈ ≈

Dear Rob,

I requested information from the U.S. Military
Records Center in St. Louis, Missouri, to no avail.
However, your problem contained the seed for the
solution! Your father was at the Seoul Garden Hotel.
I have a large directory of hotels around the world
and I looked up the Seoul Garden. They had a fax
listed. I faxed a letter to the hotel manager and
explained that I was trying to help you find your
father.

Sixteen days later, the hotel manager faxed me
back. He knew your father personally and gave me his
address and phone number. Your father was retired,

but still living in Seoul. The manager had contacted
your father and given him my letter.
—NORMA

*The next day, Rob's father called me. When I told him that his chil-
dren were looking for him, he began sobbing. He said he had tried for
many years to locate his children, but because they had moved he
could not find them. He wanted to talk to his children immediately.
He told me that he would never lose contact with them again.*

Dear Norma,

As an eighteen-year-old soldier in Vietnam in the
1970s, you can imagine how homesick I became. I
had never been away from home before and I was
scared to death.

When I went to boot camp, I met Jack, from my
home state of Kentucky. Jack and I became the best of
friends, but were separated with our duty assignments.
Imagine the thrill I felt when he was assigned to my
unit in Vietnam. We hadn't seen each other for a
long time, but it was like being reunited with a member of my family. We were inseparable and I cared for
him like a brother.

After we got out of the service and returned
home, we lost contact. It has been fourteen years
since I have seen Jack and I would like very much to
find him and renew our friendship. I have attempted
to find him at the address I had for him fourteen years
ago, but apparently he has moved. I moved also, so if
he tried to find me, I was not there either.

Please help me find my "brother." I really have
missed him and would like to know what he has done
since I last saw him. Most of all, I'd like for him to
meet my family.
—BOB

≈ ≈ ≈

Dear Bob,

Sometimes the obvious can seem to be invisible. You knew your friend's full name, date of birth, and last known address. Almost anyone can be found with that much information! You just did not know what to do with what you had.

All I had to do was check for a vehicle registered to him. I found him in about ten minutes. I wish all my searches were this easy.

—Norma

Bob and Jack have vowed not to lose touch with one another again. The last I heard from them, they were planning to spend their vacation together. I love happy endings!

Consider the Possibilities

Many military publications exist in which you could run a classified ad. Many libraries contain service information. Each state has a list of military personnel who either enlisted or were discharged from that state. The National Archives has regional records centers around the country. There are plenty of ways to locate someone who was in the military.

Overseas searchers may be looking for an American father or friend who was stationed in a foreign country. These people may not realize that there are many sources who can help them, even if they cannot come to the United States. If someone from another country has nothing but a name, it is possible to find the name in a computer database. The Veterans of Foreign Wars, American Legion, and other organizations maintain membership lists.

If you know the name, branch of military, dates of service, places stationed, or other information about someone in the military, it is possible to find the person. It may take a lot of research, but there are various ways of locating almost anyone who is—or was—in the military.

Veterans

There are approximately 27 million living veterans, including 100,000 veterans of World War I, more than 9 million veterans of World War II, 5 million veterans of the Korean War, and more than 8 million veterans of the Vietnam War who are still living.

Some government agencies, such as Social Security, Internal Revenue Service, and the Veterans' Administration may have a current address for your missing military person. There may be an office of disclosure within one of these agencies that, upon written request, will forward a letter to a relative.

To have a letter forwarded, you will need to prepare two separate letters. One will be sent to the office of disclosure requesting the enclosed letter be forwarded. Explain briefly your relationship to the veteran, with as much identifiable information as possible about yourself and the veteran. If possible, include some form of identification, such as a birth certificate. Enclose the second letter in an unsealed, stamped envelope with the name and service I.D. number of the veteran written on the front of the envelope. You will be notified if your veteran cannot be identified or if the post office is unable to deliver your letter. Before trying to have a letter forwarded, it is advisable to contact one of the regional offices of the VA to verify if a death benefit has been paid or a claim filed. If the VA regional office furnishes you information, include this with your letter. Make your letter simple and straightforward.

When requesting information pertaining to veterans, it is advisable to obtain the correct mailing address for the office. To contact the nearest VA regional office call (800) 827-1000 and you will be automatically connected. You may verify that a

veteran is listed in their files before you mail your correspondence. The more information you can provide, the easier it will
be for someone to locate your missing person. If you do not
have a full name, date of birth, branch of service, the city and
state where the person entered the service, and/or Social
Security or service I.D. number, ask if the person you seek has
filed a claim. If so, ask for the claim number, which is usually
the service I.D. number or the Social Security number.

The VA has addresses—current at the time of application
for or receipt of benefits—of veterans who have applied for
benefits, such as educational assistance, medical care, disability,
pensions, loans, insurance, and death. VA insurance offices
have information that is not available to the regional offices.

> Veterans' Administration
> Dept. of Veterans' Affairs
> P.O. Box 13399
> Philadelphia, PA 19101
> (800) 669-8477
> To contact the VA office nearest you, call (800)
> 827-1000.

For veterans who have been separated for less than five
years, contact:
> OSGLI
> 213 Washington Street
> Newark, NJ 07102-2999
> (201) 802-7676

To have a letter forwarded to a veteran:
> Dept. of Veterans' Affairs
> Veterans' Benefits Administration
> Administrative Support Staff (20A52)
> 810 Vermont Ave., NW
> Washington, DC 20420

A list of regional VA offices can be found in Chapter Fourteen.

Military Rosters

The VA National Personnel Records Center (NPRC) in St. Louis, Missouri, is responsible for researching rosters of large groups of veterans. The charge is about $2 per name to be researched, payable to Department of Veterans' Affairs. When requesting information, include the veteran's name and service number. If you do not have the service number, try to provide one or more of these pieces of identifying information: full name; date of birth; Social Security number; city and state of enlistment; and branch of service.

The records center will provide you with the following information for each name you submit: VA file or claim number; VA regional office where file is located; If death benefits were applied, the date of death; If no benefits were applied for, notification that no record exists; No information if you did not provide correct information, or they could not locate a record based on the facts you submitted.

The VA claim number, file number, service I.D. number, or Social Security number may be the same. Since June 1974, the VA has used one's Social Security number as the VA claim number.

The National Personnel Records Center

The National Personnel Records Center (NPRC) may forward a letter to a veteran if the requestor qualifies under the following permissible purposes:

1. Requestor's VA/Social Security benefits are dependent on contacting the veteran (dependent relative).
2. Veteran's benefits will be affected.
3. The letter to be forward is in the best interest of the veteran, as in probating a will or settling an estate in which the veteran may be involved.
4. A legitimate effort to claim a debt by a financial institution.

A fee of $3.50 will be charged if the correspondence is not in the veteran's interest, such as debt collection.

If the NPRC forwards your letter to the veteran and it is not delivered, you will not be notified.

A federal court decision in 1990 directed the NPRC to forward letters to the last known address of veterans who may have fathered illegitimate children who are members of an organization called War Babes. (These children were fathered by U.S. servicemen while in Great Britain during World War II.)

In 1973, a fire at the NPRC destroyed about 80 percent of the records for army personnel discharged between November 1, 1912, and January 1, 1960. (About 75 percent of the records for air force personnel with surnames from Hubbard through Z who were discharged between September 25, 1947, and January 1, 1964, were also destroyed.)

State adjutants general and state veterans' offices keep war records, including all enlistments and discharges in that state. The state archives will also have military records. Contact:

National Personnel Records Center
9700 Page Blvd.
St. Louis, MO 63132

Army (314) 538-4261
Air Force (314) 538-4243
Navy, Marine Corps, Coast Guard
(314) 538-4141

Military Organizations

Most military, veterans', and patriotic organizations have newsletters and magazines that provide news about forthcoming reunions. They run lists of veterans who are being sought to notify them of the reunions. When requesting military information always be prepared to provide as much identifying information as possible, such as full name, date of birth, Social Security number, or service I.D. number. Usually military organizations do not charge a fee for locator services, such as forwarding a letter to present or former members.

A list of military organizations that provide locating services can be found in Chapter Fourteen.

Tips for Military Searches

1. Write the National Personnel Records Center for information. A form is provided and a fee is charged.
2. Check state war records.
3. Contact military locating offices for active duty personnel.
4. The National Archives regional library branches contain military records.
5. An information broker can possibly find this person with a name only.
6. With a Social Security number, try a computer database.

12

The Buck Stops Here: Deadbeat Dads and Other People Who Owe Money

~

THE MAJORITY OF parents who don't pay child support are fathers, but it is understood that both fathers and mothers may owe back child support. I will refer to the father as the person who owes child support to keep this simple, but that isn't always the case.

Most fathers are not hardened criminals, and they feel they got a bad deal. They either cannot or will not pay their obligations. They disappear to avoid legal complications.

Of course, absent fathers are not the only kinds of people who owe money. All sorts of people who have debts to pay may try their hand at disappearing.

Dear Norma,

My husband owes me more than $18,000 in back child support. I have a court order for his arrest if he can be located. I'm sure he has a good job and can afford to pay this, but he has chosen to deny his responsibility. I have had to struggle to support our children.

I have waited for the local child-support collection office to find him for five years, but nothing has happened. It seems like they are not even trying to find him or do anything. In our state, once a father fails to pay back child support, he is subject to arrest until the debt is paid.

Sincerely,
—BARBARA

~ ~ ~

Dear Barbara,

Although the numbers will vary according to population, if you use your city of approximately 500,000 people as an example, there could be as many as 50,000 other mothers in your city experiencing the same problem.

With the information you furnished, I was able to locate your former husband in two days. I even found where he was employed and delivered a copy of the warrant for his arrest to the local sheriff's office. Your former husband was picked up and taken to jail from his office. Within three hours, his parents had paid all back child support and bailed him out of jail.

Sincerely,
—NORMA

This man could have paid what he owed, but he chose not to. He had almost all of his assets, including his home, bank accounts, vehicles, and other property in his parents' names. He tried to hide so no one could force him to pay, but it did not work. If he had not had the assets, or his family had not helped him, he would have remained in jail indefinitely until the debt was paid.

The typical missing father probably has moved to another state hoping he is safe. He may try not to leave a paper trail but will continue to live a normal lifestyle. He may own a home, a car, be employed, attend church, have credit cards, be a member of a club or organization, have friends, and visit or contact relatives. How does he pay rent? Utilities? Does he live with someone? Is he self-employed, employed, disabled, or unemployed?

This type of missing person will maintain contact with someone. He is cautious about returning for fear a warrant will be served on him. He feels safe as long as he is far away. There is a chance (however slight) that he will change his identity. He will most likely have an unlisted telephone, use a post office box for mail, and have his property in someone else's name, but he will still use his correct date of birth and Social Security number. He may even remarry and have a new family. Whatever interests and hobbies he once enjoyed, he will continue to enjoy. This missing person will not expect to be caught and will be completely off guard if you do not ask too many questions or talk to anyone who might tip him off. This type of person will run the minute he thinks someone is looking for him. Extreme caution must be taken so that the missing person is unaware someone is looking for him. This can be done in various ways.

One method is to have someone get close to his best friend or closest relative and be very nonthreatening. Without asking direct questions, it is possible to learn much information. Asking the right questions takes a lot of planning and skill. It is possible to talk to someone about something totally unrelated and casually mention something that will make the person you are talking to volunteer the information you are really after.

Until you are proficient in this technique, I do not recommend that you use it. Develop the skill with practice and experience. Talk to people you know. See how much information they will tell you without your asking directly for it. Learn to push the buttons of the person you are talking to. Learn to ask indirect questions that will result in the answers you actually seek.

The parent who has skipped out without paying child support will probably have a driver's license with his correct name and date of birth on it. You should always take a look at the missing person's driving history. Perhaps there has been a traffic violation or an accident. This information could divulge the person's whereabouts. The vehicle that was driven before the disappearance could be the same vehicle being driven now. While it may have a new license plate, the vehicle identification number will remain the same no matter where the missing person goes. By obtaining a copy of the missing person's vehicle title and registration you can also obtain the vehicle's identification number. This number can be traced to a new license number and a new address. It may be possible to obtain this information with only a name.

Not every state will accommodate searchers, but the majority will. You may write one letter and have it photocopied fifty times, then mail each state a request for a search for that vehicle identification number. Each state that offers this service will charge a small fee, usually less than $10.

Some people who owe money never intended to have a financial problem. Thus they were emotionally unprepared when it hit; they panicked and saw no way out except to run. This is often the case with a deadbeat dad. He may be in debt to begin with. When the court orders him to pay child support, he may have to take on an extra job. If he still cannot come up with the money, he risks going to jail.

Whatever his reason for not paying, he probably won't be able to see his child because of the financial default. Children are always the victims of divorce. And when money comes between them and their fathers, they lose again. Not only have they lost a two-parent home, now they've lost the security, stability, love, and nurturing that their father can provide, even if they do not see him on a daily basis.

> *When Dad runs away, Mom loses money, but the kids lose their father.*

Dear Norma,

I represent a client who owns a carpet business. My client extended credit of more than $10,000 to a man named Ken Roberts, who remodeled homes. Mr. Roberts gave false information on his credit application and my client failed to verify the information.

Mr. Roberts has disappeared. Efforts to contact him at the address furnished on his application proved to be unsuccessful as the address was a vacant lot. The phone number was a pay phone booth. Nothing on his application was true, except his name.

With only a name to work with, is it possible to locate Mr. Roberts?

Sincerely,
—K. JONES, ATTORNEY

≈ ≈ ≈

Dear Mr. Jones,

It seems that for every pound of lies therein lies at least an ounce of truth. Such is the case with K. Roberts. He used his correct name.

Because your client has a judgment against Mr. Roberts, and I am actually being paid directly by your client, and because Mr. Roberts signed a release for checking his credit, I obtained a copy of Mr. Roberts' credit report.

From Mr. Roberts' credit report, I learned that a recent inquiry was made from a car dealer near Atlanta, Georgia. I contacted the car dealer and located a salesman who recently sold him a vehicle. The salesman was kind enough to check his records to identify Mr. Roberts' employer.

With this information, I contacted the employer
and verified employment, so you can garnishee Mr.
Roberts' wages.
Sincerely,
—NORMA

*Because Roberts is a fairly common name, I chanced that I could
find him in my computer with a surname search. Thus I was able to
find his new address in Alpharetta, Georgia, and Mr. Jones was able
to collect his judgment.*

A Breed unto Themselves

Deadbeat dads and skiptracers are missing persons who are
deliberately hiding because they owe money. They usually leave
a trail, or at least a few good clues, because they are not professional criminals, although some of them may be borderline
crooks.

Individuals like this continue to survive despite the fact that
they owe money. To do so, they require an income. Identifying
this source of revenue may be almost impossible, especially if
they are self-employed, which is common with this particular
group. They may have a business license accessible only by the
name of the business.

The person who owes money will try to hide to avoid being
found and made to pay. This sort of missing person probably
fears that every time he answers the phone or opens the door it
will be a bill collector, a process server, or even the Internal
Revenue Service.

---

*Missing persons take their habits and hobbies
with them. These activities may provide clues.*

Leaving a Paper Trail

The person who disappears owing money is a voluntary missing person. Not being a professional criminal, this type of person does not know how to avoid leaving a paper trail. The missing person simply moves away and tries to start over. Nevertheless, he is probably going to become lax after a while. Once he gets comfortable in his new life, he begins to leave a new trail. As long as no one has bothered him, he eventually begins to feel secure.

Voluntary missing persons work, own a car, buy a home, and act like everyone else. There is nothing different about these people, other than the fact that they owe someone money and cannot or will not pay it back. Finding their paper trail begins with clues from information known about them before they disappeared. For them to live normally, they have to have certain necessities, which may include: driver's license; vehicle registration; voter's registration; taxes assessed on property owned; financial records; contact with relatives and friends; recreational activities and hobbies; clubs, groups, organizations, and religious institutions.

Whatever the reason for their departure, missing people who owe money have to eat, find shelter, and be transported from one place to another. Unless they've changed their Social Security number and/or date of birth (which involves some fairly risky dealings) or failed to use it, they are trackable.

Tips for Finding People Who Owe Money

1. Learn the full correct name of your target person.

2. Get the date of birth (for discovering driving history).

3. Obtain a Social Security number (and hope it is correct!). That number is a universal tracking number and one of the keys to various databases. Maybe your target will use it for credit purposes in another state.

4. Did he own a vehicle? If so, obtain the title and registration. The vehicle identification number remains with the vehicle and is a good tracking number. Your insurance agent possibly can check an insurance database to see if the missing person has any kind of insurance. If an agent can help you, look for medical claims, automobile insurance, and life insurance.

5. A former girlfriend or spouse who is angry at the target will be an excellent source of information. His enemies are your best friends!

6. Unsuspecting relatives may know of the debtor's whereabouts but probably will not cooperate. It is up to you to find a friendly, nonthreatening way to make contact with a relative or friend. The indirect approach is best.

7. Neighbors and former business associates may provide new clues.

8. Other persons may also be looking for him for collection purposes. Maybe by pooling your resources and sharing and comparing information, everyone involved will have a better chance of locating the person and claiming their money.

13

Tracing Your Family Tree

~

TRACING YOUR family tree can be as much fun as a treasure hunt. You never know where you might have to look to
find your treasure: information about your family.

When you begin to trace your family tree, it is important to
realize the value of every piece of information, no matter how
insignificant it may seem. Each piece will lead to another piece.
Every single name, address, date of birth, place of birth, place of
death, and all survivors must be carefully examined and ana-
lyzed.

Dear Norma,

After watching you on the "Sally Jessy Raphael"
show, I thought you could help me. I am in the
process of tracing my family tree and would appreciate any help or advice that you could offer. I have
already traced my mother's family history back to our
Jewish ancestors in Europe, but I would like to continue my search.
Please contact me if you can assist me in any way.
Sincerely,
—TERRI

151

No matter how little information you have, take time to start a log or record with each name. See how much other information you can list pertaining to that name. Depending on the time period you are working with, perhaps there was a will or an estate involved. There may have been property, so a deed and tax records might exist at the state archives and library.

Obviously the logical place to begin your family tree is with your birth certificate. I realize some people do not have one. Often the only record is the family Bible, because births and deaths were not recorded publicly until around the turn of the twentieth century. Church records and family Bibles also contain listings of baptisms, marriages, and deaths.

Original documents are the primary source of accurate genealogical information because they are records that were created at the time of important events in your ancestors' lives. For example, a local church or the local government may have recorded your ancestors' births, christenings/baptisms, marriages, and deaths/burials. In addition to civil and church records, original documents may also include census, military, immigration, land, and court records.

Dear Mrs. Tillman,

I have recently returned from Virginia. A friend there showed me a book that listed old Virginia families. There were many people on that list with my maiden name, which is an unusual one. My father's family is from Illinois, so I was surprised to find such a large group of them in Virginia. American history is a hobby of mine, and now I'm wondering if my family dates back to the American Revolution and the thirteen colonies. How can I find out?

I've enclosed a self-addressed, stamped envelope

for any information you might have about tracing
genealogies. Thanks.
     Sincerely,
     —NICOLE

Everyone wants to know something about his or her ancestry. All children, including adoptees and those living with their
natural parents, have a difficult time forming their identity. The
struggle is more complicated and fraught with anxiety for those
whose ancestry is unknown to them. At some time or other,
everyone asks the same questions: Who am I? Where did I
come from? What makes me the way I am?

As you can see from the sample of letters I've received, people from many backgrounds want to know more about their
families, their ancestors, and their cultural heritage. Whatever
you know about yourself is your starting point. If you know who
your parents are and where they were from, you can begin to
search backward from there.

Once you have a record of your birth, use this information
to look for your parents' birth records. If no birth records exist,
there are other effective methods.

If your plan A does not work, don't worry; there is a plan B,
a plan C, and maybe even a plan D. Searching for information
may be time consuming, expensive, and frustrating, but eventually it is rewarding.

Remember my motto: Every problem contains the seed for
the solution. All you have to do is learn to recognize the seed.

Genealogical research involves asking the following five
basic questions over and over again:

1. What do I know about my family?
2. What do I want to learn about my family?
3. What records are available at the library?
4. How do I obtain a record?
5. What do I do next?

Organize your records for easy access. Record your information on a chart and keep a research log of all records you locate. Make and file copies of key documents.

In genealogical research, you must evaluate each new piece of information and then decide where this information might lead you. One of the most valuable contacts is the county historian or the historical society of the community in which you are searching. The historical society primarily consists of people who are natives to the area and are knowledgeable about families who lived there. This is especially true of a small town in which the residents were not transient. Historians will know local private family cemeteries and who maintains them and their records. You can get a list of county historians at a public library or state archives. Once you have this list, you may want to write a letter, telephone, or visit the historian, requesting information about the family you are researching.

Here are a few more valuable sources for your genealogical search:

Birth Certificates and Death Records

The Bureau of the Census does not issue birth certificates, nor does it keep files or indexes of birth records. These are maintained by the Office of Vital Statistics in the states or areas where the births occurred.

The National Archives has records of births at U.S. Army facilities in the states and territories for 1884 to 1912, with some records dated as late as 1928. It will search the records if provided with: name of child, names of his/her parents, place of birth, and month and year of birth. *Military Service Records in the National Archives of the United States* has details. The leaflet is available free of charge from Publication Services, National Archives and Records Administration, Washington, DC 20408.

The value of death records is that they give the date of birth as well as the date of death, the place of birth, and the names of other family members. If you do not live in a city with a library, it may be possible to request a search by mail. Some libraries allow you to bring your own computer disk and download the information at no charge. Copies may cost only a dime or quarter. When requesting information by mail, always include a large, self-addressed, stamped envelope. When actually visiting a library, always bring lots of change for copies.

Another source for obtaining death records is through an information broker, who will have access to a computer network of all deaths (1940–1993) from the Social Security master death index.

If you do not have the time or are unable to actually conduct your own genealogical search, you may prefer to hire a professional genealogical searcher. Some searches may take years and become quite expensive.

Census Records

Census records are released every ten years, but they must be seventy years old before they are made public. If you are searching for someone who was born prior to 1920, there is a good chance the family will be listed in the census of 1920 or earlier. The census lists all persons living in a household, even nonfamily members such as boarders or tenants. Census records are recorded on microfilm and are available at a state archives and library and often at a main public library.

Census schedules for 1790 through 1920 in the custody of the National Archives are distributed on microfilm to many libraries and other users and are open to the public. Title 44, U.S. Code, allows the public to use the National Archives' census record holdings after seventy-two years. The archives will not research census records, but will copy them (and provide certification, if necessary) for a fee, if given the exact volume and page citation.

The 1890 census is limited to fragments from Alabama, the District of Columbia, Georgia, Illinois, Minnesota, New Jersey,

New York, North Carolina, Ohio, South Dakota, and Texas, in addition to the special 1890 schedules covering Union veterans of the Civil War and their widows.

There are federal decennial census schedules, other than for population and principally from the nineteenth century, that contain some information about individuals or their activities and living conditions. These records deal with agriculture, manufacturing, mining, mortality, and such social concerns as schools, libraries, and wages. The National Archives has some of these records on microfilm; others are in collections in state archives.

Since the Bureau of the Census was established as a permanent organization in 1902, it has had continual requests for information from individuals interested in history and genealogy and for certified transcripts of census records for use in court proceedings and for other purposes. Many states did not register births until after 1900 and some still did not begin such documentation until the late 1920s. Civil War veterans were among the first to need census transcripts (showing their ages) to support their pension claims.

Legislation affecting employment of children, various states' pension laws, mobilization of men and women for defense employment in which proof of citizenship was required, and the need to prove age and citizenship to travel abroad all increased the volume of requests for personal information recorded in the census.

The Bureau of the Census formed a special searching section in the late 1920s. After the national Social Security law was enacted in 1936, demands for help from people who found they had to have evidence of their age and had nowhere else to turn increased from 60,000 in 1937 to more than 700,000 a year during World War II. Because of the need for additional space, the searching section (now named the Personal Census Service Branch) moved to Pittsburg, Kansas, in August 1958. The present volume of age search requests runs about 50,000 a year.

The United States was the first nation to write census-taking into its constitution (Article I, Section 2) and in doing so to create a series of statistical records about its people. In 1790, and every ten years since then, a federal population census has told how many persons there were in a certain age group, of a particular race, male or female, and so on. The "manuscript census schedules," as they are called, at first showed only the name of each family head, but added later was the name of every individual (to make certain no one was missed or counted twice), together with data about that household or person. Some of the schedules were subsequently lost or burned, such as in the War of 1812. Most of the remaining ones, and those collected in later years, were bound into volumes and stored. Most of the 1890 schedules were lost in a fire in 1921. Beginning in the 1920s, all remaining schedules were microfilmed. The originals that were open to the public were offered to state and other archives, such as the Daughters of the American Revolution, or were destroyed by congressional order to save space.

Thus the federal population censuses are a major source of information about individuals over spans of years and generations. Some of this information is available to the public, but most is deemed confidential by law.

The exact questions asked in each of the censuses, together with the enumerators' instructions, appear in a U.S. Bureau of the Census publication, *200 Years of U.S. Census Taking: Population and Housing Questions, 1790-1990* (Washington DC, Government Printing Office, 1989).

Although a population census has been taken in the United States every ten years since 1790, the bureau holds only the records for 1900 through 1990. The Personal Census Service Branch (PCSB), in Pittsburg, Kansas, maintains and searches these records, which are confidential by law. Information from them is available only to the named individuals, their heirs, or legal representatives. The PCSB also will tabulate (on a reimbursable basis) statistics not already published in census reports. This is done in such a way that no individual or household can be identified.

Census records are on microfilm and are arranged by geographic location—state, county, place, enumeration district (ED), ward, and the like. Within these, a street address may appear in urban areas. The listings on the record pages are in the order of the census-takers' house-to-house visits or, in recent years, the addresses to which census questionnaires were sent by mail. Thus an address—or in the case of a rural location, the distance and direction from a known place—is needed to find a record. There are ED maps for all states from 1930 on, with some for previous censuses dating back to 1880. There also are indexes to street addresses arranged by EDs on microfilm and microfiche for some years. (The National Archives has maps and address indexes available for public use and sale.) The Pittsburg staff also maintains a library of city directories, alphabetic indexes, and a special index file called Soundex, which groups together surnames of the same or similar sounds but of variant spellings.

The Bureau of the Census does not make any distinction on its questionnaires between natural or adopted children.

There are microfilm indexes for 1880 (all states and territories, but only for households with children), 1900, 1910 (twenty-one states, principally those in the South), 1920, and 1930 (partial). The National Archives has 1880, 1900, and 1910 indexes, which are available to the public. (The Bureau of the Census has indexes for 1900 through 1930, but only for internal use.)

In addition, there are ongoing projects to compile alphabetical indexes to the federal population census records. Some may cover entire states; others are only for certain counties and particular years. Any checklist of these indexes would be incomplete, but researchers may wish to consult the latest edition of *Genealogical and Local History Books in Print* (three volumes, paperback, $32.50), where such indexes are listed.

The National Archives has on microfilm all of the available census schedules (1790-1920) and the indexes to those for 1880, 1900, and 1910. Copies are available at a moderate cost per roll of film. The archives' publications—*Federal Population Censuses, 1790-1890, 1900; Federal Population Census;* and the *1910 Federal Population Census*—contain roll listings and indicate the price for each roll. They will be mailed on request. Direct inquiries to:

> Publication Orders
> National Archives and Records
> Administration
> 7th & Pennsylvania Ave., NW
> Washington, DC 20408
> (202) 523-3181

Knowing one's identity is vital to human development.

These microfilmed census schedules are also available for use in reference rooms at the National Archives and Records Administration, Reference Service Branch (NNRM), and at the archives' regional branches (check the list in the Reference Section). These branches also have copy facilities for their patrons and at some locations provide a request for information form, which may be mailed.

Copies (certified, if requested) of specifically identified pages of the federal population schedules may be ordered from the National Archives' headquarters. Provide the name of the individual listed, page number, census year, state and county; and for the 1880 through 1920 censuses, the enumeration district.

Many public and academic libraries, state archives, and historical and genealogical societies have reference collections of census microfilm. Most local libraries have lists of such sources;

the principal one is *Federal Population and Mortality Schedules, 1790-1920,* in the National Archives and the *States, Special List Number 24* (microfiche) (National Archives and Records Administration, 1986).

Individual users also may borrow the microfilm through some libraries and research institutions. Microfilm rolls of 1790 to 1910 population schedules also can be rented directly by contacting:

Census Microfilm Program
P. O. Box 30
Annapolis Junction, MD 20701-0030
(301) 604-3699

Within political boundaries, such as counties and cities, census records often are arranged by ED number. Beginning in 1880, some enumerators carried ED maps that showed their census assignments—prior to that, their assigned areas were simply described in their commissions—and they marked the houses and routes on them. The National Archives' Cartographic and Architectural Branch, in Alexandria, Virginia, has a collection of these maps. The archives produced indexes on microfilm or microfiche that relate street address ranges to enumeration districts for some census years.

Some states took their own censuses after the year 1790 to serve constitutional provisions for apportioning representatives to their legislatures. Territorial censuses were taken by territorial organizations and usually represented attempts to establish eligibility for admission into the Union as a state. These records are in the custody of the secretary of state in the state in which the census was taken.

The 1920 census is the most recent record released. However, all states may not be indexed. In some states your research must begin with the 1900 census, which is indexed for all states.

You must know at least your ancestor's full name and state or territory of residence to begin research in the 1900, 1910, or

1920 census. Although not absolutely necessary, it is helpful to know the full name of the head of the household in which your ancestor lived. It is possible to search with a surname only, but because it involves the process of elimination, it takes longer.

The Library of Congress has cadastral and fire maps that may be useful in pinpointing the locations of households listed in the censuses.

Family tree books may be available through Halberts Inc., 3699 Ira Road, Bath, OH 44210.

Subscribe to *Everton's Genealogical Helper.* It is full of helpful information (check your local library or bookstore).

Immigration and Naturalization Records

With the exception of Native Americans, all of us have fore-fathers who immigrated to this country. There is a computer situated on Ellis Island in New York City that has a record of any-one who arrived in that port. There are also excellent records available at most National Archives branches of all passenger lists of ships arriving in the United States. Passenger lists contain the following information: passenger's name, age, race, sex, occupation, and marital status; name and address of nearest for-eign relative; last residence; port of arrival; and final destination.

This information is kept on microfilm at the National Archives. To obtain microfilm data about a particular immi-grant, request several original copies of NATF Form 81, "Order for Copies of Ship and Passenger Arrival Records." A small fee is charged when the information is located.

If you have reason to believe that the person you are look-ing for may have been an immigrant, two types of citizenship records will be available: documentation of becoming a U.S. citizen and naturalization records. The latter usually include declaration of intention, a petition, and a certificate of natural-ization.

Three separate sets of these records are issued for every new citizen who entered the United States after 1906. One copy is given to the citizen. The second is filed with the court of jurisdiction, usually in the county where the individual first established residency. The third copy is retained by the U.S. Immigration and Naturalization Service (INS). These records typically include name and address of applicant, nationality and country of immigration, age and or birthdate, marital status, and names of spouse and children.

Write to:

Immigration and Naturalization Service (INS)
U.S. Dept. of Justice
425 I St. NW
Washington, DC 20536

To obtain a copy of the birth certificate of a U.S. citizen in a foreign country, request an original Form FS-240 from:

Passport Services
Correspondence Branch
U.S. Dept. of State
Washington, DC 20007

If you are looking for a death record of a U.S. citizen who died in a foreign country, write to the above address for Passport Services and request an original Form OF-180, "Report of the Death of an American Citizen Abroad."

The National Archives offers the catalog Immigrant and Passenger Arrivals. If your local library does not have a copy, send a $2 money order to:

Catalog
Dept. G05
National Archives
Washington, DC 20408

This catalog indexes reels of microfilm in an easily under-stood format. Reels can be purchased for $23 each. Check with your local library and/or Mormon Family History Center to see which reels are available locally.

The Civil Reference Branch (NNRC) of the National Archives has passenger arrival lists and immigration passenger lists. These lists may also be found in the reference sections of many other libraries. The MOT (Marine Ocean Terminal), Building 22, Bayonne, NJ 07002-5388, (201) 823-7252, has a form by which a request for information may be submitted by mail.

Libraries

The best genealogical library belongs to the Church of Jesus Christ of Latter-day Saints in Salt Lake City, Utah. Since its beginning in 1894, the main library has become the largest of its kind in the world. It has a collection of more than 1 million rolls of microfilm, 150,000 books, 8 million family records, and many other records.

Most of the main library's records have been acquired through an extensive microfilming program started in 1938. At present, more than one hundred microfilmers are filming origi-nal documents in courthouses, churches, and other archives throughout the world. The microfilmers send the rolls of film to Salt Lake City where they are preserved in a vault in the moun-tains nearby. Microfilm copies can be ordered and sent to a branch library in your area.

Workers in the branch libraries are volunteers who can help you order and use the main library's records. They can't do research for you, but they can assist you with your own research. Call ahead to determine the library's schedule and to inquire whether you need to reserve a microfilm reader.

Updated catalogs and indexes on microfilm and microfiche are available to help you search for your ancestors. There are also reference aids, research papers, and other related publications.

Native American Ancestry

The census schedules for 1860 through 1920 and many other records concerning Native Americans, chiefly those who maintained their tribal status, are available to the public at the Civil Reference Branch of the National Archives, archives' regional branches, and at some libraries in various parts of the country. Also available at the National Archives and on microfilm are the Native American census rolls, 1885 to 1940. For detailed holdings, see *American Indians, A Select Catalog of National Archives Microfilm Publications* (National Archives Trust Fund Board, 1984) and *Guide to Genealogical Research in the National Archives* (National Archives Trust Fund Board, 1982).

The Tribal Affairs Division (U.S. Bureau of Indian Affairs, Washington, DC 20245) will not provide lists of names, but will search its records for verification of Native American ancestry if given the tribe's specific name, name of the person, and date and place of birth.

Reference Section

~

This chapter may be the most important, most useful, most valuable part of the entire text!

The preceding chapters are built around a single theme—searches for mothers, fathers, children, or other specific cases. In this reference section, you'll find names, addresses, suggestions, and options for further investigation. They could apply to virtually any search; when combined with other information, they may lead you to the person you've been seeking and to that reunion you've been dreaming about.

I hope you'll find your search as exciting as a treasure hunt or a real-life mystery adventure. And if you're missing some clues, you just may find them in the pages that follow.

Finding a missing person is an awesome experience, one that can forever change your life by filling a void and making you feel complete. At last you can put a closure to living with the unknown and have peace of mind. I know that many of you are afraid of what you might find. Let me assure you that what you find is better than not knowing, even if it is not what you hoped for.

As you embark on your search, I urge you to think positive and be persistent—don't give up or get discouraged. Have realistic expectations and be prepared to accept whatever you find.

Don't procrastinate. There is no time better than now to begin. I know you can do it. Don't fear the unknown and don't be afraid of the truth.

Once your search is completed, you might even consider helping another person with his or her search. I'm living proof that searching can become addictive! Helping someone find a missing loved one is one of the most challenging and rewarding experiences in the world.

When your search is complete, write me a letter and tell me all about it. Please send me a picture of you and your loved one. I wish I could be there for your reunion.

Best wishes for your successful search and reunion.

CHECK INFORMATION KNOWN

☐ FULL NAME _____
☐ MAIDEN NAME _____
☐ MARRIED NAME _____

☐ LAST KNOWN ADDRESS _____
☐ CITY/ STATE _____

☐ DATE OF BIRTH _____

☐ APPROXIMATE AGE IF EXACT DATE OF BIRTH
IS NOT KNOWN _____

☐ PLACE OF BIRTH _____

☐ RELIGION _____

☐ HOSPITAL OF BIRTH _____

☐ SOCIAL SECURITY NUMBER _____

☐ MILITARY BRANCH OF SERVICE _____

☐ SCHOOL(S) _____

☐ RELATIVES _____
_____
_____
_____
_____

☐ EMPLOYER OR OCCUPATION _____

☐ OTHER INFORMATION YOU MAY KNOW ABOUT THE
PERSON YOU ARE SEARCHING FOR: _____
_____
_____
_____

CHECK INFORMATION DESIRED

☐ FULL NAME _____
☐ MAIDEN NAME _____
☐ MARRIED NAME _____

☐ LAST KNOWN ADDRESS _____
☐ CITY/ STATE _____

☐ DATE OF BIRTH _____

☐ APPROXIMATE AGE IF EXACT DATE OF BIRTH
IS NOT KNOWN _____

☐ PLACE OF BIRTH _____

☐ RELIGION _____

☐ HOSPITAL OF BIRTH _____

☐ SOCIAL SECURITY NUMBER _____

☐ MILITARY BRANCH OF SERVICE _____

☐ SCHOOL(S) _____

☐ RELATIVES _____
_____
_____
_____
_____

☐ EMPLOYER OR OCCUPATION _____

☐ OTHER INFORMATION YOU MAY WANT TO KNOW
ABOUT THE PERSON YOU ARE SEARCHING FOR: _____
_____
_____
_____

WHERE TO LOOK FOR ADDITIONAL INFORMATION

LOCAL RECORDS

COURTHOUSE

Marriage	Probate (Wills)	Liens
Divorce	Registrar of deeds	Criminal
Voters	Judgments	Business licenses
Property owners	Lawsuits	Adoption records
Assessors		

Ask where old records are stored. There may be a local archives.

PUBLIC LIBRARY REFERENCE SECTION

Obituaries/death notices	Telephone directories
School yearbooks	Genealogy reference materials
City/suburban directories	Birth records
Crisscross directories	Census records
Microfilm/microfiche/CD-ROM	Old newspapers/periodicals

State room (Almost every state has a library with a room devoted to state historical information.)

STATE RECORDS

Birth certificates	Military enlistments/discharges
Death certificates	Adoption records
Marriage records	Professional licenses
Driving records	Corporation records
Vehicle registration	

STATE ARCHIVES

Census records	Old telephone directories
Birth index	Genealogical records
Military records	Immigration passenger lists
Military enlistments/discharges	Microfilm/microfiche
Old newspapers	Old county courthouse records
Old city/suburban directories	Adoption records
Old yearbooks	

FEDERAL RECORDS & RESOURCES

Military records	National Archives & branches
Social Security master death index	Offices of Disclosure
Bankruptcy records	IRS
Veterans' Administration	Social Security
Military Locating Services	Immigration & Naturalization Office

OTHER RECORDS

Family Bibles	
Family genealogical records	Church records & directories
Mormon Church libraries	Membership
Genealogists	Baptismal/marriage/death
Everton's Genealogical Helper	Cemetery & funeral home records
School records	Veterans' organizations
Civic organizations	Embassies of other countries
Professional associations	Adoption search & support groups
Historical society	Adoption agencies
County historian	Adoption records/social workers
Family cemeteries	

*Not all records are available in every state.

National Archives and Regional Branches

National Archives Headquarters
7th & Pennsylvania Ave. NW
Washington, DC 20408
(202) 501-5400

National Archives/Northwest
   Region
6125 Sand Point Way, NE
Seattle, WA 98115
(206) 526-6507

National Archives/New England
   Region
654 W. 3rd Ave.
Waltham, MA 02154
(907) 271-2441

National Archives/Alaska
380 Trapelo Rd.
Anchorage, AK 99501
(617) 647-8100

National Archives/Pacific
   Southwest
P.O. Box 25307
Laguna Niguel, CA 92677
(303) 236-0817

National Archives/Mountain
   States
24000 Avila Rd.
Denver, CO 80225
(714) 643-4241

National Archives/Pacific Sierra
1000 Commodore Dr.
San Bruno, CA 94066
(415) 876-9009

National Archives/Central Plains
2312 E. Bannister Rd.
Kansas City, MO 64131
(816) 026-6272

National Archives/Southwest/Gulf
   Region
P.O. Box 6216
Fort Worth, TX 76115
(817) 334-5525

National Archives/Southeast
   Region
1557 St. Joseph Ave.
East Point, GA 30344
(404) 763-7477

National Archives/Great Lakes
   Region
7358 S. Pulaski Rd.
Chicago, IL 60629
(312) 581-7816

National Archives/Northeast
   Region
Building #22
MOT (Marine Ocean Terminal),
   Bayonne
Bayonne, NJ 07002
(201) 823-7545

National Archives/Mid-Atlantic
   Region
9th & Market Sts.
Room 1350
Philadelphia, PA 19107
(215) 597-3000

Federal Agencies

Here are some federal agencies that might be sources of information in your search:

Congress:
House (202) 225-3121
Senate (202) 224-3121
Department of Commerce:
(202) 377-2000
Department of Defense (all military branches): (202) 545-6700
Department of Justice:
Inmate Monitoring Service:
(202) 307-3036
Inmate Locate Service:
(202) 307-3126
Drug Enforcement Administration:
Drug Registration:
(202) 307-3126
Federal Aviation Administration:
(202) 267-3484
Aircraft Registration:
(405) 680-3205
Pilot Certification:
(405) 680-3205
Federal Election Commission:
(202) 219-3420; (800) 424-9530
General Services Administration:
(202) 535-0800
Government Printing Office:
(202) 512-0000
Interpol (International Child Abduction): (202) 272-8383
Library of Congress:
(202) 707-5000
National Reference:
(202) 707-5522
Military Locators (active):
Air Force: (512) 652-5774
Navy: (703) 614-3155
Army: (317) 542-4211
Marines: (703) 640-3942

Military Personnel Records (all branches): (314) 263-3901
National Archives:
(202) 501-5402
National Center for Missing & Exploited Children:
(800) 843-5678
National Institute of Standards & Technology: (301) 975-2000
National Ocean & Atmospheric Administration: (301) 443-8330
National Transportation Safety Board: (202) 382-6600
U.S. Coast Guard Locators:
Active: (202) 267-1615
Reserves: (202) 267-0547
Retired: (202) 267-0547
U.S. Department of State (country desks): (202) 647-4000
U.S. Merchant Marine Locators (U.S. Coast Guard):
(202) 267-4000
U.S. Patent & Trademark Office:
(202) 557-5168
Veterans' Pension Information:
(202) 233-2044
White House (liaison):
(202) 456-7486
For catalog information write:
Consumer Information Center
P.O. Box 100
Pueblo, CO 81002
(719) 948-3334

Information USA
P.O. Box 15700
Chevy Chase, MD 20815
(301) 657-1200

Congressional Government
Judiciary
Mt. Vernon, VA 22121
(703) 765-3400

Superintendent of Documents
U.S. Government Printing Office
N. Capitol & H St. NW

Washington, DC 20402
(202) 275-2051

Washington Researchers
2612 P St., NW
Washington, DC 20007
(202) 333-3499

State Unclaimed Property Offices

ALABAMA
Alabama Dept. of Revenue
Unclaimed Property Sec.
P.O. Box 1191
Montgomery, AL 36130
(205) 242-9614

ALASKA
Alaska Dept. of Revenue
Unclaimed Property Sec.
1111 W. 8th St., Room 106
Juneau, AK 99801
(907) 465-4653

ARIZONA
Arizona Dept. of Revenue
Unclaimed Property
1600 W. Monroe
Phoenix, AZ 85007-2650
(602) 542-4643

ARKANSAS
Auditor of State
Unclaimed Property Div.
230 State Capitol
Little Rock, AR 72201
(501) 324-9670

CALIFORNIA
Controller of the State
Div. of Unclaimed Property
P.O. Box 942850
Sacramento, CA 94250-5873
(916) 445-8318

COLORADO
Colorado State Treasury
Unclaimed Property Div.
1560 Broadway, Suite 630
Denver, CO 80202
(303) 894-2443

CONNECTICUT
Unclaimed Property Div.
Connecticut State Treasury
20 Trinity St.
Hartford, CT 06106
(203) 566-5516

DELAWARE
Delaware State Escheator
P.O. Box 8931
Wilmington, DE 19899
(302) 577-3349

DISTRICT OF COLUMBIA
Dept. of Finance and Revenue
Unclaimed Property Unit
300 Indiana Ave. NW
Room 5008
Washington, DC 20001
(202) 727-0063

FLORIDA
State Comptroller
Unclaimed Property Sec.
State Capitol
Tallahassee, FL 32399-0350
(904) 487-0510

GEORGIA
Dept. of Revenue
Property Tax Div.
Unclaimed Property Sec.
270 Washington St. SW
Room 405
Atlanta, GA 30334
(404) 656-4244

HAWAII
Unclaimed Property Branch
Dept. of Budget and Finance
P.O. Box 150
Honolulu, HI 96810
(808) 586-1589

IDAHO
Unclaimed Property
State Tax Commission
P.O. Box 36
Boise, ID 83722

ILLINOIS
Dept. of Financial Institutions
Unclaimed Property Div.
500 Iles Park Pl.
Suite 510
Springfield, IL 62718
(217) 782-6692

INDIANA
Office of Attorney General
Unclaimed Property Div.
219 State House
Indianapolis, IN 46204-2794
(317) 232-6348

IOWA
Treasurer of State
Great Iowa Treasure Hunt
Hoover Bldg.
Des Moines, IA 50319
(515) 281-5366

KANSAS
State Treasurer
Unclaimed Property Div.
900 S.W. Jackson, Suite 201
Topeka, KS 66612-1235
(913) 296-4165

KENTUCKY
Revenue Cabinet
Abandoned Property Unit
Station 62
Frankfort, KY 40620
(502) 564-2100

LOUISIANA
Unclaimed Property Sec.
Dept. of Revenue
P.O. Box 201
Baton Rouge, LA 70821
(504) 925-7425

MAINE
Abandoned Property Div.
Treasury Dept.
State Office Bldg.
Station Space 39
Augusta, ME 04333
(207) 289-2771

MARYLAND
Comptroller of the Treasury
Unclaimed Property Sec.
301 W. Preston St.
Baltimore, MD 21201
(301) 225-1700

MASSACHUSETTS
Treasury Dept.
Abandoned Property Div.
1 Ash Burton Pl., 12th Floor
Boston, MA 02108
(617) 367-0400

MICHIGAN
Michigan Dept. of Treasury
Escheats Division
Lansing, MI 48910
(517) 334-6550

MINNESOTA
Dept. of Commerce
Unclaimed Property
133 E. 7th St.
St. Paul, MN 55101
(612) 296-2568

MISSISSIPPI
Unclaimed Property Div.
Mississippi Treasury Dept.
P.O. Box 138
Jackson, MS 39205
(601) 359-3600

MISSOURI
Unclaimed Property Section
Harry S. Truman Bldg.
P.O. Box 1272
Jefferson City, MO 65102
(314) 751-0840

MONTANA
Dept. of Revenue
Abandoned Property Sec.
Mitchell Bldg.
Helena, MT 59620
(406) 444-2425

NEBRASKA
Office of the State Treasurer
State Capitol
P.O. Box 94788
Lincoln, NE 68509-4788
(402) 471-3130

NEVADA
Dept. of Commerce
Unclaimed Property Div.
State Mail Room
Las Vegas, NV 89158
(702) 486-4140

NEW HAMPSHIRE
State Treasury
Dept. of Abandoned Property
Room 121
State House Annex
Concord, NH 03301
(603) 271-2649

NEW JERSEY
Dept. of Treasury
Unclaimed Property
CN-214
Trenton, NJ 08646
(609) 292-9200

NEW MEXICO
Taxation and Revenue Dept.
Unclaimed Property Unit
P.O. Box 630
Santa Fe, NM 87504-0630
(505) 827-0767

NEW YORK
Office of the State Comptroller
Office of Unclaimed Funds
9th Floor
A. E. Smith Bldg.
Albany, NY 12236
(518) 473-0824

NORTH CAROLINA
NC Dept. of State Treasurer
Escheat & Unclaimed Property
   Program
325 N. Salisbury St.
Raleigh, NC 27603-1388
(919) 733-6876

NORTH DAKOTA
Unclaimed Property Div.
P.O. Box 5523
Bismarck, ND 58502-5523
(701) 224-2805

OHIO
Div. of Unclaimed Funds
77 S. High St.
Columbus, OH 43266-0545
(614) 466-4433

OKLAHOMA
Oklahoma Tax Commission
Unclaimed Property
2501 Lincoln Blvd.
Oklahoma City, OK 73194-0010
(405) 521-4280

OREGON
Div. of State Lands
Unclaimed Property Sec.
775 Summer St. NE
Salem, OR 97310
(503) 378-3805

PENNSYLVANIA
Pennsylvania Dept. of Revenue
Bureau of Administrative Services
Abandoned & Unclaimed
   Property Div.
2850 Turnpike Industrial Dr.
Middletown, PA 17057
(717) 986-4640

PUERTO RICO
Consumer Affairs Div.
437 Ponce De Leon Ave.
11th Floor
Hato Rey, PR 00918
(809) 751-7479

RHODE ISLAND
Unclaimed Property Div.
P.O. Box 1435
Providence, RI 02901-1435
(401) 277-6505

SOUTH CAROLINA
South Carolina Tax Commission
Abandoned Property Div.
P.O. Box 125
Columbia, SC 29214
(803) 737-4771

SOUTH DAKOTA
Unclaimed Property Div.
State Treasury
500 E. Capitol Ave.
Pierre, SD 57501-5070
(605) 773-3378

TENNESSEE
Unclaimed Property Div.
Andrew Jackson Bldg.
11th Floor
Nashville, TN 37243-0242
(615) 741-6499

TEXAS
Unclaimed Property
P.O. Box 17728
Austin, TX 78760
(512) 444-7833

UTAH
Unclaimed Property Div.
Treasurer, State of Utah
341 S. Main
5th Floor
Salt Lake City, UT 84111
(801) 533-4101

VERMONT
State Treasurer
Abandoned Property Div.
133 State St.
Montpelier, VT 05633-6200
(802) 828-2301

VIRGINIA
Div. of Unclaimed Property
P.O. Box 3-R
Richmond, VA 23207
(804) 225-2393

WASHINGTON
Dept. of Revenue
Miscellaneous Tax Div.
Unclaimed Property
P.O. Box 448
Olympia, WA 98507
(206) 586-2736

WEST VIRGINIA
State Treasurer's Office
Div. of Unclaimed Property
State Capitol
Charleston, WV 25305
(304) 343-4000

WISCONSIN
Office of State Treasurer
Unclaimed Property Div.
P.O. Box 2114
Madison, WI 53701-2114
(608) 267-7977

WYOMING
Wyoming State Treasurer's Office
Unclaimed Property Div.
State Capitol
Cheyenne, WY 82002
(307) 777-7408

Veterans' Administration State Offices

All letters should be addressed to VA Regional Office.

ALABAMA
474 S. Court St.
Montgomery, AL 36104
(205) 262-7781

ALASKA
235 E. 8th Ave.
Anchorage, AK 99501
(907) 279-6116

ARIZONA
3225 N. Central Ave.
Phoenix, AZ 85012
(602) 263-5411

ARKANSAS
P.O. Box 1280
North Little Rock, AR 72115
(501) 370-3800

CALIFORNIA
Federal Bldg.
11000 Wilshire Blvd.
Los Angeles, CA 90024
(310) 479-8900

2022 Camino Del Rio N.
San Diego, CA 92108
(619) 297-8220

211 Main St.
San Francisco, CA 94105
(415) 495-8900

COLORADO
P.O. Box 25126
Denver, CO 80225
(303) 980-1300

CONNECTICUT
450 Main St.
Hartford, CT 05103
(203) 278-3230

DELAWARE
1601 Kirkwood Hwy.
Wilmington, DE 19805
(302) 998-0191

DISTRICT OF COLUMBIA
941 N. Capitol St. NE
Washington, DC 20421
(202) 872-1151

FLORIDA
144 1st Ave. S.
St. Petersburg, FL 33701
(612) 898-2121

GEORGIA
730 Peachtree St. NE
Atlanta, GA 30365
(404) 881-1776

HAWAII
P.O. Box 50188
Honolulu, HI 96850
(808) 541-1000

IDAHO
550 W. Fort St.
Boise, ID 83724
(208) 334-1010

ILLINOIS
P.O. Box 8136
Chicago, IL 60680
(312) 663-5510

INDIANA
575 N. Pennsylvania St.
Indianapolis, IN 46204
(317) 226-5566

IOWA
210 Walnut St.
Des Moines, IA 50309
(515) 284-0219

KANSAS
550 E. Kellogg
Wichita, KS 67218
(316) 264-9123

KENTUCKY
600 Martin Luther King, Jr.
Louisville, KY 40202
(502) 584-2231

LOUISIANA
701 Loyola Ave.
New Orleans, LA 70113
(504) 589-7191

MAINE
Route 17 E.
Togus, ME 04330
(207) 623-8000

MARYLAND
31 Hopkins Plaza
Baltimore, MD 21201
(410) 685-5454

MASSACHUSETTS
JFK Federal Bldg.
Boston, MA 02203
(617) 227-4600

MICHIGAN
477 Michigan Ave.
Detroit, MI 48226
(313) 964-5110

MINNESOTA
Federal Bldg., Fort Snelling
St. Paul, MN 55111
(612) 726-1454

MISSISSIPPI
100 W. Capitol St.
Jackson, MS 39269
(601) 965-4873

MISSOURI
1520 Market St.
St. Louis, MO 63103
(314) 342-1171

MONTANA
Fort Harrison, MT 59636
(406) 447-7975

NEBRASKA
5631 S. 48th St.
Lincoln, NE 68516
(402) 437-5001

NEVADA
1201 Terminal Way
Reno, NV 89520
(702) 329-9244

NEW HAMPSHIRE
275 Chestnut St.
Manchester, NH 03101
(603) 666-7785

NEW JERSEY
20 Washington Pl.
Newark, NJ 07102
(201) 645-2150

NEW MEXICO
500 Gold Ave. SW
Albuquerque, NM 87102
(505) 766-3361

NEW YORK
111 W. Huron St.
Buffalo, NY 14202
(716) 846-5191

252 7th Ave./24th St.
New York, NY 10001
(212) 620-6901

NORTH CAROLINA
251 N. Main St.
Winston-Salem, NC 27155
(919) 748-1800

NORTH DAKOTA
2101 N. Elm St.
Fargo, ND 58102
(701) 293-3656

OHIO
1240 E. 9th St.
Cleveland, OH 44199
(216) 621-5050

OKLAHOMA
125 S. Main St.
Muskogee, OK 74401
(918) 687-2500

OREGON
1220 SW 3rd Ave.
Portland, OR 97204
(503) 221-2431

PENNSYLVANIA
P.O. Box 8079
Philadelphia, PA 19101
(401) 273-4910

PUERTO RICO
GPO Box 4867
San Juan, PR 00936
(809) 766-5141

SOUTH CAROLINA
1801 Assembly St.
Columbia, SC 29201
(803) 765-5861

SOUTH DAKOTA
P.O. Box 5046
Sioux Falls, SD 57117
(605) 336-3496

TENNESSEE
110 9th Ave. S.
Nashville, TN 37203
(615) 736-5251

TEXAS
2515 Murworth Dr.
Houston, TX 77054
(713) 664-4664

1400 N. Valley Mills Dr.
Waco, TX 76799
(817) 772-3060

UTAH
P.O. Box 11500
Salt Lake City, UT 84147
(801) 524-5960

VERMONT
N. Hartland Rd.
White River Junction, VT 05001
(802) 296-5177

VIRGINIA
210 Franklin Rd. SW
Roanoke, VA 24011
(703) 982-6440

WASHINGTON
915 2nd Ave.
Seattle, WA 98174
(206) 624-7200

WEST VIRGINIA
640 4th Ave.
Huntington, WV 25701
(304) 529-5720

WISCONSIN
5000 W. National Ave.
Bldg. 6
Milwaukee, WI 53295
(414) 383-8680

WYOMING
2360 E. Pershing Blvd.
Cheyenne, WY 82001
(307) 778-7396

State Motor Vehicle Registration Offices

(For information on automobile licenses, registrations, or titles.)

ALABAMA
Title Section
2721 Gunter Park Dr.
P.O. Box 1331
Montgomery, AL 36102
(205) 271-3250

ALASKA
Dept. of Public Safety
Motor Vehicle Div.
Attn: Research
5700 E. Tudor Rd.
Anchorage, AK 99507
(907) 269-5559

ARIZONA
Motor Vehicle Div.
Title Records
1801 W. Jefferson Ave.
Phoenix, AZ 85007

ARKANSAS
Off. of Motor Vehicles
P.O. Box 1272
Little Rock, AR 72203

CALIFORNIA
Dept. of Motor Vehicles
P.O. Box 944247
Sacramento, CA 94244-2470
(916) 732-7243

COLORADO
Title Section
140 W. Sixth Ave.
Denver, CO 80204
(303) 620-4108

CONNECTICUT
Div. of Motor Vehicles
60 State St.
Wethersfield, CT 06109
(203) 566-4410

DELAWARE
Div. of Motor Vehicles
Attn: Correspondence Pool
P.O. Box 698
Dover, DE 19903
(302) 736-3147

DISTRICT OF COLUMBIA
Bur. of Motor Vehicle Services
301 C St. NW
Washington, DC 20001
(202) 727-6680

FLORIDA
Div. of Motor Vehicles
Neil Kirkman Bldg.
Tallahassee, FL 32301
(904) 488-4127

GEORGIA
Motor Vehicle Div.
126 Trinity-Washington Bldg.
Atlanta, GA 30334
(404) 656-4100

HAWAII
Div. of Motor Vehicle Licensing
1455 S. Beretania St.
Honolulu, HI 96814
(808) 955-8221

IDAHO
Transportation Dept.
Vehicle Research
P.O. Box 34
Boise, ID 83707
(208) 334-8663

ILLINOIS
Sec. of State
Vehicle Records Inquiry Sec.
4th Fl., Centennial Bldg.
Springfield, IL 62756
(217) 782-6992

INDIANA
Bur. of Motor Vehicles
401 State Off. Bldg.
100 N. Senate Ave.
Indianapolis, IN 46204
(317) 232-2798

IOWA
Dept. of Transportation
Off. of Vehicle Registration
Lucas State Off. Bldg.
Des Moines, IA 50319
(515) 281-7710

KANSAS
Dept. of Revenue
Div. of Vehicles
State Off. Bldg.
Topeka, KS 66626
(913) 296-3621

KENTUCKY
Dept. of Vehicle Regulation
Motor Vehicle Licensing
New State Off. Bldg.
Frankfort, KY 40622
(502) 564-7570

LOUISIANA
Off. of Motor Vehicles
Dept. of Public Safety
P.O. Box 64886
Baton Rouge, LA 70896
(504) 925-6146

MAINE
Dept. of State
Motor Vehicle Div.
State House Station #29
Augusta, ME 04333
(207) 287-3071

MARYLAND
Motor Vehicle Administration
6601 Ritchie Hwy., NE
Glen Burnie, MD 21062
(410) 768-7000

MASSACHUSETTS
Registrar of Motor Vehicles
100 Nashua St.
Boston, MA 02114
(617) 727-3700

MICHIGAN
Dept. of State
Bur. of Driver & Vehicle Services
Dept. of State
7064 Crowner Dr.
Lansing, MI 48918
(517) 322-1166

MINNESOTA
Dept. of Public Safety
Driver & Vehicle Services Div.
Transportation Bldg.
St. Paul, MN 55155
(612) 296-6911

MISSISSIPPI
State Tax Commission
Dept. of Motor Vehicles
Title Division
P.O. Box 1140
Jackson, MS 39205
(601) 359-1248

MISSOURI
Motor Vehicle Bur.
P.O. Box 100
Jefferson City, MO 65701
(314) 751-4509

MONTANA
Registrar's Bur.
925 Main St.
Deer Lodge, MT 58722
(406) 846-1423

NEBRASKA
Dept. of Motor Vehicles
P.O. Box 94789
Lincoln, NE 68509
(402) 471-2281

NEVADA
Dept. of Motor Vehicles
Registration Div.
Carson City, NV 89711
(702) 855-5370

NEW HAMPSHIRE
Dept. of Safety
Div. of Motor Vehicles
J. H. Hayes Bldg.
Concord, NH 03305
(603) 271-2251

NEW JERSEY
Bur. of Off. Services
Certified Info. Unit
25 S. Montgomery St.
Trenton, NJ 08666
(609) 292-4102

NEW MEXICO
Motor Vehicles Div.
P.O. Box 1028
Santa Fe, NM 87504
(505) 827-2173

NEW YORK
Dept. of Motor Vehicles
Empire Plz.
Albany, NY 12228
(518) 474-2121

NORTH CAROLINA
Vehicle Registration
Div. of Motor Vehicles
1100 New Bern Ave.
Raleigh, NC 27697
(919) 733-3025

NORTH DAKOTA
Motor Vehicles Dept.
Capitol Grounds
Bismarck, ND 58505
(701) 224-2725

OHIO
Dept. of Highway Safety
Bur. of Motor Vehicles
P.O. Box 16520
Columbus, OH 43216
(614) 752-7500

OKLAHOMA
Motor Vehicle Div.
2501 Lincoln Blvd.
Oklahoma City, OK 73194
(405) 521-3221

OREGON
Motor Vehicle Div.
1905 Lana Ave., NE
Salem, OR 97314
(503) 371-2200

PENNSYLVANIA
Bur. of Motor Vehicles
Transportation & Safety Bldg.
Harrisburg, PA 17122
(717) 787-3130

PUERTO RICO
Dept. of Transportation &
    Public Works
Motor Vehicles Area
P.O. Box 41243
Minillar Station
Santurce, PR 00940
(809) 723-9607

RHODE ISLAND
Registrar of Motor Vehicles
State Off. Bldg.
Providence, RI 02903
(401) 277-2970

SOUTH CAROLINA
Motor Vehicle Div.
Dept. of Highway & Public
    Transportation
Columbia, SC 29216
(803) 737-1114

SOUTH DAKOTA
Dept. of Rev.
118 W. Capitol
Pierre, SD 57501
(605) 773-3541

TENNESSEE
Motor Vehicle Div.
500 Deaderick St.
Nashville, TN 37242
(615) 741-3101

TEXAS
Motor Vehicle Div.
Dept. of Highway & Public
    Transportation
40th and Jackson Ave.
Austin, TX 78779
(512) 465-7611

UTAH
State Tax Comm.
Motor Vehicle Div.
State Fair Grounds
1095 Motor Ave.
Salt Lake City, UT 84116
(801) 538-8300

VERMONT
Dept. of Motor Vehicles
120 State St.
Montpelier, VT 05603
(802) 828-2000

VIRGINIA
Dept. of Motor Vehicles
P.O. Box 27412
Richmond, VA 23269
(804) 367-0523

WASHINGTON
Dept. of Licensing
P.O. Box 9909
Olympia, WA 98504
(206) 753-6946

WEST VIRGINIA
Dept. of Motor Vehicles
State Capitol Complex, Bldg. 3
Charleston, WV 25317
(304) 348-3900

WISCONSIN
Registration Files
Dept. of Transportation
P.O. Box 7909
Madison, WI 53707
(608) 266-1466

WYOMING
Dept. of Revenue
Motor Vehicle Div.
122 W. 25th St.
Cheyenne, WY 82002
(307) 777-6511

Vital Statistics State Offices

ALABAMA
State Registrar
Center for Health Statistics
Dept. of Public Health
572 E. Patton Ave.
Montgomery, AL 36111
(205) 242-5033

ALASKA
Chief
Bur. of Vital Statistics
Dept. of Health & Social Services
P.O. Box 110675
Juneau, AK 99811
(907) 465-3393

ARIZONA
Assistant State Registrar
Off. of Vital Records
Dept. of Health Services
2727 W. Glendale Ave.
Phoenix, AZ 85051
(602) 255-2501

ARKANSAS
Registrar
Vital Records Div.
Dept. of Health
4815 W. Markham St.
Little Rock, AR 72205
(501) 661-2371

CALIFORNIA
Chief
Vital Statistics Branch
Dept. of Health Services
P.O. Box 730241
Sacramento, CA 94244
(916) 445-1719

COLORADO
Dir.
Health Policy Div.
Dept. of Health
4300 Cherry Creek Dr., S.
Denver, CO 80222
(303) 692-2930

CONNECTICUT
Registrar
Vital Records
Div. of Health Statistics
Dept. of Health Services
150 Washington St.
Hartford, CT 06101
(203) 566-6545

DELAWARE
Vital Statistics Off.
Div. of Public Health
P.O. Box 637
Dover, DE 19903
(302) 739-4701

DISTRICT OF COLUMBIA
Chief
Research & Statistics Div.
Dept. of Human Services
425 I St. NW, Rm. 3001
Washington, DC 20001
(202) 727-0682

FLORIDA
Chief
Off. of Vital Statistics
Dept. of Health & Rehabilitative
    Services
P.O. Box 210
Jacksonville, FL 32231
(904) 359-6970

GEORGIA
Dir.
Vital Records Div.
Dept. of Human Resources
47 Trinity Ave. SW
Atlanta, GA 30334
(404) 656-4750

HAWAII
Acting Chief
Research & Statistics Off.
Dept. of Health
1250 Punchbowl St.
Honolulu, HI 96813
(808) 586-4526

IDAHO
State Registrar & Chief
Center for Health Statistics
Dept. of Health & Welfare
450 W. State St.
Boise, ID 83720
(208) 334-5976

ILLINOIS
Chief
Div. of Vital Records
Dept. of Public health
605 W. Jefferson
Springfield, IL 62761
(217) 782-6554

INDIANA
Registrar
Vital Records Section
State Board of Health
1330 W. Michigan St., Rm. 111
Indianapolis, IN 46206
(317) 633-0695

IOWA
Bur. Chief
Vital Records & Statistics
Dept. of Public Health
Lucas State Off. Bldg.
Des Moines, IA 50319
(515) 281-6762

KANSAS
State Registrar
Off. of Vital Statistics
Dept. of Health & Environment
Landon Off. Bldg., 1st Fl.
Topeka, KS 66612
(913) 296-1400

KENTUCKY
Assistant Dir.
Div. of Vital Records & Health
    Development
Cabinet for Human Resources
275 E. Main St.
Frankfort, KY 40621
(502) 564-4212

LOUISIANA
Dir. of Vital Statistics
Off. of Preventive & Public Health
    Services
P.O. Box 60630
New Orleans, LA 70160
(504) 568-8353

MAINE
Dir.
Div. of Vital Records & Statistics
Dept. of Human Services
State House Station #11
Augusta, ME 04333
(207) 624-5445

MARYLAND
Deputy Chief
Div. of Vital Records
Dept. of Health & Mental Hygiene
4201 Patterson Ave..
Baltimore, MD 21215
(410) 764-3028

MASSACHUSETTS
Registrar
Vital Statistics
Dept. of Public Health
150 Tremont St.
Boston, MA 02111
(617) 727-2700

MICHIGAN
State Registrar
Vital & Health Statistics
Dept. of Public Health
P.O. Box 30195
Lansing, MI 48909
(517) 335-8676

MINNESOTA
State Registrar
Vital Records Services Sec.
Dept. of Health
717 Delaware St. SE
Minneapolis, MN 55440
(612) 623-5121

MISSISSIPPI
State Registrar
Vital Records
Dept. of Health
2423 N. State St.
Jackson, MS 39216
(601) 960-7982

MISSOURI
Vital Records Administrator
Bur. of Vital Records
Dept. of Health
1738 E. Elm
P.O. Box 570
Jefferson City, MO 65102
(314) 751-6383

MONTANA
Chief
Vital Statistic Bur.
Dept. of Health & Environmental
    Services
Cogswell Bldg.
Helena, MT 59620
(406) 444-2614

NEBRASKA
Dir.
Bur. of Vital Statistics
Dept. of Health
P.O. Box 95007
Lincoln, NE 68509
(402) 471-2871

NEVADA
Mgr.
State Off. of Vital Records
Dept. of Human Resources
505 E. King St.
Carson City, NV 89710
(702) 687-4740

NEW HAMPSHIRE
Acting Dir.
Bur. of Vital Records & Health
    Statistics
Dept. of Health & Welfare
Hazen Dr.
Concord, NH 03301
(603) 271-4651

NEW JERSEY
Registrar
Vital Statistics
Dept. of Health
S. Warren & Market Sts., CN370
Trenton, NJ 08625
(609) 292-4087

NEW MEXICO
Chief
Vital Statistics Bur.
Public Health Div.
Dept. of Health
1190 St. Francis Dr.
Santa Fe, NM 87503
(505) 827-0121

NEW YORK
Dir.
Vital Records
Dept. of Health
733 Broadway
Albany, NY 12207
(518) 474-3055

NORTH CAROLINA
Head
Vital Records Branch
Dept. of Human Resources
225 N. McDowell St.
Raleigh, NC 27603
(919) 733-3000

NORTH DAKOTA
Data Processing Coordinator
Vital Records
Dept. of Health
600 E. Boulevard Ave.
Bismarck, ND 58505
(701) 224-2360

OHIO
Chief
Div. of Vital Statistics
Dept. of Health
65 S. Front St., Rm. G-20
Columbus, OH 43266
(614) 466-2533

OKLAHOMA
Dir.
Vital Records Div.
Dept. of Health
1000 NE 10th St.
P.O. Box 53551
Oklahoma City, OK 73152
(405) 271-4040

OREGON
State Registrar
Center for Health Statistics
Dept. of Human Resources
800 NE Oregon St.
Portland, OR 97201
(503) 229-6558

PENNSYLVANIA
Chief
Div. of Vital Statistics
Dept. of Health
P.O. Box 1528
New Castle, PA 16103
(412) 656-3100

RHODE ISLAND
Chief
Vital Statistics
Dept. of Health
75 Davis St.
Providence, RI 02908
(401) 277-2812

SOUTH CAROLINA
Dir.
Vital Records & Public Health
Health & Environmental Control
2600 Bull St.
Columbia, SC 29201
(803) 734-4810

SOUTH DAKOTA
Sec.
Dept. of Health
445 E. Capitol Ave.
Pierre, SD 57501
(605) 773-3361

TENNESSEE
Dir.
Div. of Vital Records
Dept. of Health
Tenn. Towers
Nashville, TN 37247
(615) 532-2600

TEXAS
Chief
Bur. of Vital Statistics
Dept. of Health
1100 W. 49th St.
Austin, TX 78756
(512) 458-7111

UTAH
Dir.
Bur. of Health Statistics
Dept. of Health
P.O. Box 16700
Salt Lake City, UT 84116
(801) 538-6186

VERMONT
Supervisor
Vital Records Div.
Dept. of Health
P.O. Box 70
Burlington, VT 05402
(802) 863-7275

VIRGINIA
Dir.
Div. of Vital Records
Dept. of Health
400 Madison Bldg.
Richmond, VA 23219
(804) 786-6202

WASHINGTON
Acting Dir.
Center for Health Statistics
Dept. of Health
1112 Quince St.
Olympia, WA 98504
(206) 753-5936

WEST VIRGINIA
Dir.
Vital Registration Off.
Bur. of Public Health
Bldg. 3, Rm. 516
1900 Kanawha Blvd. E.
Charleston, WV 25305
(304) 558-2931

WISCONSIN
Dir.
Center for Health Statistics
Dept. of Health & Social Services
P.O. Box 309
Madison, WI 53701
(608) 266-1334

WYOMING
Deputy State Registrar
Vital Records
Dept. of Health
Hathaway Bldg.
Cheyenne, WY 82002
(307) 777-7591

State Archives

ALABAMA
Dir.
Dept. of Archives & History
624 Washington Ave.
Montgomery, AL 36130
(205) 242-4361

ALASKA
State Archivist
Dept. of Education
141 Willoughby Ave.
Juneau, AK 99811
(907) 465-2275

ARIZONA
Dir.
Dept. of Library, Archives &
    Public Records
1700 W. Washington, Rm. 200
Phoenix, AZ 85007
(602) 542-4035

ARKANSAS
State Historian
History Comm.
One Capitol Mall
Little Rock, AR 72201
(501) 682-6900

CALIFORNIA
State Archivist
1020 O St.
Sacramento, CA 95814
(916) 445-4293

COLORADO
Dir.
Archives & Public Records Div.
Dept. of Administration
1313 Sherman St., Rm. 1B-20
Denver, CO 80203
(303) 866-2055

CONNECTICUT
State Archivist
State Library
213 Capitol Ave.
Hartford, CT 06106
(203) 566-5650

DELAWARE
State Archivist
Div. of Historical & Cultural
    Affairs
Hall of Records
P.O. Box 1401
Dover, DE 19903
(302) 739-5318

DISTRICT OF COLUMBIA
Archivist
1300 Naylor Ct. NW
Washington, DC 20001
(202) 727-2052

FLORIDA
Chief
Bur. of Archives & Records
    Management
Dept. of State

411 E. Bloxham St.
Tallahassee, FL 32399
(904) 487-2073

GEORGIA
Dir.
Dept. of Archives & History
330 Capitol Ave., SW
Atlanta, GA 30334
(404) 656-2358

HAWAII
State Archivist
Dept. of Accounting & General
    Services
Iolani Palace Grounds
Honolulu, HI 96813
(808) 586-0329

IDAHO
State Archivist
State Historical Society
Dept. of Administration
325 W. State
Boise, ID 83702
(208) 334-3890

ILLINOIS
Dir.
State Archives & Records Div.
Archives Bldg.
Springfield, IL 62756
(217) 782-4682

INDIANA
Dir.
Comm. on Public Records
IGC-South, Rm. W472
402 W. Washington
Indianapolis, IN 46204
(317) 232-3373

IOWA
State Archivist
Dept. of Cultural Affairs
Capitol Complex
Des Moines, IA 50319
(515) 281-3007

KANSAS
State Archivist
Research Collections
State Historical Society
120 W. Tenth
Topeka, KS 66612
(913) 296-4792

KENTUCKY
State Archivist
Public Records Div.
Dept. of Library & Archives
P.O. Box 537
Frankfort, KY 40602
(502) 875-7000

LOUISIANA
Sec. of State
Dept. of State
P.O. Box 94125
Baton Rouge, LA 70804
(504) 922-1000

MAINE
State Archivist
State House Station #84
Augusta, ME 04333
(207) 287-5790

MARYLAND
State Archivist
350 Rowe Blvd.
Annapolis, MD 21401
(410) 974-3867

MASSACHUSETTS
Archivist
Off. of Sec. of State
220 Morrissey Blvd.
Boston, MA 02125
(617) 727-2816

MICHIGAN
State Archivist
Dept. of State History Bur.
717 W. Allegan
Lansing, MI 48918
(517) 373-0510

MINNESOTA
State Archivist
State Historical Society
345 Kellogg Blvd., W.
St. Paul, MN 55102
(612) 296-6980

MISSISSIPPI
Dir.
Dept. of Archives & History
P.O. Box 571
Jackson, MS 39205
(601) 359-6850

MISSOURI
State Archivist
Off. of Sec. of State
P.O. Box 778
Jefferson City, MO 65102
(314) 751-4717

MONTANA
Head
Library & Archives Program
State Historical Society
225 N. Roberts St.
Helena, MT 59601
(406) 444-4787

NEBRASKA
Dir.
State Historical Society
P.O. Box 82554
Lincoln, NE 68501
(402) 471-4745

NEVADA
Administrator
Div. of Archives & Records
State Library & Archives
100 Stewart St.
Carson City, NV 89710
(702) 687-8317

NEW HAMPSHIRE
Dir. & State Archivist
Records Management & Archives
Dept. of State
71 S. Fruit St.
Concord, NH 03301
(603) 271-2236

NEW JERSEY
Dir.
Div. of Archives & Records
    Management
Dept. of State
2300 Stuyvesant Ave., CN307
Trenton, NJ 08625
(609) 530-3200

NEW MEXICO
Administrator
State Records Center & Archives
404 Montezuma Ave.
Santa Fe, NM 87503
(505) 827-8860

NEW YORK
State Archivist
State Archives & Records
    Management
Dept. of Education
10D45 Cultural Education Center
Albany, NY 12230
(518) 474-1195

NORTH CAROLINA
Dir.
Div. of Archives & History
Dept. of Cultural Resources
109 E. Jones St.
Raleigh, NC 27601
(919) 733-7305

NORTH DAKOTA
State Archivist
State Historical Society
North Dakota Heritage Center
612 E. Boulevard Ave.
Bismarck, ND 58505
(701) 224-2668

OHIO
Dir.
Historical Society
1982 Velma Ave.
Columbus, OH 43211
(614) 297-2300

OKLAHOMA
Dir.
Dept. of Libraries
200 NE 18th St.
Oklahoma City, OK 73105
(405) 521-2502

OREGON
State Archivist
Archives Div.
Off. of Sec. of State
800 Summer St. NE
Salem, OR 97310
(503) 373-0701

PENNSYLVANIA
Ex. Dir.
State Historical & Museum
    Comm.
P.O. Box 1026
Harrisburg, PA 17108
(717) 787-2891

RHODE ISLAND
State Archivist
Off. of Sec. of State
337 Westminister St.
Providence, RI 02903
(401) 277-2353

SOUTH CAROLINA
Dir.
Dept. of Archives & History
1430 Senate St.
P.O. Box 11669
Columbia, SC 29211
(803) 734-8577

SOUTH DAKOTA
State Archivist
State Historical Society
900 Governors Dr.
Pierre, SD 57501
(605) 773-3804

TENNESSEE
State Librarian & Archivist
State Library & Archives
403 Seventh Ave. N
Nashville, TN 37243
(615) 741-2451

TEXAS
State Archivist
P.O. Box 12927
Austin, TX 78711
(512) 463-5455

UTAH
Dir. of State Archives
    State Archives & Records
    Service
Archives Bldg.
State Capitol
Salt Lake City, UT 84114
(801) 538-3012

VERMONT
State Archivist
    Off. of Sec. of State
Pavilion Off. Bldg.
109 State St.
Montpelier, VT 05609
(802) 828-2369

VIRGINIA
State Librarian
    State Library & Archives
11th St. at Capitol Sq.
Richmond, VA 23219
(804) 786-2332

WASHINGTON
State Archivist
Archives & Records
Management Div.
Off. of Sec. of State
P.O. Box 40238
Olympia, WA 98504
(206) 753-5485

WEST VIRGINIA
Dir.
Archives & History Div.
Div. of Culture & History
Cultural Center
Capitol Complex
Charleston, WV 25305
(304) 558-0230

WISCONSIN
State Archivist
State Historical Society
816 State St.
Madison, WI 53706
(608) 262-7304

WYOMING
Dir.
Div. of Parks & Cultural Res.
Dept. of Commerce
Barrett Bldg.
Cheyenne, WY 82002
(307) 777-7013

State Adoption Search and Support Groups

ALABAMA
Jo Beth Smith
Adoptees Liberty Movement
Association
P.O. Box 55063
Birmingham, AL 35255

Virginia Womack
Concerned United Birthparents
Rt. 3, Box 579
Trussville, AL 35173

Searchline of Texas Chapter
3902 29th St. NE
Tuscaloosa, AL 35404

ALASKA
Joanne Lewis
Adoptees Liberty Movement
Association

P.O. Box 873573
Wassilla, AK 99510

Jana Shedlock
Concerned United Birthparents
7105 Shooreson Cir.
Anchorage, AK 99504

Ted Scott
P.O. Box 372
Glenallen, AK 99588

ARKANSAS
Clorinda Kraiger
Arkansas Adoption Triad
1912 Sanford Dr., #2
Little Rock, AR 72207

Orphan Train Heritage Society of
America
Rt. 4, Box 656
Springdale, AR 71901

Searchline
Rt. 5, Box 29-B
Huntville, AR 72740

ARIZONA
Alice Syman
Orphan Voyage of Arizona
P.O. Box 8245
Scottsdale, AZ 85252

Flagstaff Research & Support
P.O. Box 1031
Flagstaff, AZ 85002

Martha Shidler
Rt. 8, Box 305
Flagstaff, AZ 86009

Parents & Adoptees Uplifted
Rt. 1, Box 71
Williams, AZ 86046

Gari-Sue Greene
Tracers Ltd.
P.O. Box 18511
Tucson, AZ 85732

Charles Wollin
1402 Bethany Home Rd.
Phoenix, AZ 85013

Adoptees Liberty Movement
Association
P.O. Box 25966
Tempe, AZ 85282

Angelo Gurnett
2111 S. Farwell
Tucson, AZ 86711

Bonnie Rice
Adoptees Liberty Movement
Association
P.O. Box 36016
Tucson, AZ 86704

Arizona Adoption Support
Network
2238 S. McClintock
Tempe, AZ 86002

Karen Tinkham
Search Triad, Inc.
P.O. Box 1432
Litchfield Park, AZ 95340

Evelyn Loudat
Adoptees Liberty Movement
Association
P.O. Box 1445
Bullhead City, AZ 86430

CALIFORNIA
Emily Carter
Adoptees Liberty Movement
Association
P.O. Box 2341
Alameda, CA 94501

Barbara Mae Specht
4501 Riverside Ave., SP 47
Anderson, CA 96001

Ann Spanel
Roots/Bakersfield Crisis Pregnancy
4212 Starling Dr.
Bakersfield, CA 93309

Adoptsearch
1940 Los Angeles St.
Berkeley, CA 94707

Rainbow City/Wordworks
Helen Harvey
P.O. Box 8447
Berkeley, CA 94707

Maurice Weitman
Post Adoption Center for
    Education and Research
1634 Walnut
Berkeley, CA 94704

Nancy O'Neill
1430 Sacramento, #8
Berkeley, CA 94702

Janine Baer
Chain of Life
P.O. Box 8081
Berkeley, CA 94707

Toni Nason
P.O. Box 2355
Beverly Hills, CA 90213

Alberta Sorenson
Family Search Services
    Adoptees/Birthparents
    Association
P.O. Box 587, or P.O. Box 33
Camarillo, CA 93011

Betty Hanlon
P.O. Box 2569
Canoga Park, CA 91306

Ed Noonan
Adoptee-Birth Family Registry
3128 Mamand St.
P.O. Box 803
Carmichael, CA 95608

Carol Mogenroth
Worldwide Tracers
P.O. Box 1309
Chester, CA 96020

Danielle Collins
Concerned United Birthparents
14170 S. Evening View Dr.
Chino, CA 91709

Carol Hodemaker
6127 Seven Oaks St.
Chino Hills, CA 91709

Helen Gallagher
Independent Search Consultants
P.O. Box 10192
Costa Mesa, CA 92627

Jean Gold, L.C.S.W.
Golden West Radiology
P.O. Box 6029
Cypress, CA 90630

Concerned United Birthparents
3374 Aztec Rd., #35C
Doraville, CA 90240

Pat Miller
7751 Deacosta St.
Downey, CA 90240

Jim Shinn
536 Lenrey Ave.
El Centro, CA 92243

Cindy Shacklett
Concerned United Birthparents
P.O. Box 816
El Toro, CA 92630

Currie Wolfe
Search Consultants Adoption
   Network
P.O. Box 230643
Encinitas, CA 92023

Jo Kuhlman
2134 W. Alluvial
Fresno, CA 93711

Pat Treadway
Severed Strings
P.O. Box 2203
Fullerton, CA 92633

Daniel Millward, Detective
Millward & Associates
878 Neptune Ave.
Leukadia, CA 92024

Carol Longoria
Independent Search Consultant
5 Stratford Pl.
Gilroy, CA 95020

Rex W. Molitor
Rex W. Molitor Investigations
1900 Broadview Dr.
Glendale, CA 91208

Susan Bott
Central Coast Adoption Support
94 Manchester Pl.
Goleta, CA 93117

Hal Aigner
Paradigm Press
127 Greenbrae Boardwalk
Greenbrae, CA 94904

Karyn Medansky
Independent Search Consultant
1718 Longbranch
Grover City, CA 93433

Marilyn Miller
South Coast Adoption Research &
   Support
P.O. Box 39
Harbor City, CA 90710

Mrs. Maj. Leslie Hood
Coordinator, Missing Persons Div.
Salvation Army
900 W. 9th St.
P.O. Box 15899/Del Valle Station
Los Angeles, CA 90015-0899

Eva Torres
Menlo Lake Adoption Triad
P.O. Box 487
Hopland, CA 95449

Judy Albert, M.A.
17610 Beach Blvd, #38
Huntington Beach, CA 92647

Anne Sturdivant
5051 Alton Pkwy.
Irvine, CA 92714

Adoptive Parents for Open
  Records
P.O. Box 18242
Irvine, CA 92712

Patsy Hankins, M.S.W., L.C.S.W.
930 Enterprise St.
Inglewood, CA 90303

Family Life Institute
457 Westbourne St.
La Jolla, CA 92037

Kathleen Lawson
Open Heritage Society
2127 Foothill Blvd.
La Verne, CA 91750

Nancy Verrier
Psychologist
919 Village Center #9
Lafayette, CA 94549

James T. Kepley
California Genealogical Alliance
19765 Grand Ave.
Lake Elsinore, CA 92330

Mary Ann Rothschild
Independent Search Consultant
People Finders
840 W. 29th St.
Long Beach, CA 90805

J. Nelson
312 Glendora
Long Beach, CA 90803

Dean Watt
5855 Naples Plaza, #306
Long Beach, CA 90803

Reaching Out
P.O. Box 42749
Los Angeles, CA 90042

Tennessee Adoptees in Search
  (California)
4598 Rosewood
Montclair, CA 91763

Don Fordham
P.O. Box 1702
Monterey, CA 93942

Adoptees Research Association
P.O. Box 304
Montrose, CA 91020

Christian Frazier
25841 Paseo Pacifico
Moreno Valley, CA 92388

Chris Zapasnick
Zapasnick Adoption Search
25184 Vanessa Ct.
Moreno Valley, CA 92553

Sandra Lexington
P.O. Box 212
Mount Herman, CA 95041

Adoptee-Birth Parent Locators
18645 Sunburst St.
Northridge, CA 91324

Lydee D. Hensen, Ph.D.
351 Hospital Rd., #420
Newport Beach, CA 92263

Post Adoption Center for
  Education & Research
30 Lomba Vista
Novato, CA 94947

Concerned United Birthparents
4453 Pleasant Valley Ct.
Oakland, CA 94611

Sarah Crystal
Concerned United Birthparents
467 42nd St.
Oakland, CA 94609

Merrit Sielski
33 N. Glassel
Orange, CA 92666

Post Adoption Center for
    Education & Research
P.O. Box 309
Orinda, CA 94563

Lori Carangelo
Americans for Open Records
P.O. Box 401
Palm Desert, CA 92261

Patty Prickett
Suzanne Kauffman
Concerned United Birthparents
686 S. Arroyo Pkwy., #106
Pasadena, CA 91110

Thada Wachtel
Concerned United Birthparents
1420 N. White Ave.
Pomona, CA 91768

Judi Meye
Concerned United Birthparents
P.O. Box 3265
2369 Mt. Vernon Pl.
Quail Valley, CA 92380

Bexie Elliott
5851 W. Bowles
Raisin City, CA 93652

Missing Persons Dir.
Salvation Army
30840 Hawthorne Blvd.
Rancho Palos Verdes, CA 90274

Sherry Champagne
P.O. Box 1338
Redway, CA 95560

Attorney Martin Brandfon
Adoption Search
255 Shoreline Dr., Ste. 420
Redwood City, CA 94065

Mary Ann Alam
Concerned United Birthparents
20510 Claremont Ave.
Riverside, CA 92587

La County Adoption Search
    Association
P.O. Box 1461
Roseville, CA 95661

Search & Find
P.O. Box 8765
Riverside, CA 92515

Carol & Gray McDowell
Adoptees Liberty Movement
    Association
P.O. Box 8081
Sacramento, CA 95818

Larry & Cindy Martin
1713 Vermont Ave.
West Sacramento, CA 95691

Trish McAleer
Independent Search Consultant
Concerned United Birthparents
306 Ave. Costanso
San Clemente, CA 92672

Khari Lamarca
4791-95 Mansfield St.
San Diego, CA 92116

Nancy Hale
Reunite of California
P.O. Box 7524
San Diego, CA 92167

Karyl Ketchum
Adoptees Liberty Movement
    Association
12052 Camino Campana
San Diego, CA 92128

Bridie Kelly
Adoptees Liberty Movement
    Association
P.O. Box 880335
San Diego, CA 92108

Mary Medlin
Concerned United Birthparents
P.O. Box 171302
San Diego, CA 92174

Concerned United Birthparents
P.O. Box 40065
San Diego, CA 92164

Kate Burke
American Adoption Congress
1053 Filbert St.
San Francisco, CA 94183

Randa Phillips
Bay Area Relinquishing Mothers
    Association
75 Elsie St.
San Francisco, CA 941110

Jeanne Paredes
Paredes & Paredes
5276 Hollister Ave.
Santa Barbara, CA 93111

Women's Adoptee Support Group
    of Santa Cruz
197 Hammond Ave.
Santa Cruz, CA 95062

Deborah Kantor
2431 2nd St.
Santa Monica, CA 90405

Pat Rutherford
Worldwide Tracers
115 Calle de Industrias, #100
P.O. Box 4495
San Clemente, CA 92674

Concerned United Birthparents
1787 Michon Dr.
San Jose, CA 95106

Doreen Alegrete
Dorothy Yturriaga
P.O. Box 24095
San Jose, CA 95154

Sandra Marshall
Concerned United Birthparents
2925 Fourth, #15
Santa Monica, CA 90405

Triad Research
300 Golden W.
Shafter, CA 93263

Mary Lou Kozub
Independent Search Consultant
2027 Finch Ct.
Simi Valley, CA 90302

Gayle E. Beckstead
Adoption Reality
2180 Clover St.
Simi Valley, CA 93065

Gloria Lucas
Snoop Sisters
P.O. Box 129
Soulsbyville, CA 95372

The Family Network
P.O. Box 1995
Studio City, CA 91614

Neil Kelly
Adoptees Identity Discovery
P.O. Box 2159
Sunnyvale, CA 94087

J. Dillon Ross & Co.
2745 Ynez Rd., #175
Temecula, CA 92591

Tricia Cleland
Roots
10997 Rd. 252
Terra Bella, CA 93270

Patty Bybee
Hand in Hand
391 Teasdale St.
Thousand Oaks, CA 91360

Ann Fisher
Families by Adoption
1405 Marcelina, Ste. 101
Torrance, CA 90501

Carol Carmagno
Concerned United Birthparents
13661 Fairmont Way
Tustin, CA 92680

Concerned United Birthparents
2214 Walnut Ave.
Venice, CA 90291

Adoption Family Services
7137 Darnock Way
West Hills, CA 91307

Susanne Wood
Independent Search Consultant
8310 Wells Rd.
Westminster, CA 92683

Mary Jo Rillera
Triadoption, Inc.
P.O. Box 638
Westminster, CA 92684

COLORADO
Michael & Debbie Paris
Adoption & Family Search
    Consultants
P.O. Box 1038
Boulder, CO 89005

Jean Patton
The Open Records Movement,
    USA
Orphan Voyage
2141 Rd. 2300
Cedaredge, CO 81413

Lisa Botsko
Adoptees in Search
Contract Station #27
P.O. Box 323
Lakewood, CO 80212

Victoria Ransler
Concerned United Birthparents
10511 W. 104th Ave.
Broomfield, CO 80020

Jane Eckels-McGrath
Birthparents Adoption Trinity
P.O. Box 16512
Colorado Springs, CO 80935

Reunion
P.O. Box 112
Salinda, CO 81201

Mary Ann Wilself
Lambs in Search
35780 Parkmoor Village Dr.
Colorado Springs, CO 80935

CONNECTICUT
Jane Servadio
Ties That Bind
P.O. Box 3119
Milford, CT 05460

Carol Chandler Founds
Adoption Healing
288 Rowayton Ave.
Rowayton, CT 06853

Concerned United Birthparents
8 Homestead Rd.
South Glastonbury, CT 06073

Birthparent Support Group
9 Whitney Rd.
Columbia, CT 06237

National Adoption Reunion
  Registry
P.O. Box 2494
Danbury, CT 06813

Natalie Oliver
989 Ott Dr.
Cheshire, CT 06410

Karen Waggoner
Concerned United Birthparents
P.O. Box 558
Bethel, CT 06801

Nancy Sitterly
Adoptees Search Connection
120 Hill St.
Suffield, CT 06028

Wilma Cogliantry
44 Christian Lane
Berlin, CT 06037

DELAWARE
Trialog
2005 Baynard Blvd.
Wilmington, DE 19802

Finders Keepers
P.O. Box 748
Bear, DE 19701

DISTRICT OF COLUMBIA
Adoptee-Birthparent Support
  Network
3421 M St. NW, Ste. 328
Washington, DC 20007

American Adoption Congress
1000 Connecticut Ave. NW, #9
Washington, DC 20036

Kinship, Inc.
232 2nd St. SE
Washington, DC 20003

FLORIDA
Sandy Musser
Musser Foundation
1105 Cape Coral Pkwy.
P.O. Box 1860
Cape Coral, FL 33910

Tallahassee Adoption Support
   Group
275 John Knox Rd., #F-104
Tallahassee, FL 32303
Mid-Florida Adoption Reunions
P.O. Box 3474
Belleview, FL 32620

James & Marilyn George
Orphan Voyage
1130 NE 92nd St.
Miami Shores, FL 33138

Kathryn Spragg
2605 W. Aleuts Dr.
Beverly Hills, FL 32655

Adoption Consultants, Inc.
9329 SW 170th St.
Miami, FL 33157

Joanne Steenbergen
16208 Marshfield Dr.
Tampa, FL 33624

Debbie Raiford
1501 Garvin Rd.
Jacksonville, FL 32225

Orphan Voyage
P.O. Box 10909
Jacksonville, FL 32247

Anne Slagle
Adoptees Liberty Movement
   Association
P.O. Box 4358
Ft. Lauderdale, FL 33338

Concerned United Birthparents
455 Branan Field Dr.
Middleberg, FL 32068

Search Light, Inc.
1032 Veronica St.
Fort Charlotte, FL 33952

Orphan Voyage
P.O. Box 312
Oklawawa, FL 32679

Susan Schweitzer
Adoption Search Support
420 Gails Way
Merritt Island, FL 32953

Don Woods
Adults Separated by Adoption
75280 Greensboro Dr., #3
West Melbourne, FL 32904

Mary Hicks
Rt. 3, Box 127
Chipley, FL 33335

Peggy McCall
6459 Oak Shore Dr.
Panama City, FL 32404

Oasis
P.O. Box 31612
St. Petersburg, FL 33732

Judy Collins
2905 Arrow Ct.
Tallahassee, FL 32308

Julie Breton
1305 Dorado Dr.
Kissimmee, FL 32741

Oasis
P.O. Box 11
Valrico, FL 33594

Charles Eckert
2425 Brengle Ave. 28
Orlando, FL 32808

Diana Edwards Person
Clarity Network
P.O. Box 1117
St. Augustine, FL 32055

Lorraine Boiselle
The Adoption Center
500 N. Maitland Ave.
Maitland, FL 32751

Chris Adamac
1921 Ohio St. NE
Palm Bay, FL 32907

Jone Carlson
People Searching News
P.O. Box 22611
Ft. Lauderdale, FL 33335

Adoptees Liberty Movement
    Association
P.O. Box 4358
Ft. Lauderdale, FL 33338

Jay Swearingen
Orphan Voyage
3986 Pepperell Dr.
Tampa, FL 33624

Orphan Voyage
13505 SE 110 Ct.
Miami, FL 33176

Georgia D. Humphrey
1022 Everglade Dr.
Niceville, FL 32578

Orphan Voyage
12094 Old Country Rd.
West Palm Beach, FL 33411

Rachel Rivers
Organized Adoption Search
    Information Service
P.O. Box 53-0761
Miami Shores, FL 33153

Paula J. Hausman
Oasis
214 Golden Sands Dr.
Sarasota, FL 33578

GEORGIA
Georgiann Holt
Adoption Beginnings
P.O. Box 440121
Kennesaw, GA 30144

Larry Neil Daniel
P.O. Box 1847
Dublin, GA 31040

Kay D. Russell
Caring Hearts
P.O. Box 2260
Stone Mountain, GA 30086

Joanne Howards
Concerned United Birthparents
3374 Aztec Rd., #34-C
Doraville, GA 30340

Adoptees Liberty Movement
    Association
62 Park Gate Dr.
Atlanta, GA 30328

Diana Brown
Independent Search Consultant
1103 Riverbend Club NE
Atlanta, GA 30339

HAWAII
Martha Hulbert
Adoption Support Group
55 Niuki Cir.
Honolulu, HI 96821

Adoption Circle of Hawaii
4614 Kilauea Ave., #431
Honolulu, HI 96816

Adoptees Liberty Movement
    Association
58-250 (C) Kam Hwy.
Haleiva, HI 96712

John Rogers
524-B Olive Ave.
Wahiwa, HI 96786

IDAHO
Joyce Krummes
Searchfinders of Idaho
P.O. Box 7941
Boise, ID 83707

Adopted Child
P.O. Box 9362
Moscow, ID 83843

Adoption Support
Ann Williams
P.O. Box 1435
Ketchum, ID 83304

Margaret Sisson
Rt. 1, Box 19-A
Cataldo, ID 83810

Lavonne Morris
P.O. Box 219
Priest River, ID 83854

Karen Westergard
P.O. Box 1033
Sandpoint, ID 83864

Patricia Jones
1311 E. Commercial
P.O. Box 226
Wesler, ID 83672

Jean Van Pelt
9023 Garvendale Dr.
Boise, ID 83702

Martha Haumann
3802 Targee
Boise, ID 83705

Beverly Weeks
Adoptees Liberty Movement
  Association
5057 Valley St.
P.O. Box 4281
Boise, ID 83704

Marianne Brandy
2011 Victory View Cir.
Boise, ID 83708 ·

Joan Babel
3400 Beverly St.
Boise, ID 83709

Patricia Tulles
965 E. 14th
Idaho Falls, ID 83401

Donalee Velvick
Rt. 1, Box 1374
Napa, ID 83651

Barbara Cannon
2412 12th Ave.
Lewiston, ID 83654

ILLINOIS
Healing Hearts, Inc.
P.O. Box 606
Normal, IL 61761

Missing Pieces
P.O. Box 7541
Springfield, IL 62791

Susan Dudish
Concerned United Birthparents
1455 N. Sandburg, #702
Chicago, IL 60610

Adoption Triangle
13 Hemlock
P.O. Box 384
Park Forest, IL 60466

Sue Lentz
Adoptees Liberty Movement
  Association
P.O. Box 81
Barrington, IL 60438

Karen Shults
18921 Creekview
Mokena, IL 60448

Protect the Children, Inc.
P.O. Box 49
Steger, IL 60475

Margie Gibson
1812 W. Hood
Chicago, IL 60660

Adoptees Liberty Movement
  Association
P.O. Box 5935
Chicago, IL 60659

Paula Randant
101 S. Pine St., #2
Mt. Prospect, IL 60058

Lynda Brown
2010 S. Arlington Heights Rd.
Arlington Heights, IL 60005

Mark Sellin
18521 Oakley
Lansing, IL 60438

Truth Seekers in Adoption
P.O. Box 366
Prospect, IL 60070

Concerned United Birthparents
110 W. Circle Dr.
Lockport, IL 60441

Cyndi Almada
9462 Bay Colony, 3-N
Des Plaines, IL 60018

People Searching for People
1539 22nd Ave.
Rock Island, IL 61201

Hidden Birthright
3241 Saxony Rd.
P.O. Box 1651
Springfield, IL 62705

Concerned United Birthparents
156 W. Burton Pl.
Chicago, IL 60610

Woody Mitchell
Adoptees Liberty Movement
   Association
P.O. Box 74
Lebanon, IL 62254

Elaine Morris
Adoptees Liberty Movement
   Association
P.O. Box 59345
Chicago, IL 60659

INDIANA
Betty Heide
Adoptees Identity Doorway
   Reunion Registry of Indiana
51537 Myrtle Ave.
P.O. Box 361
South Bend, IN 46637

Mickey Carty
P.O. Box 1062
Richmond, IN 47374

Coping with Adoption
P.O. Box 1058
Peru, IN 46970

Susan Singleton
P.O. Box 187
Sharpsville, IN 46069

Search for Tomorrow, Inc.
Martha Barrow, Independent
   Search Consultant
241 Twillo Run
P.O. Box 441
New Haven, IN 46774

Indiana Adoption Coalition
   Support of Search
P.O. Box 1292
Kokomo, IN 46901

Lafayette Adoption Search Service
   Organization
5936 Lookout Dr.
West Lafayette, IN 47906

Karen Bolen
Concerned United Birthparents
4501 Farnsworth
Indianapolis, IN 46241

Search-Adoption Identity
P.O. Box 1202
Elkhart, IN 46515

Seek
213 Breamwold
Michigan City, IN 46360

Support of Search
P.O. Box 1292
Kokomo, IN 46901

Oasis
P.O. Box 3031
Kokomo, IN 46901

Full Circle
1701 N. Madison, #E-5
Anderson, IN 46901

Adoptees Liberty Movement
  Association
P.O. Box 207
Chalmers, IN 47929

Nancy Vanderhoose
Greater Love Adoption Decision
P.O. Box 9105
Evansville, IN 47710

Search Committee of Madison
  County Historical Society
P.O. Box 523
Anderson, IN 46901

IOWA
Concerned United Birthparents
2000 Walker St.
Des Moines, IA 50217

Family Search Counseling
436 S. 1st Ave.
Council Bluffs, IA 51501

Iowa Reunion Registry
P.O. Box 8
Blairsburg, IA 50034

Judy Wilkins
Concerned United Birthparents
130 33rd Ave. SW
Cedar Rapids, IA 52404

Orphan Voyage
P.O. Box 21
Cedar, IA 52543

Adoptees Quest
408 Buresh
Iowa City, IA 53340

Adoptive Experience Group
1105 Fremont
Des Moines, IA 50316

Iowa Referral Reunion Library
P.O. Box 9191
Cedar Rapids, IA 52409

KANSAS
Wichita Adult Adoptees
4551 S. Osage St.
Wichita, KS 67217

Adoption Concerns Triangle
1427 N. Harrison
Topeka, KS 66608

Adoption Support Group
1425 New York St.
Lawrence, KS 66044

Adoptees Liberty Movement
  Association
P.O. Box 532
Leavenworth, KS 66048

Reunions Ltd.
2611 E. 25th
Topeka, KS 66605

KENTUCKY
Linda Cecil
Locators Unlimited
P.O. Box 1218
Nicholasville, KY 40340-1218

Susan Monroe
Concerned United Birthparents
140 Molly St.
Versailles, KY 40383

Adoption Awareness
P.O. Box 23019
Anchorage, KY 40223

Sandy Rogers
Concerned United Birthparents
P.O. Box 22795
Louisville, KY 40222

Adoptees Looking in Kentucky
P.O. Box 866
Lexington, KY 40587

Susan Secchi
Concerned United Birthparents
2159 Lansil Rd.
P.O. Box 13033
Lexington, KY 40583

LOUISIANA
Gloria Veillon
Johnny Kocurek
Adoption Triad, Inc.
P.O. Box 2932
Lafayette, LA 70502

Adoption Connection of Louisiana
7301 W. Judge Perez, Ste. 311
Arabi, LA 70032

Adoption Triad Network
511 Blue Bell
Port Allen, LA 70605

Adoption Triad, Inc.
P.O. Box 324
Swartz, LA 71281

Adoption Triad Network
P.O. Box 1140
Morgan City, LA 70381

Adoption Triad Network
P.O. Box 6175
Lake Charles, LA 70605

MAINE
Patricia Yates
Concerned United Birthparents
Rt. 1, Box 1017
West Paris, ME 04289

Adoption Support Group of
    Penobscot Bay
Taylor's Point
Tenant's Harbor, ME 05860

Lois Thurston
P.O. Box 14
Gardiner, ME 04345

Adoption Search Consultants of
    Maine
10 Meadow Way
P.O. Box 2793
South Portland, ME 04106

Concerned United Birthparents
RFD 2, Hiltons Lane
North Berwick, ME 03906

Mina Bicknell
Independent Search Consultant
19 Myrtle Ave.
South Portland, ME 04106

Orphan Voyage
P.O. Box 104
West Bethel, ME 04286

MARYLAND
Laura Lewis
14914 Nighthawk Lane
Bowie, MD 20716

Adoption Connection Exchange
1301 Park Ave.
Baltimore, MD 21217

Adoptees in Search
P.O. Box 41016
Bethesda, MD 20824

Maryland Mutual Consent
 Registry
311 W. Sarasota St.
Baltimore, MD 20201

Robin Quinter
Independent Search Consultant
3308 Gold Mine Rd.
Brookeville, MD 20830

Adoption Connection Exchange
P.O. Box 2724
Laurel, MD 20708

Carol Setola
Independent Search Consultant
P.O. Box 441
Glen Dale, MD 20769

Adoptees Search Organization
P.O. Box 55298
Ft. Washington, MD 20744

Alan Talbert
110 Parkside Rd.
Silver Spring, MD 20910

MASSACHUSETTS
Jean Rumbo
American Adoption Congress
85 Hosmer, Unit B-1
Actin, MA 01720

Jo Devlin
34 Pleasant
Stoneham, MA 01280

Cape Cod Adoption Connection
P.O. Box 336
Brewster, MA 02631

The Adoption Connection, Inc.
Susan Darke
The O'Shea Bldg.
11 Peabody Sq., #6
Peabody, MA 01960

Birth Mother Support Group
Univ. of Massachusetts
Wilder Hall
Amherst, MA 01003

David Zoffoli
Independent Search Consultant
429 Cabot St.
Beverly, MA 01915

Adoptees Liberty Movement
    Association
P.O. Box 595
North Andover, MA 01845

Cape Cod Association for Truth in
    Adoption
P.O. Box 606
Woods Hole, MA 02543

Concerned United Birthparents
45 Holyoke St.
North Quincy, MA 02171

Concerned United Birthparents
Harvard Sq.
P.O. Box 396
Cambridge, MA 02238

MICHIGAN
Adoption Insight
P.O. Box 171
Portage, MI 49081

Mary Louise Foess
Bonding by Blood Unlimited
4710 Cottrell Rd., RR 5
Vassar, MI 48768

Mary Louise Lee
2316 Calumet
Flint, MI 48503

Charlene Palmer
2310 Calumet
Flint, MI 48503

Roots & Reunions
Ellen Cosner
P.O. Box 121
Scandia, MI 49885

Amy Smith
2342 Nichols Rd.
Flushing, MI 48433

Kathy Unger
1265 W. Thompson Rd.
Fenton, MI 48430

Eleanor Wilson
5007 Sandalwood
Grand Blanc, MI 48439

Norma Preston
Adoptees Liberty Movement
    Association
4082 Harbor Pt. Dr.
Muskegon, MI 49441

Adoptees Search for Knowledge
P.O. Box 752
East Lansing, MI 48823

Peg Richer
Adoption Identity Movement
P.O. Box 9265
Grand Rapids, MI 49509

Jo Anne Swanson
Birth Connections
Birco Publishing
P.O. Box 341
Gladstone, MI 49837

Post Adoption Support Services
1221 Minnesota Ave.
Gladstone, MI 49837

Brenda Engstrom
Independent Search Consultant
P.O. Box 1390
Muskegon, MI 49443

Adoption Identity Movement
P.O. Box 134
Traverse City, MI 49685

Irma Amore
4615 Western Rd., Lot 76
Flint, MI 48506

Mary Ahrens
524 Westchester
Saginaw, MI 49081

Christine Nueher
1270 Grosvenor Way
Palmyra, MI 49268

Dave & Linda Clark
2431 Roanoke
Ypsilanti, MI 48197

Adoptees Search for Knowledge
4227 S. Belsay Rd.
Burton, MI 48519

Adoption Identity Movement
136 Podunk
Cedar Springs, MI 49319

Adoption Triangle
1261 Witham Rd., A
Muskegon, MI 49445

Paths Reunited
2720 Burlingame SW
Wyoming, MI 49509

Adoption Insight
P.O. Box 153
Otsego, MI 49078

Concerned United Birthparents
801 Granger Ave.
Ann Arbor, MI 48104

Inheritance Research
P.O. Box 349
Calumet, MI 49913

Parent Finders
18968 Woodside Dr.
Harper, MI 48225

Adoption Identity Movement
P.O. Box 9265
Grand Rapids, MI 49509

Concerned United Birthparents
Truth in Adoption
8107 Webster Rd.
Mt. Morris, MI 48458

John Keller
Independent Search Consultant
4197 E. Cedar Lake Dr.
Greenbush, MI 48738

Bob Schafer
Adoption Reform Movement of
 Michigan
95 Whites Bridge Rd.
Belding, MI 48809

Chris Spurr
Independent Search Consultant
1602 Cole
Birmingham, MI 48008

Adoption Identity Movement
P.O. Box 812
Hazel Park, MI 48030

Patti Packhorn
304 W. Morgan
Battlecreek, MI 49017

Patti Vanderband
Roots & Reunions
412 Cedar St.
Sault St. Marie, MI 49783

MINNESOTA
Sandy Sperazza
6429 Mendelssohn Lane
Edine, MN 55343

Olewnik
P.O. Box 104
Mantorville, MN 53955

Sheryl Hall
Liberal Education for Adoption
    Reform
Minnesota Reunion Registry
23247 Lofton Ct.
North Scandia, MN 55073

Joan Grabe
Concerned United Birthparents
609 W. Summit Ave.
Fergus Falls, MN 56537

Adoptees Liberty Movement
    Association
7048 Progress Rd.
Hugo, MN 55038

Pat Slattery
Concerned United Birthparents
9450 Wellington Lane
Osseo, MN 55369

MISSISSIPPI
Adoption Information Network
P.O. Box 4154
Meridian, MS 39304

Adoptees Liberty Movement
    Association
P.O. Box 212
Columbus, MS 39701

MISSOURI
Support Open Records
4589 Hopewell Rd.
Wentzville, MO 63385

Bill & Kathy Young
Adoptees Liberty Movement
    Association
P.O. Box 3704
Kirkwood, MO 63122

Kansas City Adult Adoptees
P.O. Box 11828
Kansas City, MO 64138

Southwestern Missouri Adult
    Adoptees
Rt. 5, Box 172
Joplin, MO 64801

Concerned United Birthparents
Susan Fogelsong
7000 Jackson
Kansas City, MO 64132

Connecting Adoptees through
    Research & Education
P.O. Box 30252
Kansas City, MO 64112

Southwestern Adult Adoptees
3138 Kissimme Ct.
Springfield, MO 65801

MONTANA
Jo Glass
20034 Pacific Coast Hwy. S.
Seattle, WA 98198

NEBRASKA
Nancy Sullivan
Midwest Adoption Triad
P.O. Box 37272
Omaha, NE 68137

Linda Arteman-Wilshusen
9305 Carmen Ave.
Omaha, NE 68134

NEVADA
International Soundex Reunion
   Registry
Tony Villardi
P.O. Box 2312
Carson City, NV 89702

Marsha L. Reinhart
4478 Casa Blanca
Las Vegas, NV 89121

NEW HAMPSHIRE
Concerned United Birthparents
Vesselrock Road
P.O. Box 233
Gilsum, NH 03488

Concerned United Birthparents
Susan Daggett
P.O. Box 64
Merrimack, NH 03054

Darlene Roschow
P.O. Box 26
Bristol, NH 03222

Concerned United Birthparents
595 Central Ave.
Dover, NH 03820

Circle of Hope
P.O. Box 127
Somersworth, NH 03878

NEW JERSEY
Carol Gustavson
Adoptive Parents for Open
   Records
9 Marjorie Dr.
Hackettstown, NJ 07840

Ruth Ann Morris
4 Michelle Dr.
Middletown, NJ 07748

Marsha Ribe
Mary Ann Cohen
Origins
45 Hunters Glen Dr., Bldg. 5
Plainsboro, NJ 08536

Origins
P.O. Box 556
Whippany, NJ 07981

Adoptees Liberty Movement
   Association
P.O. Box 627-M
Morristown, NJ 07960

Rebecca Adams
50 Dawson Dr.
Bridgton, NJ 08032

Attorney Harold Cassidy
Foundation for Social Justice
225 Broad St.
P.O. Box 896
Red Bank, NJ 07701

Sue Wright
Origins
49 Richardson
New Brunswick, NJ 08901

Jane C. Nast
Adoptive Parents for Open
    Records
3 Harding Terrace
Mendham Township, Cr. 32
Morristown, NJ 07960

Birthdates
117 Nelson Ave.
Jersey City, NJ 07307

West Central Search Support of
    New Jersey
P.O. Box 3604
Trenton, NJ 08629

Adoption Support Group of
    Central New Jersey
500-4B Auten Rd.
Somerville, NJ 08876

NEW MEXICO
Sally File
Operation Identity, Inc.
13101 Blackstone NE
Albuquerque, NM 87111

Cheryl Block
1411 Los Lentes NE
Los Lunas, NM 87031

Leonie D. Boehmer
805 Alvarado NE
Albuquerque, NM 87108

Vonda Cheshire
Triad Adoption Services
4004 Carlisle Blvd. NE, #A
Albuquerque, NM 87107

NEW YORK
Florence Fisher
Adoptees Liberty Movement
    Association
P.O. Box 154
Washington Bridge Station
New York, NY 10033

Adoption Crossroads
Joe Soll
401 E. 74th St., Ste. 17-D
New York, NY 10021

Adoption Circle-Putnam
Sally McCracked
19 Lindy Dr.
Carmel, NY 10512

Joyce Bahr
Manhattan Birthparents Group
P.O. Box 2017
Cherokee Station
New York, NY 10028

Candid Adoption Talk
175-A Fawn Hill Rd.
Tuxedo, NY 10987

Always Support for Adopted
    People
12 Sunset Ave. S.
Farmingdale, NY 11735

Birthparents United in Support
Marsha Cohen
39 Tidd Ave.
Farmington, NY 11425

Birthmoms in Recovery thru
   Healing
7 Cheryl Pl.
Massapequa, NY 11758

Adoption Connection
P.O. Box 492
Northville, NY 12134

Triangle of Truth
P.O. Box 2039
Liverpool, NY 13089

Kinquest
P.O. Box 873
Bowling Green Station
New York, NY 10274

Kinquest
Evensong Futon Shop
159 Park Ave.
Amityville, NY 11701

Gretchen Hoffman
Concerned United Birthparents
2 Stemmer Lane
Suffern, NY 10901

Denise McCarty
42 Morris St.
Auburn, NY 13021

Barbara Kats-Rothman
827 E. 21st St.
Brooklyn, NY 11210

Rosalie Schwab
3 Townhouse Cir.
Great Neck, NY 11021

Attorney Dirck Brown
American Adoption Congress
P.O. Box 57
Orient, NY 11957

Adoptee Information Service
19 Marion Ave.
Mt. Vernon, NY 10552

Patti Van Wahner
Greiner, Inc.
3 Marcus Blvd., #102
Albany, NY 12205

NE Adoption Association
112 Parkwood Blvd.
Schenectedy, NY 13210

Birthparent Support Network
232 Front St.
Schenectedy, NY 12305

Kimlee Butterfield
Concerned United Birthparents
215 Edgemont Dr.
Syracuse, NY 13214

Center for Reuniting Families
1479 Kensington Ave., #202
Buffalo, NY 14215

Susan Kelsey
Adoptees Liberty Movement
   Association
6101 Slocum Rd.
Ontario, NY 14519

Vickie Luzia
Adoption Coalition, Inc.
P.O. Box 92181
Rochester, NY 14692

Diane Mees
Adoption Circle
31 Bartels Pl. (New Rochelle)
P.O. Box 311
Shenrock, NY 10587

Adoptees Liberty Movement
    Association
P.O. Box 10441
Rochester, NY 14610

Adoptees Liberty Movement
    Association
P.O. Box 809
Beacon, NY 12508

Always in Me
P.O. Box 809
Orchard Park, NY 14126

Gail Davenport, C.S.W.
Birthparent Support Network
11 Rockledge
P.O. Box 120
North White Plains, NY 10602

Far Horizons
P.O. Box 621
Cortland, NY 13045

Joan Wheeler
580 Breckenridge St.
Buffalo, NY 14222

Adoption Friendship Circle
P.O. Box 125
Bible School Park, NY 13717

Adoption Task Force
P.O. Box 1576
Southhampton, NY 11968

Marie P. Lamarche
Right to Know
P.O. Box 52
Old Westbury, NY 11568

Susan Burrows
Concerned United Birthparents
102 N St.
Manilus, NY 13104

The Adoption Circle
3 Townhouse Cir., #2-A
Great Neck, NY 11021

Adoption Friendship Circle
P.O. Box 7067
Endicott, NY 13760

Eileen McCarthy
1365 Chelsea Rd.
Wantagh, NY 11793

William Gage
2300 Ocean Ave.
Brooklyn, NY 11229

National Adoption Search
    Registry, Inc.
P.O. Box 2051
Great Neck, NY 11022

Suffolk Adoption Search and
    Support
10 Janice Lane
Selden, NY 11784

Adoption Circle
401 E. 74th St., #17-D
New York, NY 10021

Birthparent Support Network
669 Coney Island Ave.
Brooklyn, NY 11218

Birthparent Support Network
P.O. Box 34
Old Bethpage, NY 11804

Lee Beeman
Adoptees Liberty Movement
    Association
P.O. Box 808
Bolton Landing, NY 12814

Concerned United Birthparents
457 E. Maine Rd.
Johnson City, NY 13790

Carol Whitehead
37 Sylvia Lane
Plainview, NY 11803

NORTH CAROLINA
Concerned United Birthparents
4916 Brentwood Dr.
Durham, NC 27713

Marvin Hardison
Hardison Detective Agency
Rt. 1
La Grange, NC 28551

Adoption Information Exchange
46 Fairfax Ave.
Asheville, NC 28806

Adoption Information Exchange
800-54 Whiteside Rd.
Gastonia, NC 28052

Adoptees Liberty Movement
    Association
P.O. Box 901
Madison, NC 27025

Adoption Information Exchange
P.O. Box 1
Cumberland, NC 28331

Adoptees Together
P.O. Box 16532
Greensboro, NC 27406

Lynn Giddens
Adoption Information Exchange
P.O. Box 4153
Chapel Hill, NC 27515

Adoption Information Exchange
8539 Monroe Rd.
Charlotte, NC 28212

Adoption Information Exchange
Adoption Search Consultants
P.O. Box 1917
Matthews, NC 28106

Amy & Dennis Bergman
115 Slatestone Dr.
P.O. Box 768
Vanceboro, NC 28586

NORTH DAKOTA
Susan Lovett
2802 Syler
Hutchinson, KS 67504

OHIO
Birthparents Today
3423 Blue Rock
Cincinnati, OH 45239

Adoption Connection
7770 Cooper Rd.
Cincinnati, OH 45242

Adoption Triangle Unity
2714 Albion
Toledo, OH 43610

Adoption Network
302 Overlook Pk. Dr.
Cleveland, OH 44110

John Weiss
4309 Hamilton Ave., #22
Cincinnati, OH 45223

Carol Colon
Concerned United Birthparents
5-561 Ann Ave.
Wauseon, OH 43567

Carol Hunter
Concerned United Birthparents
5248 York Rd. SW
Rataska, OH 43062

Concerned United Birthparents
2544 Bonnie Lane
Maumee, OH 43537

Joanne Gall
Chosen Children
311 Springbrook, #B-1
Dayton, OH 45405

Adoptees Search Rights
P.O. Box 2249
Cleveland, OH 44102

Sunshine Reunion
1175 Virginia Ave.
Akron, OH 44036

Lost & Found Search & Support
    Group
P.O. Box 1033
Cayahoga Falls, OH 44223

Adoptees Search Rights
P.O. Box 8713
Toledo, OH 43623

Dominic Telesco
P.O. Box 694
Reynoldsburg, OH 43068

Search
P.O. Box 360074
Stringsville, OH 44136

Birthright
6779 Manchester Rd.
Clinton, OH 44216

Janet Crawley
Independent Search Consultant
1147 Shady Brook Dr.
Akron, OH 44312

Catherine Oatis
Concerned United Birthparents
2434 N. 4th
Columbus, OH 43202

OKLAHOMA
Lynda Lu Reed
Adoptees as Adults
8220 NW 114th St.
Oklahoma City, OK 73132

Oklahoma Adoption Triad
P.O. Box 2503
Broken Arrow, OK 74103

Willows Graduates
RR 8, Box 324
Claremore, OK 74017

OREGON
Ginni D. Snodgrass
9203 SW Cree Cir.
Tualatin, OR 97062

Sarah Atkins
11505 SW Duchess
Beaverton, OR 97005

Oregon Adoptive Rights
   Association
P.O. Box 1332
Beaverton, OR 97520

Kathy Brown
1076 Queens Branch Rd.
Rogue River, OR 97537

Family Ties
3185 Lincoln
Eugene, OR 97405

Kathlyn Krautscheld
Independent Search Consultant
P.O. Box 7271
Aloha, OR 97009

Dads against Discrimination
P.O. Box 8504
Portland, OR 97207

Jeanne McComber
Independent Search Consultant
1533 Grand Ave.
Medford, OR 97504

Oregon Adoptive Rights
   Association
P.O. Box 882
Portland, OR 97207

Southern Oregon Adoptee Rights
   Association
P.O. Box 202
Grants Pass, OR 97526

Family Ties
4537 Souza
Eugene, OR 97402

Nancy J. Finley
5236 SW Nebraska
Portland, OR 97219

Birthparents in Oregon
P.O. Box 17521
Portland, OR 97405

Norma Benjamin
14394 Ehlen Rd.
Aurora, OR 97002

Sue Farrer
Footprints
P.O. Box 764
Phoenix, OR 97535

Anne Ballis
P.O. Box 9084
Portland, OR 97207

Chris Bronson
410 Sodaville Rd.
Lebanon, OR 97355

Southern Oregon Adoptee Rights
492 Willow
Ashland, OR 97520

PENNSYLVANIA
John Goldberg
Adoption Forum
4719 Springfield
Philadelphia, PA 19143

Pennsylvania Open Records
    Coalition
P.O. Box 83
Oreland, PA 19025

Pittsburgh Adoption Connection
P.O. Box 4564
Pittsburgh, PA 15205

Birthparents for Life
P.O. Box 334
Chester Heights, PA 19017

Catholics for Open Records
P.O. Box 83
Oreland, PA 19025

Glenda Shay
37 Edgecliff
Carnegie, PA 15106

Carol Bravin
Adoption Lifeline
414 28th Ave.
Altoona, PA 16601

Sheila Grossholz
PA Adoptee Search Team
1210 Taki Dr.
Erie, PA 16505

Penny Partridge
Adoption Forum
525 S. 4th St., Ste. 3645
Philadelphia, PA 19147

Concerned United Birthparents
P.O. Box 7673
Pittsburgh, PA 15214

Pittsburgh Adoption Lifeline
P.O. Box 52
Gibsonia, PA 15044

Concerned United Birthparents
P.O. Box 1156
Bryn Mawr, PA 19109

Concerned United Birthparents
Chris Frank
2800 W. Chestnut Ave.
Altoona, PA 16603

Claudia Reynolds
Adoptees Liberty Movement
    Association
P.O. Box 207
New Brighton, PA 15066

RHODE ISLAND
Linda Brown
96 Everett Ave.
Providence, RI 02906

Parents of Adoptees Library of
    Rhode Island
861 Mitchells Lane
Middletown, RI 02840

Paul V. Zecchino
Search Ltd.
35 E. Pond Rd.
Narrangansett, RI 02882

Yesterday's Children
77 Homer St.
Providence, RI 02903

Search Ltd.
RFD 1, Box 337
Ashaway, RI 02804

SOUTH CAROLINA
Adoptees Birthparents in Search
P.O. Box 5551-Cayce W.
West Columbia, SC 29171

Adoptees Birthparents in Search
P.O. Box 4883
Florence, SC 29502

Pollie Robinson
263 Lemonade Rd.
Pacolet, SC 29372

Cyndi Walters
Adoption Search for Life
303 Brighton Rd.
Anderson, SC 29621

Lynn Zillmer
2571 Mt. Gallant Rd.
Rock Hill, SC 29611

Adoptees in Search
P.O. Box 6426-B
Greenville, SC 29506

Triad, Inc.
P.O. Box 4778
Columbia, SC 29240

SOUTH DAKOTA
Shirley Shinneman
Adoptees Liberty Movement
   Association
1325 S. Bahnson
Sioux Falls, SD 57103

TENNESSEE
Denny Glad
Independent Search Consultant
5108 Oak Meadow Ave.
Memphis, TN 38134

Tennessee Right to Know
P.O. Box 34334
Memphis, TN 38134

Norma Tillman
Unlimited Facts Obtained, Inc.
P.O. Box 290333
Nashville, TN 37229

Jalena Bowling
5150 Chiswood Cove
Memphis, TN 38134

Adult Adoptees & Birthparents in
   Search
P.O. Box 3572
Chattanooga, TN 37404

Jamie Johnson
Adoptees Liberty Movement
   Association
P.O. Box 15064
Chattanooga, TN 37415

Roots
P.O. Box 363
Strawberry Plains, TN 37871

Group for Openness in Adoption
518 General George Patton Rd.
Nashville, TN 37221

Roots
7110 Westway Ctr.
Knoxville, TN 37919

Nancy Kvapil
Independent Search Consultant
6636 Ferncrest
Memphis, TN 38134

Tennessee Searchers for Truth
7721 Whites Creek Pike
Joelton, TN 37080

Tennessee Adoptees in Search
P.O. Box 8684
Chattanooga, TN 37411

Family Finders
122 Bass Dr.
Mt. Juliet, TN 37122

TEXAS
Linda Crenwelge
1305 Augustine Ct.
College Station, TX 77840

Adoption Knowledge Affiliates
P.O. Box 402033
Austin, TX 78704

Jim Rockwell
Adoptees Liberty Movement
   Association
706 Gresham
Smithville, TX 78958

Adoptees Adoptive/Birth Parents
   in Search
4208 Roxbury
El Paso, TX 79922

Marilyn Morris/Peace of Mind
Adoption Search & Reunite, Inc.
2404 Huntington Dr.
P.O. Box 371
Pasadena, TX 77504

Right to Know
P.O. Box 1409
Grand Prairie, TX 78209

Janelle Reitsma
Searchline of Texas
5039 Hacienda
San Antonio, TX 78233

Concerned United Birthparents
P.O. Box 1527
Plano, TX 75074

Searchline of Texas
3313 Lombard
P.O. Box 4101
Amarillo, TX 79106

Searchfinders of Texas
150 Terrell Plz., #49
San Antonio, TX 78208

Pat Palmer
Independent Search Consultant
Searchline of Texas
1516 Old Orchard
Irving, TX 75061

Adoptees Liberty Movement
Association
P.O. Box 5735
Austin, TX 78763

Orphan Voyage
5811 Southminster
Houston, TX 77035

Kim Trimble
Concerned United Birthparents
5307 Gulfway Dr., #195
Groves, TX 77619

Barbara Donnelly
Adoptees Liberty Movement
Association
P.O. Box 9263
Longview, TX 75604

Adoption Awareness Center
615 Elm at McCullough
San Antonio, TX 78415

Beckie Scott
5738 Crest Grove
Corpus Christi, TX 78415

UTAH
Carl Clyde
Cari Lakey
Adoptees Liberty Movement
Association
P.O. Box 11383
Salt Lake City, UT 84147

Interstate Genealogists
369 E. 900 S.
Salt Lake City, UT 84111

Concerned United Birthparents
P.O. Box 1613
Sandy, UT 84091

David L. Barss
Salt Lake City Legs
P.O. Box 174
North Salt Lake, UT 84054

Charlotte Staten
672 E. 2025 S.
Bountiful, UT 84010

Bonnie Cox Schulte
Independent Search Consultant
P.O. Box 41
Hopper, UT 84315

Carolyn Jones
72 Hillside Ave.
P.O. Box 8124
Salt Lake City, UT 84108

VERMONT
Carol Gile
Concerned United Birthparents
RD 1, Box 716
Bridgeport, VT 05734

Living in Search of Answers
RR, Box 462
Putney, VT 05346

B & C Search Assistance of
Vermont
RR, Box 1451
St. Albans, VT 05478

Marge Garfield
Central Vermont Adoption
   Support
RR 1, Box 83
East Calais, VT 05650

Adoption Alliance of Vermont
91 Court St.
Middlebury, VT 05753

VIRGINIA
Parents & Adoptees Together
1500 Fort Hill Dr.
Richmond, VA 23226

Adoptees Support for
   Birthmothers
8630 Granby St.
Norfolk, VA 23503

Adoptees and Natural Parents
949 Lacon Dr.
Newport News, VA 23602

Adult Adoptees in Search
P.O. Box 203
Ferrum, VA 24088

WASHINGTON
Washington Adoptees Rights
   Movement
P.O. Box 2667
Olympia, WA 99507

Ann Koch Pelto
Adoption Search &
   Reconciliation
14320 SE 170th
Renton, WA 98058

Diane Sams
Independent Search Consultant
E. 303 Paradise Rd.
Spangle, WA 99031

Pat Owen
Washington Adoptees Rights
   Movement
5950 6th Ave. S., #107
Seattle, WA 98108

Carole Slaybaugh
Rt. 1, Box 17
Pomeroy, WA 99347

Washington Adoptees Rights
   Movement
220 Kirkland Ave., #10
Kirkland, WA 98033

Nancy Carton
Independent Search Consultant
12740 Bel-Red Rd.
Bellevue, WA 98005

Marilyn Dean
Independent Search Consultant
Washington Adoptees Rights
   Movement
9901 SE Shoreland Dr.
Bellevue, WA 98004

Washington Adoptees Rights
   Movement
1119 Peacock Lane
Burlington, WA 98233

Washington Adoptees Rights
   Movement
3402 52nd Ave. NE
Tacoma, WA 98422

WEST VIRGINIA
Judi Padlow
37 21st St.
McMechen, WV 26040

Society's Triangle
411 Cabell Ct.
Huntington, WV 25703

The Lost Children
312 8th Ave.
St. Albans, WV 25177

WISCONSIN
Elton Smith
6706 Revere Ave.
Milwaukee, WI 53213

Joel Remberg
Edward Thomas
Adoption Information &
  Direction
P.O. Box 23764
Milwaukee, WI 53224

Mary Sue Wedl
Adoption Information
44 Country
Rt. 1, Box 123
Lake Mills, WI 53551

Shelley Barenson
Adoption Information &
  Direction
4511 Woodbridge Dr.
P.O. Box 8162
Eau Claire, WI 54702

Betty Sue Avila
Adoptees Liberty Movement
  Association
Rt. 1, Box 104-A
Westby, WI 54667

Adoption Information &
  Direction
P.O. Box 111
Cudahy, WI 53110

Adoption Information &
  Direction
P.O. Box 2152
Appleton, WI 54913

Adoption Information &
  Direction
13025 W. Brentwood Dr.
New Berlin, WI 53151

Mary Emery
N. 5080 17th Ave.
Mauston, WI 53948

Adoptees Information & Direction
P.O. Box 7371
Madison, WI 53707

Adoptees Information & Direction
2116 Ellis St.
Stevens Point, WI 54481

Adoptees Information & Direction
P.O. Box 1552
La Crosse, WI 54601

Carrol Duer
Independent Search Consultant
1217 Indigo Dr.
Oshkosh, WI 54901

Sharon Alverson
Independent Search Consultant
Rt. 1, Box 197-A
New Lisbon, WI 53950

Mary Niebuhr
Independent Search Consultant
4221 Tomscott Trail
Madison, WI 53074

Ginny Whitehouse
Independent Search Consultant
610 Hintze Rd.
Madison, WI 53074

WYOMING
K. T. Roes
61 Schneider
Cody, WY 82414

Debbie Fomento
100 S. 30th, #13
Laramie, WY 82070

Contact information for these groups changes frequently. The sources listed here represent the most current information available to the author at the time this book was printed.

Social Security Numbers

The first three numbers in a Social Security number tell you where the card was originally applied for:

001–003	New Hampshire	429–432	Arkansas
004–007	Maine	433–439	Louisiana
008–009	Vermont	440–448	Oklahoma
010–034	Massachusetts	449–467	Texas
035–039	Rhode Island	468–477	Minnesota
040–049	Connecticut	478–485	Iowa
050–134	New York	486–500	Missouri
135–158	New Jersey	501–502	North Dakota
159–211	Pennsylvania	503–504	South Dakota
212–220	Maryland	505–508	Nebraska
221–222	Delaware	509–515	Kansas
223–231	Virginia	516–517	Montana
232–236	West Virginia	518–519	Idaho
237–246	North Carolina	520	Wyoming
247–251	South Carolina	521–524	Colorado
252–260	Georgia	525	New Mexico
261–267	Florida	526–527	Arizona
268–302	Ohio	528–529	Utah
303–317	Indiana	530	Nevada
318–361	Illinois	531–539	Washington
362–386	Michigan	540–544	Oregon
387–399	Wisconsin	545–573	California
400–407	Kentucky	574	Alaska
409–415	Tennessee	575–576	Hawaii
416–424	Alabama	577–579	Washington, DC
425–428	Mississippi		

Vital Records

Place of event	Cost of copy	Address	Remarks
Alabama			
Birth or Death	$12.00	Center for Health Statistics State Department of Public Health P.O. Box 5625 Montgomery, AL 36103-5625	State office has had records since January 1908. Additional copies at same time are $4.00 each. Fee for special searches is $10.00 per hour. Money order or check should be made payable to Center for Health Statistics. Personal checks are accepted. To verify current fees, the telephone number is (205) 242-5033.
Marriage	$12.00	Same as Birth or Death	State office has had records since August 1936.
	Varies	See remarks	Probate Judge in county where license was issued.
Divorce	$12.00	Same as Birth or Death	State office has had records since January 1950.
	Varies	See remarks	Clerk or Register of Court of Equity in county where divorce was granted.
Alaska			
Birth or Death	$7.00	Department of Health and Social Services Bureau of Vital Statistics P.O. Box H-02G Juneau, AK 99811-0675	State office has had records since January 1913. Money order should be made payable to Bureau of Vital Statistics. Personal checks are not accepted. To verify current fees, the telephone number is (907) 465-3391. This will be a recorded message.
Marriage	$7.00	Same as Birth or Death	State office has had records since 1913.
Divorce	$7.00	Same as Birth or Death	State office has had records since 1950.

Place of event	Cost of copy	Address	Remarks
	Varies	See remarks	Clerk of Superior Court in judicial district where divorce was granted. Juneau and Ketchikan (First District), Nome (Second District), Anchorage (Third District), Fairbanks (Fourth District).
Arizona			
Birth (long form)	$8.00	Vital Records Section	State office has had records since July 1909 and abstracts of records filed in counties before then.
Birth (short form)	$5.00	Arizona Department of Health Services	
Death	$5.00	P.O. Box 3887 Phoenix, AZ 85030	Check or money order should be made payable to Office of Vital Records. Personal checks are accepted. To verify current fees, the telephone number is (602) 255-3260. This will be a recorded message. Applicants must submit a copy of picture identification or have their request notarized.
Marriage	Varies	See remarks	Clerk of Superior Court in county where license was issued.
Divorce	Varies	See remarks	Clerk of Superior Court in county where divorce was granted.
Arkansas			
Birth	$5.00	Division of Vital Records	State office has had records since February 1914 and some original Little Rock and Fort Smith records from 1881. Additional copies of death record, when requested at the same time, are $1.00 each.
Death	$4.00	Arkansas Dept. of Health 4815 West Markham Street Little Rock, AR 72201	Check or money order should be made payable to Arkansas Department of Health. Personal checks are accepted. To verify current fees, the telephone number is (501) 661-2336. This will be a recorded message.

Place of event	Cost of copy	Address	Remarks
Marriage	$5.00	Same as Birth or Death	Coupons since 1917.
	Varies	See remarks	Full certified copy may be obtained from Circuit or Chancery Clerk in county where license was issued.
Divorce	$5.00	Same as Birth or Death	Coupons since 1917.
	Varies	See remarks	Full certified copy may be obtained from Circuit or Chancery Clerk in county where divorce was granted.
California			
Birth Death	$12.00 $8.00	Vital Statistics Section Department of Health Services P.O. Box 730241 Sacramento, CA 94244-0241	State office has had records since July 1905. For earlier records, write to County Recorder in county where event occurred. Check or money order should be made payable to State Registrar, Department of Health Services or Vital Statistics. Personal checks are accepted. To verify current fees, the telephone number is (916) 445-2684.
Heirloom Birth	$31.00	Not available until further notice	Decorative birth certificate (11"x14") suitable for framing.
Marriage	$12.00	Same as Birth or Death	State office has had records since July 1905. For earlier records, write to County Recorder in county where event occurred.
Divorce	$12.00	Same as Birth or Death	Fee is for search and identification of county where certified copy can be obtained. Certified copies are not available from State Health Department.
	Varies	See remarks	Clerk of Superior Court in county where divorce was granted.

Place of event	*Cost of copy*	*Address*	*Remarks*
Colorado			
Birth or Death	$12.00	Vital Records Section Colorado Dept. of Health 4300 Cherry Creek Drive South Denver, CO 80222-1530	State office has had death records since1900 and birth records since 1910. State office also has birth records for some counties for years before 1910. Additional copies of the same record ordered at the same time are $6.00.
			Check or money order should be made payable to Colorado Department of Health. Personal checks are accepted. To verify current fees, the telephone number is (303) 756-4464. This will be a recorded message.
Marriage	See remarks	Same as Birth or Death	Certified copies are not available from State Health Department. Statewide index of records for 1900-39 and 1975 to present. Fee for verification is $12.00.
	Varies	See remarks	Copies available from County Clerk in county where license was issued.
Divorce	See remarks	Same as Birth or Death	Certified copies are not available from State Health Department. Statewide index of records for 1900-39 and 1968 to present. Fee for verification is $12.00.
	Varies	See remarks	Copies available from Clerk of District Court in county where divorce was granted.
Connecticut			
Birth or Death	$5.00	Vital Records Department of Health Services 150 Washington St. Hartford, CT 06106	State office has had records since July 1897. For earlier records, write to Registrar of Vital Statistics in town or city where event occurred.

Place of event	Cost of copy	Address	Remarks
Marriage	$5.00	Same as Birth or Death	Check or money order should be made payable to Department of Health Services. Personal checks are accepted. FAX requests are not accepted. Must have original signature on request. To verify current fees, the telephone number is (203) 566-2334. This will be a recorded message. Records since July 1897 at State Registry.
		See remarks	For older records, contact the Registrar of Vital Statistics in town where marriage occurred.
Divorce		See remarks	Applicant must contact Clerk of Superior Court where divorce was granted. State office does not have divorce decrees and cannot issue certified copies.
Delaware Birth or Death	$5.00	Office of Vital Statistics Division of Public Health P.O. Box 637 Dover, DE 19903	State office has death records since 1930 and birth records since 1920. Additional copies of the same record requested at the same time are $3.00 each.
			Check or money order should be made payable to Office of Vital Statistics. Personal checks are accepted. To verify current fees, the telephone number is (302) 739-4721.
Marriage	$5.00	Same as Birth or Death	Records since 1930. Additional copies of the same record requested at the same time are $3.00 each.
Divorce	See remarks	Same as Birth or Death	Records since 1935. Inquiries will be forwarded to appropriate office. Fee for search and verification of essential facts of divorce is $5.00 for each 5-year period searched. Certified copies are not available from State office.

Place of event	Cost of copy	Address	Remarks
	$2.00	See remarks	Prothonotary in county where divorce was granted up to 1975. For divorces after 1975 the parties concerned should contact Family Court in county where divorce was granted.
District of Columbia Birth or Death	$12.00	Vital Records Branch Room 3009 425 I Street, NW Washington, DC 20001	Office has had death records since 1855 and birth records since 1874, but no death records were filed during the Civil War. Cashiers check or money order should be made payable to DC Treasurer. To verify current fees, the telephone number is (202) 727-9281.
Marriage	$5.00	Marriage Bureau 515 5th Street, NW Washington, DC 20001	
Divorce	$2.00	Clerk, Superior Court for the District of Columbia, Family Division 500 Indiana Avenue, NW Washington, DC 20001	Records since September 16, 1956.
	Varies	Clerk, U.S. District Court for the District of Columbia Washington, DC 20001	Records before September 16, 1956.

Place of event	Cost of copy	Address	Remarks
Florida			
Birth	$9.00	Department of Health and Rehabilitative Services Office of Vital Statistics P.O. Box 210 1217 Pearl Street Jacksonville, FL 32231	State office has some birth records dating back to April 1865 and some death records dating back to August 1877. The majority of records date from January 1917. (If the exact date is unknown, the fee is $9.00 (births) or $5.00 (deaths) for the first year searched and $2.00 for each additional year up to a maximum of $50.00. Fee includes one certification of record if found or certified statement stating record not on file.) Additional copies are $4.00 each when requested at the same time.
Death	$5.00		
			Check or money order should be made payable to Office of Vital Statistics. Personal checks are accepted. To verify current fees, the telephone number is (904) 359-6900. This will be a recorded message.)
Marriage	$5.00	Same as Birth or Death	Records since June 6, 1927. (If the exact date is unknown, the fee is $5.00 for the first year searched and $2.00 for each additional year up to a maximum of $50.00. Fee includes one copy of record if found or certified statement stating record not on file.) Additional copies are $4.00 each when requested at the same time.
Divorce	$5.00	Same as Birth or Death	Records since June 6, 1927. (If the exact date is unknown, the fee is $5.00 for the first year searched and $2.00 for each additional year up to a maximum of $50.00. Fee includes one copy of record if found or certified statement stating record not on file.) Additional copies are $4.00 each when requested at the same time.

Place of event	Cost of copy	Address	Remarks
Georgia Birth or Death	$10.00	Georgia Department of Human Resources Vital Records Unit Room 217-H 47 Trinity Avenue, SW Atlanta, GA 30334	State office has had records since January 1919. For earlier records in Atlanta or Savannah, write to County Health Department in county where event occurred. Additional copies of same record ordered at same time are $5.00 each except birth cards, which are $10.00 each. Money order should be made payable to Vital Records, GA. DHR. Personal checks are not accepted. To verify current fees, the telephone number is (404) 656-4900. This is a recorded message.
Marriage	$10.00	Same as Birth or Death	Centralized State records since June 9, 1952. Certified copies are issued at State office. Inquiries about marriages occurring before June 9, 1952, will be forwarded to appropriate Probate Judge in county where license was issued.
	Varies	See remarks	Probate Judge in county where license was issued.
Divorce	$2.00 for certification plus $0.50 per page	See remarks	Centralized State records since June 9, 1952. Certified copies are not issued at State office. Inquiries will be forwarded to appropriate Clerk of Superior Court in county where divorce was granted.
		See remarks	Clerk of Superior Court in county where divorce was granted.

Place of event	Cost of copy	Address	Remarks
Hawaii			
Birth or Death	$2.00	Office of Health Status Monitoring State Department of Health P.O. Box 3378 Honolulu, HI 96801	State office has had records since 1853. Check or money order should be made payable to State Department of Health. Personal checks are accepted for the correct amount only. To verify current fees, the telephone number is (808) 586-4533. This is a recorded message.
Marriage	$2.00	Same as Birth or Death	
Divorce	$2.00	Same as Birth or Death	Records since July 1951.
	Varies	See remarks	Circuit Court in county where divorce was granted.
Idaho			
Birth Wallet card Death	$8.00 $8.00 $8.00	Vital Statistics Unit Idaho Department of Health and Welfare 450 West State Street Statehouse Mail Boise, ID 83720-9990	State office has had records since July 1911. For records from 1907 to 1911, write to County Recorder in county where event occurred.
Heirloom Birth	$30.00	Same as Birth or Death	Decorative birth certificates (8 1/2"x11" and 5"x7") are suitable for framing. Check or money order should be made payable to Idaho Vital Statistics. Personal checks are accepted. To verify current fees, the telephone number is (208) 334-5988. This is a recorded message.

Place of event	Cost of copy	Address	Remarks
Marriage	$8.00	Same as Birth or Death	Records since May 1947. Earlier records are with County Recorder in county where license was issued.
	Varies	See remarks	County Recorder in county where license was issued.
Divorce	$8.00	Same as Birth or Death	Records since May 1947. Earlier records are with County Recorder in county where divorce was granted.
	Varies	See remarks	County records in county where divorce was granted.

Illinois

Place of event	Cost of copy	Address	Remarks
Birth or Death	$15.00 certified copy $10.00 certification	Division of Vital Records Illinois Department of Public Health 605 West Jefferson Street Springfield, IL 62702-5097	State office has had records since January 1916. For earlier records and for copies of State records since January 1916, write to County Clerk in county where event occurred (county fees vary). The fee for a search of the State files is $10.00. If the record is found, one certification is issued at no additional charge. Additional certifications of the same record ordered at the same time are $2.00 each. The fee for a full certified copy is $15.00. Additional certified copies of the same record ordered at the same time are $2.00 each.

Money orders, certified checks, or personal checks should be made payable to Illinois Department of Public Health. To verify current fees, the telephone number is (217) 782-6553. This will be a recorded message. |
| Marriage | $5.00 | Same as Birth or Death | Marriage Index since January 1962. Selected items may be verified (fee $5.00). Certified copies are not available from State office. |

Place of event	Cost of copy	Address	Remarks
			For certified copies, write to the County Clerk in county where license was issued.
Divorce	$5.00	Same as Birth or Death	Divorce Index since January 1962. Selected items may be verified (fee $5.00). Certified copies are not available from State office.
			For certified copies, write to the Clerk of Circuit Court in county where divorce was granted.
Indiana Birth Death	$6.00 $4.00	Vital Records Section State Department of Health 1330 West Michigan Street P.O. Box 1964 Indianapolis, IN 46206-1964	State office has had birth records since October 1907 and death records since 1900. Additional copies of the same record ordered at the same time are $1.00 each. For earlier records, write to Health Officer in city or county where event occurred. Check or money order should be made payable to Indiana State Department of Health. Personal checks are accepted. To verify current fees, the telephone number is (317) 633-0274.
Marriage	See remarks	Same as Birth or Death	Marriage index since 1958. Certified copies are not available from State Health Department.
	Varies	See remarks	Clerk of Circuit Court or Clerk of Superior Court in county where license was issued.
Divorce	Varies	See remarks	County Clerk in county where divorce was granted.

Place of event	Cost of copy	Address	Remarks
Iowa			
Birth or Death	$6.00	Iowa Department of Public Health Vital Records Section Lucas Office Bldg. 321 East 12th Street Des Moines, IA 50319-0075	State office has had records since July 1880. Check or money order should be made payable to Iowa Department of Public Health. To verify current fees, the telephone number is (515) 281-4944. This will be a recorded message.
Marriage	$6.00	Same as Birth or Death	State office has had records since July 1880.
Divorce	See remarks	Same as Birth or Death	Brief statistical record only since 1906. Inquiries will be forwarded to appropriate office. Certified copies are not available from State Health Department.
	$6.00	See remarks	Clerk of District Court in county where divorce was granted.
Kansas			
Birth Death	$10.00 $7.00	Office of Vital Statistics Kansas State Department of Health and Environment 900 Jackson Street Topeka, KS 66612-1290	State office has had records since July 1911. For earlier records, write to County Clerk in county where event occurred. Additional copies of same record ordered at same time are $5.00 each. Check or money order should be made payable to State Registrar of Vital Statistics. Personal checks are accepted. To verify current fees, the telephone number is (913) 296-1400. This will be a recorded message.
Marriage	$7.00	Same as Birth or Death	State office has had records since May 1913.
	Varies	See remarks	District Judge in county where license was issued.

Place of event	Cost of copy	Address	Remarks
Divorce	$7.00	Same as Birth or Death	State office has had records since July 1951.
	Varies	See remarks	Clerk of District Court in county where divorce was granted.
Kentucky			
Birth	$7.00	Office of Vital	State office has had records since
Death	$6.00	Statistics Department for Health Services 275 East Main Street Frankfort, KY 40621	January 1911 and some records for the cities of Louisville, Lexington, Covington, and Newport before then.
			Check or money order should be made payable to Kentucky State Treasurer. Personal checks are accepted. To verify current fees, the telephone number is (502) 564-4212.
Marriage	$6.00	Same as Birth or Death	Records since June 1958.
	Varies	See remarks	Clerk of County Court in county where license was issued.
Divorce	$6.00	Same as Birth or Death	Records since June 1958.
	Varies	See remarks	Clerk of Circuit Court in county where decree was issued.
Louisiana			
Birth (long form)	$10.00	Vital Records Registry	State office has had records since July 1914. Birth records for City of New
Birth (short form)	$7.00	Office of Public Health	Orleans are available from 1892. Death records are available since
Death	$5.00	325 Loyola Avenue New Orleans, LA 70112	1942. Older birth, death, and marriage records are available through the Louisiana State Archives, P.O. Box 94125, Baton Rouge, LA 70804.

Place of event	Cost of copy	Address	Remarks
			Check or money order should be made payable to Vital Records. Pesonal checks are accepted. To verify current fees, the telephone number is (504) 568-5152.
Marriage Orleans Parish	$5.00	Same as Birth or Death	
Other Parishes	Varies	See remarks	Certified copies are issued by Clerk of Court in parish where license was issued.
Divorce	Varies	See remarks	Clerk of Court in parish where divorce was granted.
Maine			
Birth or Death	$10.00	Office of Vital Statistics Maine Department of Human Services State House Station 11 Augusta, ME 04333-0011	State office has had records since 1892. Records for 1892-1922 are available at the Maine State Archives. For earlier records, write to the municipality where the event occurred. Additional copies of same record ordered at same time are $4.00 each.
			Check or money order should be made payable to Treasurer, State of Maine. Personal checks are accepted. To verify current fees, the telephone number is (207) 289-3184.
Marriage	$10.00	Same as Birth or Death	Same as Birth or Death.
Divorce	$10.00	Same as Birth or Death	Same as Birth or Death.
	Varies	See remarks	Clerk of District Court in judicial division where divorce was granted.

Place of event	Cost of copy	Address	Remarks
Maryland			
Birth or Death	$4.00	Division of Vital Records Department of Health and Mental Hygiene Metro Executive Building 4201 Patterson Ave. P.O. Box 68760 Baltimore, MD 21215-0020	State office has had records since August 1898. Records for City of Baltimore are available from January 1875. Will not do research for genealogical studies. Must apply to State of Maryland Archives, 350 Rowe Blvd., Annapolis, MD 21401, (301) 974-3914. Check or money order should be made payable to Division of Vital Records. Personal checks are accepted. To verify current fees, the telephone number is (301) 225-5988. This will be a recorded message.
Marriage	$4.00	Same as Birth or Death	Records since June 1951.
	Varies	See remarks	Clerk of Circuit Court in county where license was issued or Clerk of Court of Common Pleas of Baltimore City (for licenses issued in City of Baltimore).
Divorce Verification only	No fee	Same as Birth or Death	Records since January 1961. Certified copies are not available from State office. Some items may be verified.
	Varies	See remarks	Clerk of Circuit Court in county where divorce was granted.
Massachusetts			
Birth or Death	$6.00 (In person) $11.00 (Mail request)	Registry of Vital Records and Statistics 150 Tremont Street Room B-3 Boston, MA 02111	State office has records since 1901. For earlier records, write to The Massachusetts Archives at Columbia Point, 220 Morrissey Boulevard, Boston, MA 02125 (617) 727-2816.

Place of event	Cost of copy	Address	Remarks
	$3.00 (State Archives)		Check or money order should be made payable to Commonwealth of Massachusetts. Personal checks are accepted. To verify current fees, the telephone number is (617) 727-7388. This will be a recorded message.
Marriage	Same as Birth or Death	Same as Birth or Death	Records since 1901.
Divorce	See remarks	Same as Birth or Death	Index only since 1952. Inquirer will be directed where to send request. Certified copies are not available from State office.
	$3.00	See remarks	Registrar of Probate Court in county where divorce was granted.
Michigan Birth or Death	$13.00	Office of the State Registrar and Center for Health Statistics Michigan Dept. of Public Health 3423 North Logan Street Lansing, MI 48909	State office has had records since 1867. Copies of most records since 1867 may also be obtained from County Clerk in county where event occurred. Detroit records may be obtained from the City of Detroit Health Department for births occurring since 1893 and for deaths since 1897.
			Check or money order should be made payable to State of Michigan. Personal checks are accepted. To verify current fees, the telephone number is (517) 335-8655. This will be a recorded message.
Marriage	$13.00	Same as Birth or Death	Records since April 1867.
	Varies	See remarks	County Clerk in county where license was issued.

Place of event	Cost of copy	Address	Remarks
Divorce	$13.00	Same as Birth or Death	Records since 1897.
	Varies	See remarks	County Clerk in county where divorce was granted.
Minnesota			
Birth	$11.00	Minnesota Dept.	State office has had records since
Death	$8.00	of Health Section of Vital Statistics 717 Delaware Street, SE P.O. Box 9441 Minneapolis, MN 55440	January 1908. Copies of earlier records may be obtained from Local Registrar in county where event occurred or from the St. Paul City Health Department if the event occurred in St. Paul. Additional copies of the birth record when ordered at the same time are $5.00 each. Additional copies of the death record when ordered at the same time are $2.00 each.
			Check or money order should be made payable to Treasurer, State of Minnesota. Personal checks are accepted. To verify current fees, the telephone number is (612) 623-5121.
Marriage	See remarks	Same as Birth or Death	Statewide index since January 1958. Inquiries will be forwarded to appropriate office. Certified copies are not available from State Department of Health.
	$8.00	See remarks	Local Registrar in county where license was issued. Additional copies of the marriage record when ordered at the same time are $2.00 each.
Divorce	See remarks	Same as Birth or Death	Index since January 1970. Certified copies are not available from State office.
	Varies	See remarks	Local Registrar in county where divorce was granted.

Place of event	Cost of copy	Address	Remarks
Mississippi			
Birth	$12.00	Vital Records	State office has had records since 1912.
Birth (short form)	$7.00	State Department of Health	Full copies of birth certificates obtained within one year after the event are
Death	$10.00	2433 North State St. Jackson, MS 39216	$7.00. Additional copies of same record ordered at same time are $3.00 each for birth; $2.00 each for death and marriage.
			For out-of-state requests only bank or postal money orders are accepted and should be made payable to Mississippi State Department of Health. Personal checks are accepted only for in-state requests. To verify current fees, the telephone number is (601) 960-7981. A recorded message may be reached on (601) 960-7450.
Marriage	$10.00	Same as Birth or Death	Statistical records only from January 1926 to July 1, 1938, and since January 1942.
	$3.00	See remarks	Circuit Clerk in county where license was issued.
Divorce	See remarks	Same as Birth or Death	Records since January 1926. Certified copies are not available from State office. Index search only available at $6.00 for each 5-year increment. Book and page number for county record provided.
	Varies	See remarks	Chancery Clerk in county where divorce was granted.

Place of event	Cost of copy	Address	Remarks
Missouri			
Birth or Death	$10.00	Missouri Dept. of Health Bureau of Vital Records 1730 East Elm P.O. Box 570 Jefferson City, MO 65102-0570	State office has had records since January 1910. If event occurred in St. Louis (City), St. Louis County, or Kansas City before 1910, write to the City or County Health Department. Copies of these records are $3.00 each in St. Louis City and $5.00 each in St. Louis County. In Kansas City, $6.00 for first copy and $3.00 for each additional copy ordered at same time.
			Check or money order should be made payable to Missouri Department of Health. Personal checks are accepted. To verify current fees on birth certificates and death records, the telephone number is (314) 751-6400.
Marriage	No fee	Same as Birth or Death	Indexes since July 1948. Correspondent will be referred to appropriate Recorder of Deeds in county where license was issued.
	Varies	See remarks	Recorder of Deeds in county where license was issued.
Divorce	No fee	Same as Birth or Death	Indexes since July 1948. Certified copies are not available from State Health Department. Inquiries will be forwarded to appropriate office.
	Varies	See remarks	Clerk of Circuit Court in county where divorce was granted.

Place of event	Cost of copy	Address	Remarks
Montana			
Birth or Death	$10.00	Bureau of Records and Statistics State Dept. of Health and Environmental Sciences Helena, MT 59620	State office has had records since late 1907. Check or money order should be made payable to Montana Department of Health and Environmental Sciences. Personal checks are accepted. To verify current fees, the telephone number is (406) 444-2614.
Marriage	See remarks	Same as Birth or Death	Records since July 1943. Some items may be verified. Inquiries will be forwarded to appropriate office. Apply to county where license was issued if known. Certified copies are not available from State office.
	Varies	See remarks	Clerk of District Court in county where license was issued.
Divorce	See remarks	Same as Birth or Death	Records since July 1943. Some items may be verified. Inquiries will be forwarded to appropriate office. Apply to court where divorce was granted if known. Certified copies are not available from State office.
	Varies	See remarks	Clerk of District Court in county where divorce was granted.
Nebraska			
Birth Death	$8.00 $7.00	Bureau of Vital Statistics State Dept. of Health 301 Centennial Mall South P.O. Box 95007 Lincoln, NE 68509-5007	State office has had records since late 1904. If birth occurred before then, write the State office for information. Check or money order should be made payable to Bureau of Vital Statistics. Personal checks are accepted. To verify current fees, the telephone number is (402) 471-2871. This is a recorded message.

Place of event	Cost of copy	Address	Remarks
Marriage	$7.00	Same as Birth or Death	Records since January 1909.
	Varies	See remarks	County Court in county where license was issued.
Divorce	$7.00	Same as Birth or Death	Records since January 1909.
	Varies	See remarks	Clerk of District Court in county where divorce was granted.
Nevada			
Birth	$11.00	Division of Health-	State office has records since July
Death	$8.00	Vital Statistics Capitol Complex 505 East King Street #102	1911. For earlier records, write to County Recorder in county where event occurred.
		Carson City, NV 89710	Check or money order should be made payable to Section of Vital Statistics. Personal checks are accepted. To verify current fees, the telephone number is (702) 687-4480.
Marriage	See remarks	Same as Birth or Death	Indexes since January 1968. Certified copies are not available from State Health Department. Inquiries will be forwarded to appropriate office.
	Varies	See remarks	County Clerk in county where license was issued.
Divorce	See remarks	Same as Birth or Death	Indexes since January 1968. Certified copies are not available from State Health Department. Inquiries will be forwarded to appropriate office.
	Varies	See remarks	County Clerk in county where divorce was granted.

Place of event	Cost of copy	Address	Remarks
New Hampshire			
Birth or Death	$10.00	Bureau of Vital Records Health and Welfare Building 6 Hazen Drive Concord, NH 03301	State office has had records since 1640. Copies of records may be obtained from State office or from City or Town Clerk in place where event occurred. Additional copies ordered at the same time are $6.00 each.
			Check or money order should be made payable to Treasurer, State of New Hampshire. Personal checks accepted. To verify current fees, the telephone number is (603) 271-4654. This will be a recorded message.
Marriage	$10.00	Same as Birth or Death	Records since 1640.
	$10.00	See remarks	Town Clerk in town where license was issued.
Divorce	$10.00	Same as Birth or Death	Records since 1808.
	Varies	See remarks	Clerk of Superior Court where divorce was granted.
New Jersey			
Birth or Death	$4.00	State Department of Health Bureau of Vital Statistics South Warren and Market Streets CN 370 Trenton, NJ 08625	State office has had records since June 1878. Additional copies of same record ordered at same time are $2.00 each. If the exact date is unknown, the fee is an additional $1.00 per year searched.

Place of event	Cost of copy	Address	Remarks
		Archives and History Bureau State Library Division	For records from May 1848 to May 1878.
		State Department of Education Trenton, NJ 08625	Check or money order should be made payable to New Jersey State Department of Health. Personal checks are accepted. To verify current fees, the telephone number is (609) 292-4087. This will be a recorded message.
Marriage	$4.00	Same as Birth or Death	If the exact date is unknown, the fee is an additional $1.00 per year searched.
	$2.00	Archives and History Bureau State Library Div. State Department of Education Trenton, NJ 08625	For records from May 1848 to May 1878.
Divorce	$1.00	Public Information Center CN 967 Trenton, NJ 08625	The fee is for a certified Blue Seal copy. Make check payable to Clerk of the Superior Court.
New Mexico			
Birth	$10.00	Vital Statistics	State office has had records since
Death	$5.00	New Mexico Health Services Division P.O. Box 26110 Santa Fe, NM 87502	1920 and delayed records since 1880. Check or money order should be made payable to Vital Statistics. Personal checks are accepted. To verify current fees, the telephone number is (505) 827-2338. This will be a recorded message.
Marriage	Varies	See remarks	County Clerk in county where license was issued.
Divorce	Varies	See remarks	Clerk of Superior Court where divorce was granted.

Place of event	Cost of copy	Address	Remarks
New York (except New York City)			
Birth or Death	$15.00	Vital Records Section State Department of Health Empire State Plaza Tower Building Albany, NY 12237-0023	State office has had records since 1880. For records before 1914 in Albany, Buffalo, and Yonkers, or before 1880 in any other city, write to Registrar of Vital Statistics in city where event occurred. For the rest of the State, except New York City, write to State office.
			Check or money order should be made payable to New York State Department of Health. Personal checks are accepted. To verify current fees, the telephone number is (518) 474-3075. This will be a recorded message.
Marriage	$5.00	Same as Birth or Death	Records from 1880 to present.
	$5.00	See remarks	For records from 1880-1907 and licenses issued in the cities of Albany, Buffalo, or Yonkers, apply to— Albany: City Clerk, City Hall, Albany, NY 12207; Buffalo: City Clerk, City Hall, Buffalo, NY 14202; Yonkers: Registrar of Vital Statistics, Health Center Building, Yonkers, NY 10701.
Divorce	$15.00	Same as Birth or Death	Records since January 1963.
	Varies	See remarks	County Clerk in county where divorce was granted.

Place of event	Cost of copy	Address	Remarks
New York City			
Birth or Death	$15.00	Division of Vital Records New York City Dept. of Health P.O. Box 3776 New York, NY 10007	Office has birth records since 1910 and death records since 1949 for those occurring in the Boroughs of Manhattan, Brooklyn, Bronx, Queens, and Staten Island. For birth records prior to 1910 and death records prior to 1949, write to Archives Division, Department of Records and Information Services, 31 Chambers Street, New York, NY 10007.
			Certified check or money order should be made payable to New York City Department of Health. To verify current fees, the telephone numbers are (212) 619-4530 or (212) 693-4637. These are recorded messages.
Marriage			
Bronx Borough	$10.00	City Clerk's Office 1780 Grand Concourse Bronx, NY 10457	Records from 1847 to 1865: Archives Division, Department of Records and Information Services, 31 Chambers Street, New York, NY 10007, except Brooklyn records for this period,
Brooklyn Borough	$10.00	City Clerk's Office Municipal Building Brooklyn, NY 11201	which are filed with County Clerk's Office, Kings County, Supreme Court Building, Brooklyn, NY 11201. Additional copies of same record
Manhattan Borough	$10.00	City Clerk's Office Municipal Building Manhattan, NY 10007	ordered at same time are $5.00 each. Records from 1866 to 1907: City Clerk's Office in the borough of bride's residence; nonresidents write to City Clerk's Office in borough
Queens Borough	$10.00	City Clerk's Office 120–55 Queens Blvd. Kew Gardens, NY 11424	where license was obtained. Records since May 13, 1943: City Clerk's Office in borough where license was issued.

Place of event	Cost of copy	Address	Remarks
Staten Island (no longer called Richmond)	$10.00	City Clerk's Office Staten Island Borough Hall Staten Island, NY 10301	
Divorce			See New York State
North Carolina			
Birth or Death	$10.00	Department of Environment, Health, and Natural Resources Division of Epidemiology Vital Records Section 225 North McDowell Street P.O. Box 29537 Raleigh, NC 27626-0537	State office has had birth records since October 1913 and death records since January 1, 1946. Death records from 1913 through 1945 are available from Archives and Records Section, 109 East Jones Street, Raleigh, NC 27611. Additional copies of the same record ordered at the same time are $5.00 each. Check or money order should be made payable to Vital Records Section. Personal checks are accepted. To verify current fees, the telephone number is (919) 733-3526.
Marriage	$10.00	Same as Birth or Death	Records since January 1962.
	$3.00	See remarks	Registrar of Deeds in county where marriage was performed.
Divorce	$10.00	Same as Birth or Death	Records since January 1958.
	Varies	See remarks	Clerk of Superior Court where divorce was granted.

Place of event	Cost of copy	Address	Remarks
North Dakota			
Birth	$7.00	Division of Vital	State office has had some records
Death	$5.00	Records	since July 1893. Years from 1894 to
		State Capitol	1920 are incomplete. Additional
		600 East Boulevard	copies of birth records are $4.00
		Avenue	each; death records are $2.00 each.
		Bismarck, ND 58505	
			Money order should be made payable to Division of Vital Records. To verify current fees, the telephone number is (701) 224-2360.
Marriage	$5.00	Same as Birth or Death	Records since July 1925. Requests for earlier records will be forwarded to appropriate office. Additional copies are $2.00 each.
	Varies	See remarks	County Judge in county where license was issued.
Divorce	See remarks	Same as Birth or Death	Index of records since July 1949. Some items may be verified. Certified copies are not available from State Health Department. Inquiries will be forwarded to appropriate office.
	Varies	See remarks	Clerk of District Court in county where divorce was granted.
Ohio			
Birth or Death	$7.00	Bureau of Vital Statistics Ohio Department of Health P.O. Box 15098 Columbus, OH 43215-0098	State office has had birth records since December 20, 1908. For earlier birth and death records, write to the Probate Court in the county where the event occurred. The State Office has death records after December 31, 1936. Death records for December 20, 1908–December 31, 1936, can be obtained from the Ohio Historical Society, Archives Library Division, 1985 Velma Avenue, Columbus, OH 43211-2497.

Place of event	Cost of copy	Address	Remarks
			Check or money order should be made payable to State Treasury. Personal checks are accepted. To verify current fees, the telephone number is (614) 466-2531. This will be a recorded message.
Marriage	See remarks	Same as Birth or Death	Records since September 1949. All items may be verified. Certified copies are not available from State Health Department. Inquiries will be forwarded to appropriate office.
	Varies	See remarks	Probate Judge in county where license was issued.
Divorce	See remarks	Same as Birth or Death	Records since September 1949. All items may be verified. Certified copies are not available from State Health Department. Inquiries will be forwarded to appropriate office.
	Varies	See remarks	Clerk of Court of Common Pleas in county where divorce was granted.
Oklahoma Birth or Death	$5.00	Vital Records Section State Department of Health 1000 Northeast 10th Street P.O. Box 53551 Oklahoma City, OK 73152	State office has had records since October 1908. Check or money order should be made payable to Oklahoma State Department of Health. Personal checks are accepted. To verify current fees, the telephone number is (405) 271-4040.
Marriage	Varies	See remarks	Clerk of Court in county where license was issued.
Divorce	Varies	See remarks	Clerk of Court in county where divorce was granted.

Place of event	Cost of copy	Address	Remarks
Oregon			
Birth or Death	$13.00	Oregon Health Division Vital Statistics Section P.O. Box 14050 Portland, OR 97214-0050	State office has had records since January 1903. Some earlier records for the City of Portland since approximately 1880 are available from the Oregon State Archives, 1005 Broadway NE, Salem, OR 97310.
Heirloom Birth	$28.00	Same as Birth or Death	Presentation style calligraphy certificate suitable for framing. Money order should be made payable to Oregon Health Division. To verify current fees, the telephone number is (503) 731-4095. This will be a recorded message.
Marriage	$13.00	Same as Birth or Death	Records since January 1906.
	Varies	See remarks	County Clerk in county where license was issued. County Clerks also have some records before 1906.
Divorce	$13.00	Same as Birth or Death	Records since 1925.
	Varies	See remarks	County Circuit Court Clerk in county where divorce was granted. County Clerks also have some records before 1925.

Place of event	Cost of copy	Address	Remarks
Pennsylvania			
Birth	$4.00	Division of Vital	State office has had records since
Wallet	$5.00	Records	January 1906.
card		State Department	
Death	$3.00	of Health	For earlier records, write to Registrar
		Central Building	of Wills, Orphans Court, in county
		101 South Mercer	seat of county where event occurred.
		Street	Persons born in Pittsburgh from 1870
		P.O. Box 1528	to 1905 or in Allegheny City, now
		New Castle, PA	part of Pittsburgh, from 1882 to
		19103	1905 should write to Office of
			Biostatistics, Pittsburgh Health
			Department, City-County Building,
			Pittsburgh, PA 15219. For events
			occurring in City of Philadelphia from
			1860 to 1915, write to Vital Statistics,
			Philadelphia Department of Public
			Health, 401 North Broad Street,
			Room 942, Philadelphia, PA 19108.
			Check or money order should be
			made payable to Division of Vital
			Records. Personal checks are accept-
			ed. To verify current fees, the tele-
			phone number is (412) 656-3100.
Marriage	Varies	See remarks	Make application to the Marriage
			License Clerks, County Courthouse,
			in county where license was issued.
Divorce	Varies	See remarks	Make application to the
			Prothonotary, Courthouse, in county
			seat of county where divorce was
			granted.

Place of event	Cost of copy	Address	Remarks
Rhode Island			
Birth or Death	$10.00	Division of Vital Records Rhode Island Department of Health Room 101, Cannon Building 3 Capitol Hill Providence, RI 02908-5097	State office has had records since 1853. For earlier records, write to Town Clerk in town where event occurred. Additional copies of the same record ordered at the same time are $5.00 each. Money order should be made payable to General Treasurer, State of Rhode Island. To verify current fees, the telephone number is (401) 277-2811. This will be a recorded message.
Marriage	$10.00	Same as Birth or Death	Records since January 1853. Additional copies of the same record ordered at the same time are $5.00 each.
Divorce	$1.00	Clerk of Family Court 1 Dorrance Plaza Providence, RI 02903	
South Carolina			
Birth or Death	$8.00	Office of Vital Records and Public Health Statistics South Carolina Department of Health and Environmental Control 2600 Bull Street Columbia, SC 29201	State office has had records since January 1915. City of Charleston births from 1877 and deaths from 1821 are on file at Charleston County Health Department. Ledger entries of Florence City births and deaths from 1895 to 1914 are on file at Florence County Health Department. Ledger entries of Newberry City births and deaths from the late 1800s are on file at Newberry County Health Department. These are the only early records obtainable. Additional copies of the same birth records ordered at the same time of certification are $3.00.

Place of event	Cost of copy	Address	Remarks
			Check or money order should be made payable to Department of Health and Environmental Control. Personal checks are accepted. To verify current fees, the telephone number is (803) 734-4830.
Marriage	$8.00	Same as Birth or Death	Records since July 1950.
	Varies	See remarks	Records since July 1911. Probate Judge in county where license was issued.
Divorce	$8.00	Same as Birth or Death	Records since July 1962.
	Varies	See remarks	Records since April 1949. Clerk of county where petition was filed.
South Dakota			
Birth or Death	$5.00	State Department of Health Center of Health Policy and Statistics Vital Records 523 E. Capitol Pierre, SD 57501	State office has had records since July 1905 and access to other records for some events that occurred before then. Money order should be made payable to South Dakota Department of Health. Personal checks are accepted. To verify current fees, the telephone number is (605) 773-3355. This will be a recorded message.
Marriage	$5.00	Same as Birth or Death	Records since July 1905.
	Varies	See remarks	County Treasury in county where license was issued.
Divorce	$5.00	Same as Birth or Death	Records since July 1905.
	Varies	See remarks	Clerk of Court in county where divorce was granted.

Place of event	Cost of copy	Address	Remarks
Tennessee			
Birth (long form)	$10.00	Tennessee Vital Records	State office has had birth records for entire State since January 1914,
Birth (short form)	$5.00	Department of Health	for Nashville since June 1881, for Knoxville since July 1881, and for
Death	$5.00	Cordell Hull Building Nashville, TN 37247-0350	Chattanooga since January 1882. State office has had death records for entire State since January 1914. for Nashville since July 1874, for Knoxville since July 1887, and for Chattanooga since March 6, 1872. Birth and death enumeration records by school district are available for July 1908 through June 1912. Vital Records Office keeps death records for 50 years; older records are maintained by Tennessee Library and Archives, Archives Division, Nashville, TN 37243-0312. For Memphis birth records from April 1874 through December 1887 and November 1898 to January 1, 1914, and for Memphis death records from May 1848 to January 1, 1914, write to Memphis-Shelby County Health Department, Division of Vital Records, Memphis, TN 38105. Additional copies of the same birth, marriage, or divorce record, requested at the same time, are $2.00 each.
			Check or money order should be made payable to Tennessee Vital Records. Personal checks are accepted. To verify current fees, the telephone number is (615) 741-1763.
Marriage	$10.00	Same as Birth or Death	Records since July 1945.
	Varies	See remarks	County Clerk in county where license was issued.

Place of event	Cost of copy	Address	Remarks
Divorce	$10.00	Same as Birth or Death	Records since July 1945.
	Varies	See remarks	Clerk of Court in county where divorce was granted.
Texas			
Birth Death	$11.00 $9.00	Bureau of Vital Statistics Texas Department of Health 1100 West 49th Street Austin, TX 78756-3191	State office has had records since 1903. Additional copies of same record ordered at same time are $3.00 each. Check or money order should be made payable to Texas Department of Health. Personal checks are accepted. To verify current fees, the telephone number is (512) 458-7111. This is a recorded message.
Marriage	See remarks		Records since January 1966. Certified copies are not available from State office. Fee for search and verification of essential facts of marriage is $9.00 each.
	Varies	See remarks	County Clerk in county where license was issued.
Divorce	See remarks		Records since January 1968. Certified copies are not available from State office. Fee for search and verification of essential facts of divorce is $9.00 each.
	Varies	See remarks	Clerk of District Court in county where divorce was granted.

Place of event	Cost of copy	Address	Remarks
Utah			
Birth	$12.00	Bureau of Vital	State office has had records since
Death	$9.00	Records	1905. If event occurred from 1890
		Utah Department	to 1904 in Salt Lake City or Ogden,
		of Health	write to City Board of Health. For
		288 North 1460	records elsewhere in the State from
		West	from 1898 to 1904, write to County
		P.O. Box 16700	Clerk in county where event
		Salt Lake City, UT	occurred. Additional copies, when
		84116-0700	requested at the same time, are $5.00 each.
			Check or money order should be made payable to Utah Department of Health. Personal checks are accepted. To verify current fees, the telephone number is (801) 538-6105. This is a recorded message.
Marriage	$9.00	Same as Birth or Death	State office has had records since 1978. Only short form certified copies are available.
	Varies	See remarks	County Clerk in county where license was issued.
Divorce	$9.00	Same as Birth or Death	State office has had records since 1978. Only short form certified copies are available.
	Varies	See remarks	County Clerk in county where divorce was granted.
Vermont			
Birth or	$5.00	Vermont Dept.	State office has had records since
Death		of Health	1981.
		Vital Records Section	
		Box 70	Check or money order should be
		60 Main Street	made payable to Vermont Department
		Burlington, VT	of Health. Personal checks are
		05402	accepted. To verify current fees, the telephone number is (802) 863-7275.

Place of event	Cost of copy	Address	Remarks
Birth, Death or Marriage	$5.00	Division of Public Records US Route 2-Middlesex 133 State Street Montpelier, VT 05633	Records prior to 1981. To verify current fees, the telephone number is (802) 828-3286.
	$5.00	See remarks	Town or City Clerk of town where birth or death occurred.
Marriage	$5.00	Same as Birth or Death	State office has had records since 1981.
	$5.00	See remarks	Town Clerk in town where license was issued.
Divorce	$5.00	Same as Birth or Death	State office has had records since 1981.
	$5.00	See remarks	Town Clerk in town where divorce was granted.
Virginia Birth or Death	$5.00	Division of Vital Records State Health Department P.O. Box 1000 Richmond, VA 23208-1000	State office has had records from January 1853 to December 1896 and since June 14, 1912. Only the cities of Hampton, Newport News, Norfolk, and Richmond have records between 1896 and June 14, 1912. Check or money order should be made payable to State Health Department. Personal checks are accepted. To verify current fees, the telephone number is (804) 786-6228. This is a recorded message.
Marriage	$5.00	Same as Birth or Death	Records since January 1853.
	Varies	See remarks	Clerk of Court in county or city where license was issued.

Place of event	Cost of copy	Address	Remarks
Divorce	$5.00	Same as Birth or Death	Records since January 1918.
	Varies	See remarks	Clerk of Court in county or city where divorce was granted.
Washington			
Birth or Death	$11.00	Department of Health Center for Health Statistics P.O. Box 9709 Olympia, WA 98507-9709	State office has had records since July 1907. For King, Pierce, and Spokane counties copies may also be obtained from county health departments. County Auditor of county of birth has registered births prior to July 1907.
			Check or money order should be made payable to Department of Health. To verify current fees, the telephone number is (206) 753-5936.
Marriage	$11.00	Same as Birth or Death	State office has had records since January 1968.
	$2.00	See remarks	County Auditor in county where license was issued.
Divorce	$11.00	Same as Birth or Death	State office has had records since January 1968.
	Varies	See remarks	County Clerk in county where divorce was granted.
West Virginia			
Birth or Death	$5.00	Vital Registration Office Division of Health State Capitol Complex Bldg. 3 Charleston, WV 25305	State office has had records since January 1917. For earlier records, write to Clerk of County Court in county where event occurred.
			Check or money order should be made payable to Vital Registration. Personal checks are accepted. To verify current fees, the telephone number is (304) 558-2931.

Place of event	Cost of copy	Address	Remarks
Marriage	$5.00	Same as Birth or Death	Records since 1921. Certified copies available from 1964.
	Varies	See remarks	County Clerk in county where license was issued.
Divorce	See remarks	Same as Birth or Death	Index since 1968. Some items may be verified (fee $5.00). Certified copies are not available from State office.
	Varies	See remarks	Clerk of Circuit Court, Chancery Side, in county where divorce was granted.

Wisconsin

Place of event	Cost of copy	Address	Remarks
Birth Death	$10.00 $7.00	Vital Records 1 West Wilson St. P.O. Box 309 Madison, WI 53701	State Office has scattered records earlier than 1857. Records before October 1, 1907, are very incomplete. Additional copies of the same record ordered at the same time are $2.00 each.
			Check or money order should be made payable to Center for Health Statistics. Personal checks are accepted. To verify current fees, the telephone number is (608) 266-1371. This will be a recorded message.
Marriage	$7.00	Same as Birth or Death	Records since April 1836. Records before October 1, 1907, are incomplete. Additional copies of the same record ordered at the same time are $2.00 each.
Divorce	$7.00	Same as Birth or Death	Records since October 1907. Additional copies of the same record ordered at the same time are $2.00 each.

Place of event	Cost of copy	Address	Remarks
Wyoming			
Birth	$8.00	Vital Records	State office has had records since July
Death	$6.00	Services	1909.
		Hathaway Building	
		Cheyenne, WY	Money order should be made payable
		82002	to Vital Records Services. To verify current fees, the telephone number is (307) 777-7591.
Marriage	$8.00	Same as Birth or Death	Records since May 1941.
	Varies	See remarks	County Clerk in county where license was issued.
Divorce	$8.00	Same as Birth or Death	Records since May 1941.
	Varies	See remarks	Clerk of District Court where divorce took place.

REQUEST PERTAINING TO MILITARY RECORDS

Please read instructions on the reverse. If more space is needed, use plain paper.

PRIVACY ACT OF 1974 COMPLIANCE INFORMATION. The following information is provided in accordance with 5 U.S.C. 552a(e)(3) and applies to this form. Authority for collection of the information is 44 U.S.C. 2907, 3101, and 3103, and E.O. 9397 of November 22, 1943. Disclosure of the information is voluntary. The principal purpose of the information is to assist the facility servicing the records in locating and verifying the correctness of the requested records or information to answer your inquiry. Routine uses of the information as established and published in accordance with 5 U.S.C.a(e)(4)(D)

include the transfer of relevant information to appropriate Federal, State, local, or foreign agencies for use in civil, criminal, or regulatory investigations or prosecution. In addition, this form will be filed with the appropriate military record and may be transferred along with the record to another agency in accordance with the routine uses established by the agency which maintains the record. If the requested information is not provided, it may not be possible to service your inquiry.

SECTION I—INFORMATION NEEDED TO LOCATE RECORDS (Furnish as much as possible)

1. NAME USED DURING SERVICE *(Last, first, and middle)*	2. SOCIAL SECURITY NO.	3. DATE OF BIRTH	4. PLACE OF BIRTH

5. ACTIVE SERVICE, PAST AND PRESENT (For an effective records search, it is important that ALL service be shown below)

BRANCH OF SERVICE *(Also, show last organization, if known)*	DATES OF ACTIVE SERVICE		Check one		SERVICE NUMBER DURING THIS PERIOD
	DATE ENTERED	DATE RELEASED	OFFI-CER	EN-LISTED	

6. RESERVE SERVICE, PAST OR PRESENT   If "none," check here ▶ ☐

a. BRANCH OF SERVICE	b. DATES OF MEMBERSHIP		c. Check one		d. SERVICE NUMBER DURING THIS PERIOD
	FROM	TO	OFFI-CER	EN-LISTED	
			☐	☐	

7. NATIONAL GUARD MEMBERSHIP   (Check one):   a. ARMY ☐   b. AIR FORCE ☐   c. NONE ☐

d. STATE	e. ORGANIZATION	f. DATES OF MEMBERSHIP		g. Check one		h. SERVICE NUMBER DURING THIS PERIOD
		FROM	TO	OFFI-CER	EN-LISTED	
				☐	☐	

8. IS SERVICE PERSON DECEASED	9. IS (WAS) INDIVIDUAL A MILITARY RETIREE OR FLEET RESERVIST
☐ YES ☐ NO If "yes," enter date of death.	☐ YES ☐ NO

SECTION II—REQUEST

1. EXPLAIN WHAT INFORMATION OR DOCUMENTS YOU NEED; OR, CHECK ITEM 2; OR, COMPLETE ITEM 3	2. IF YOU ONLY NEED A STATEMENT OF SERVICE check here ☐

3. LOST SEPARATION DOCUMENT REPLACEMENT REQUEST (Complete a or b, and c.)

	a. REPORT OF SEPARATION (DD Form 214 or equivalent) ☐	YEAR ISSUED	This contains information normally needed to determine eligibility for benefits. It may be furnished only to the veteran, the surviving next of kin, or to a representative with veteran's signed release (Item 5 of this form).
	b. DISCHARGE CERTIFICATE ☐	YEAR ISSUED	This shows only the date and character at discharge. It is of little value in determining eligibility for benefits. It may be issued only to veterans discharged honorably or under honorable conditions; or, if deceased, to the surviving spouse.

c. EXPLAIN HOW SEPARATION DOCUMENT WAS LOST

4. EXPLAIN PURPOSE FOR WHICH INFORMATION OR DOCUMENTS ARE NEEDED	6. REQUESTER
	a. IDENTIFICATION *(check appropriate box)*
	☐ Same person identified in Section I ☐ Surviving spouse
	☐ Next of kin (relationship) _____
	☐ Other (specify)

b. SIGNATURE *(see instruction 3 on reverse side)*	DATE OF REQUEST

5. RELEASE AUTHORIZATION, IF REQUIRED *(Read instruction 3 on reverse side)*

I hereby authorize release of the requested information/documents to the person indicated at right (item 7).

VETERAN SIGN HERE ▶ _____

(If signed by other than veteran show relationship to veteran.)

7. Please type or print clearly —   COMPLETE RETURN ADDRESS

Name, number and street, city, State and ZIP code

TELEPHONE NO. *(include area code)* ▶

180-106   NSN 7540-00-142-9360

STANDARD FORM 180 (Rev. 7-86)
Prescribed by NARA (36 CFR 1228.162(a))

INSTRUCTIONS

1. Information needed to locate records. Certain identifying information is necessary to determine the location of an individual's record of military service. Please give careful consideration to and answer each item on this form. If you do not have and cannot obtain the information for an item, show "NA," meaning the information is "not available." Include as much of the requested information as you can. This will help us to give you the best possible service.

2. Charges for service. A nominal fee is charged for certain types of service. In most instances service fees cannot be determined in advance. If your request involves a service fee you will be notified as soon as that determination is made.

3. Restrictions on release of information. Information from records of military personnel is released subject to restrictions imposed by the military departments consistent with the provisions of the Freedom of Information Act of 1967 (as amended in 1974) and the Privacy Act of 1974. A service person has access to almost any information contained in his own record. The next of kin, if the veteran is deceased, and Federal officers for official purposes, are authorized to receive information from a military service or medical record only as specified in the above cited Acts. Other requesters must have the release authorization, in item 5 of the form, signed by the veteran or, if deceased, by the next of kin. Employers

and others needing proof of military service are expected to accept the information shown on documents issued by the Armed Forces at the time a service person is separated.

4. Location of military personnel records. The various categories of military personnel records are described in the chart below. For each category there is a code number which indicates the address at the bottom of the page to which this request should be sent. For each military service there is a note explaining approximately how long the records are held by the military service before they are transferred to the National Personnel Records Center, St. Louis. Please read these notes carefully and make sure you send your inquiry to the right address. Please note especially that the record is not sent to the National Personnel Records Center as long as the person retains any sort of reserve obligation, whether drilling or non-drilling.

(If the person has two or more periods of service within the same branch, send your request to the office having the record for the last period of service.)

5. Definitions for abbreviations used below:
NPRC—National Personnel Records Center　　PERS—Personnel Records
TDRL—Temporary Disability Retirement List　　MED—Medical Records

SERVICE	NOTE: (See paragraph 4 above.)	CATEGORY OF RECORDS　　—　　WHERE TO WRITE ADDRESS CODE ▼		
AIR FORCE (USAF)	*Except for TDRL and general officers retired with pay, Air Force records are transferred to NPRC from Code 1, 90 days after separation and from Code 2, 150 days after separation.*	Active members (includes National Guard on active duty in the Air Force), TDRL, and general officers retired with pay.		1
		Reserve, retired reservist in nonpay status, current National Guard officers not on active duty in Air Force, and National Guard released from active duty in Air Force.		2
		Current National Guard enlisted not on active duty in Air Force.		13
		Discharged, deceased, and retired with pay.		14
COAST GUARD (USCG)	*Coast Guard officer and enlisted records are transferred to NPRC 7 months after separation.*	Active, reserve, and TDRL members.		3
		Discharged, deceased, and retired members *(see next item)*.		14
		Officers separated before 1/1/29 and enlisted personnel separated before 1/1/15.		6
MARINE CORPS (USMC)	*Marine Corps records are transferred to NPRC between 6 and 9 months after separation.*	Active, TDRL, and Selected Marine Corps Reserve members.		4
		Individual Ready Reserve and Fleet Marine Corps Reserve members.		5
		Discharged, deceased, and retired members *(see next item)*.		14
		Members separated before 1/1/1905.		6
ARMY (USA)	*Army records are transferred to NPRC as follows: Active Army and Individual Ready Reserve Control Groups: About 60 days after separation. U.S. Army Reserve Troop Unit personnel: About 120 to 180 days after separation.*	Reserve, living retired members, retired general officers, and active duty records of current National Guard members who performed service in the U.S. Army before 7/1/72.*		7
		Active officers (including National Guard on active duty in the U.S. Army).		8
		Active enlisted (including National Guard on active duty in the U.S. Army) and enlisted TDRL.		9
		Current National Guard officers not on active duty in the U.S. Army.		12
		Current National Guard enlisted not on active duty in the U.S. Army.		13
		Discharged and deceased members *(see next item)*.		14
		Officers separated before 7/1/17 and enlisted separated before 11/1/12.		6
		Officers and warrant officers TDRL.		8
NAVY (USN)	*Navy records are transferred to NPRC 6 months after retirement or complete separation.*	Active members (including reservists on duty)—PERS and MED		10
		Discharged, deceased, retired (with and without pay) less than six months, TDRL, drilling and nondrilling reservists	PERS ONLY	10
			MED ONLY	11
		Discharged, deceased, retired (with and without pay) more than six months *(see next item)*—PERS & MED		14
		Officers separated before 1/1/03 and enlisted separated before 1/1/1886—PERS and MED		6

*Code 12 applies to active duty records of current National Guard officers who performed service in the U.S. Army after 6/30/72.
Code 13 applies to active duty records of current National Guard enlisted members who performed service in the U.S. Army after 6/30/72.*

ADDRESS LIST OF CUSTODIANS (BY CODE NUMBERS SHOWN ABOVE)—Where to write / send this form for each category of records

1	Air Force Manpower and Personnel Center Military Personnel Records Division Randolph AFB, TX 78150–6001	**5**	Marine Corps Reserve Support Center 10950 El Monte Overland Park, KS 66211–1408	**8**	USA MILPERCEN ATTN: DAPC-MSR 200 Stoval Street Alexandria, VA 22332–0400	**12** Army National Guard Personnel Center Columbia Pike Office Building 5600 Columbia Pike Falls Church, VA 22041
2	Air Reserve Personnel Center Denver, CO 80280–5000	**6**	Military Archives Division National Archives and Records Administration Washington, DC 20408	**9**	Commander U.S. Army Enlisted Records and Evaluation Center Ft. Benjamin Harrison, IN 46249–5301	**13** The Adjutant General *(of the appropriate State, DC, or Puerto Rico)*
3	Commandant U.S. Coast Guard Washington, DC 20593–0001	**7**	Commander U.S. Army Reserve Personnel Center ATTN: DARP-PAS 9700 Page Boulevard St. Louis, MO 63132–5200	**10**	Commander Naval Military Personnel Command ATTN: NMPC-036 Washington, DC 20370–5036	**14** National Personnel Records Center *(Military Personnel Records)* 9700 Page Boulevard St. Louis, MO 63132
4	Commandant of the Marine Corps (Code MMRB-10) Headquarters, U.S. Marine Corps Washington, DC 20380–0001			**11**	Naval Reserve Personnel Center New Orleans, LA 70146–5000	

FORM **BC-600**
(8-21-89)

U.S. DEPARTMENT OF COMMERCE
BUREAU OF THE CENSUS

OMB No. 0607-0117;
Approval Expires 03/31/90

APPLICATION FOR SEARCH OF CENSUS RECORDS

RETURN TO: Bureau of the Census, 1600 North Walnut Street, PITTSBURG, KANSAS 66762 *(See instruction 1 on the reverse side)*

PURPOSE FOR WHICH RECORD IS TO BE USED (MUST BE STATED HERE) *(See Instruction 1 on the reverse side)*

$ _____ (Fee)
☐ Money Order
☐ Check
☐ Other

DO NOT USE THIS SPACE

CASE NO.

| FULL NAME OF PERSON WHOSE CENSUS RECORD IS REQUESTED *(Print or type)* | FIRST NAME | MIDDLE NAME | MAIDEN NAME *(If any)* | PRESENT LAST NAME | NICKNAMES |

| DATE OF BIRTH *(If unknown, estimate)* | PLACE OF BIRTH *(City, county, State)* | | RACE | SEX |

FULL NAME OF FATHER *(Stepfather, guardian, etc.)*

FULL MAIDEN NAME OF MOTHER *(Stepmother, etc.)*

Please give FULL name of husband or wife of person whose record is requested

FIRST MARRIAGE *(Name of husband or wife)* — YEAR MARRIED *(Approximate)*

SECOND MARRIAGE *(Name of husband or wife)* — YEAR MARRIED *(Approximate)*

GIVE PLACE OF RESIDENCE FOR APPROPRIATE CENSUS DATES *(SEE INSTRUCTIONS 1 AND 5)*

CENSUS DATE	NUMBER AND STREET *(Read Instruction 3 first)*	CITY, TOWN, TOWNSHIP *(Read Instruction 3 first)*	COUNTY AND STATE	NAME OF PERSON WITH WHOM LIVING *(Head of household)*	RELATIONSHIP OF HEAD OF HOUSEHOLD
JUNE 1, 1900 *(See Instruction 2)*					
APRIL 15, 1910 *(See Instruction 3)*					
JAN. 1, 1920 *(See Instruction 2)*					
APRIL 1, 1930 *(See Instruction 3)*					
APRIL 1, 1940 *(See Instruction 3)*					
APRIL 1, 1950 *(See Instruction 3)*					
APRIL 1, 1960 *(See Instruction 3)*					
APRIL 1, 1970 *(See Instruction 3)*					
APRIL 1, 1980 *(See Instruction 3)*					

Names of brother and sisters

- If the census information is to be sent to someone other than the person whose record is requested, give the name and address, including ZIP Code, of the other person or agency.
- This authorizes the Bureau of the Census to send the record to: *(See Instruction 4)*

FEE REQUIRED: See *Instructions 5 and 6 on the reverse side.*

A check or money order (DO NOT SEND CASH) payable to "Commerce—Census," must be sent with the application. This fee covers the cost of a search of not more than two census years about one person only.

Fee required .... $ 25.00	
_____ extra copies @ $2.00 each $ _____	
_____ full schedules @ $6.00 each $ _____ (for genealogy)	
TOTAL amount enclosed _____	$ _____

I certify that information furnished about anyone other than the applicant will not be used to the detriment of such person or persons by me or by anyone else with my permission.

▶ SIGNATURE — *Do not print* *(Read Instruction 7 carefully before signing)*

PRESENT ADDRESS ▶ NUMBER AND STREET

CITY | STATE | ZIP CODE

PHONE NUMBER *(Include area code)*

IF SIGNED ABOVE BY MARK (X), TWO WITNESSES MUST SIGN HERE

SIGNATURE | SIGNATURE

NOTICE — Intentionally falsifying this application may result in a fine of $10,000 or five years imprisonment, or both (title 18, U.S. Code, section 1001).

GENERAL INFORMATION

The Application on the reverse side of this sheet is for use in requesting a search of the census records and an official copy of the personal information found which includes age, place of birth, and citizenship. This application should be filled in and mailed to BUREAU OF THE CENSUS, 1600 N. Walnut Street, PITTSBURG, KS 66762, together with a money order or check payable to "Commerce — Census."

Birth certificates, including delayed birth certificates, are not issued by the Bureau of the Census but by the Health Department or similar agency of the State in which the birth occurred. In most Federal Censuses, the census takers obtained the age at the time of the census (**not the date of birth**) and place of birth (**state, territory, or country only**) of individuals. Copies of these census records often are accepted as evidence of age, citizenship, and place of birth for employment, social security benefits, insurance, and other purposes. *Since the*

place of birth and citizenship were obtained only on a sample basis during the 1960, 1970, and 1980 Censuses, this information will not be shown on transcripts for those years.

If you authorize the Bureau of the Census to send your record to someone other than yourself, attention is called to the possibility that the information shown in the census record may not agree with that given in your application. The record must be copied exactly as it appears. Censuses are taken primarily for statistical, not legal purposes, and the records exist only on microfilm. Therefore, the Census Bureau is not in a position to make changes in them even though it realizes that enumerators may have been misinformed or made mistakes in writing down the data they collected. Those agencies that accept census transcripts as evidence of age, relationship, or place of birth usually overlook minor spelling differences, but would be reluctant to consider a record that was changed years later at an applicant's request.

INSTRUCTIONS FOR COMPLETING THIS FORM

▶ **1. Purpose**
The purpose for which the information is desired must be shown so that a determination may be made under 13 U.S.C. 8(a) that the record is required for a proper use. For proof of age, most agencies require documents closest to date of birth, therefore we suggest you complete information for the two earliest censuses after date of birth.

▶ **2. Censuses 1900—1920**
A system for filing names by sound is available for these census years. Information can be furnished in many instances when only the following information is given:

The name of the person about whom the information is desired.

The name of the city or county and State where the person resided.

The name of the head of the household with whom this person was living on the various dates of these censuses.

Additional information such as the names of brothers and sisters is helpful if it can be furnished.

▶ **3. Censuses — years 1910—1930—1940—1950—1960—1970 —1980**
The potential for finding an individual's census record is increased when the respondent provides thorough and accurate address information. If residing in a city at the time these censuses were taken, it is necessary to furnish the house number, the name of the street, city, county, and State and the name of the parent or other head of household with whom residing at the time of the census. If residing in a rural area, it is **very important** to furnish the township, district, precinct or beat **and** the direction and number of miles from the nearest town.

▶ **4. Confidential information given to other than person to whom it relates**
(a) Census information for the years 1900 and on is confidential and ordinarily will not be furnished to another person unless the person to whom it relates authorizes this in the space provided or there is other proper authorization as indicated in 4(b), 4(c), and 4(d) hereof.

(b) Minor children
Information regarding a child who has not reached legal age may be obtained upon the written request of either parent or the legal guardian.'

(c) Mentally incompetent persons
Information regarding persons who are mentally incompetent may be obtained upon the written request of the legal representative supported by a certified copy of the court order naming such legal representative.

(d) Deceased persons
If the record requested relates to a deceased person, the application must be signed by (1) a blood relative in the immediate family (parent, brother, sister, or child), (2) the surviving wife or husband, (3) the administrator or executor of the estate, or (4) a beneficiary by will, or insurance. In all cases involving deceased persons, a certified copy of the death certificate must be furnished, and the relationship to the deceased must be stated on the application. Legal representatives must also furnish a certified copy of the court order naming such legal representatives; and beneficiaries must furnish legal evidence of such beneficiary interest.

▶ **5. Fee required**
The $25.00 fee is for a search of not more than two suggested censuses about one person only. The time required to complete a search depends upon the number of cases on hand at the particular time and the difficulty encountered in searching a particular case. The normal processing time would require from two to six weeks. Since the fee covers return postage, do not send stamped self-addressed envelope with the application.

Not more than two censuses will be searched and the results furnished for one fee. Should it be necessary to search more than two censuses to find the record, you will be notified to send another fee for further searches are made. Tax monies are not available for the furnishing of the information. Accordingly, even though the information is not found, if a search has been made, the fee cannot be returned.

▶ **6. Full schedules (For Genealogy)**
Upon request, a full schedule will be furnished. There is an additional charge of $6.00 for each full schedule requested. The full schedule is the complete one-line entry of personal data recorded for the individual. The name of the head of household may also be shown, but the names of other persons will not be listed.

▶ **7. Signature**
In general, the signature should be the same as that shown on the line captioned "full name of person whose census record is requested." When the application is for the census record concerning another person, the authority of the requester must be furnished as set forth in instruction 4 above. If signed by marking (X), please indicate the name of the person whose mark it is and have witnesses sign as instructed.

Suggested Readings

Anonymous. *How to Create a New Identity*. New York: Citadel, 1983.

Asking, Hane, and Bob Oskarn. *Search*. New York: Harper & Row, 1982.

Culligan, Joseph J. *You, Too, Can Find Anybody*. North Miami, FL: Hallmark, 1991.

————*When in Doubt, Check Him Out*. North Miami, FL: Hallmark, 1993.

Doane, Gilbert H., and James R. Dell. *Searching for Your Ancestors*. Fifth Ed. Minneapolis: University of Minnesota Press, 1990.

Faron, Fay. *A Nasty Bit of Business*. San Francisco: Creighton-Morgan, 1988.

French, Scott. *The Big Brother Game*. Secaucus, NJ: Lyle Stuart, 1975.

Hauser, Greg. *So You Wanna Be a P.I., Huh Binky?* Lowell, MI: Hauser & Assoc. 1992.

Jacobson, Trudy, and Gary McClain. *State of the Art Fact-Finding*. New York: Dell. 1993.

King, Dennis. *Get the Facts on Anyone*. New York: Prentice-Hall, 1992.

Klunder, Virgil, and Troy Dunn. *The Locator*. Klunder & Dunn. 1992.

Johnson, Richard. *How to Locate Anyone Who Is or Has Been in the Military*. Fifth Ed. San Antonio: MIE, 1993.

Johnson, Richard. *The Abandoned Money Book*. San Antonio: MIE, 1992.

Lapin, Lee. *How to Get Anything on Anybody Book*. San Mateo, CA: ISECO, 1991.

Pankau, Ed. *Check It Out*. Chicago: Contemporary, 1992.

Rothfeder, Jeffrey. *Privacy for Sale*. New York: Simon & Schuster, 1992.

Sullivan, Charlene, and Robert Johnson. *Credit and Collections for Small Stores*. Washington, DC: U.S. Small Business Administration.

Thomas, Ralph. *Advanced Skip Tracing Techniques*. New York: Thomas, 1989.